A ONE-LEGGED STOOL

HOW SHAREHOLDER PRIMACY HAS BROKEN
BUSINESS (AND WHAT WE CAN DO ABOUT IT)

ED CHAMBLISS

First Edition: March 2022

Developmental Editor: Shay Totten
Copy Editor: Hugh Barker
Cover Design: Joe Montgomery
Proofreader: Kate Victory Hannisian

ISBN-13: 979-8-9854487-0-2 (paperback)
ISBN-13: 979-8-9854487-1-9 (ebook)
Library of Congress Control Number: 2021924898

Published by Best Friend Brands, LLC.
www.bestfriendbrands.com

❀ Created with Vellum

For anyone trying to help more than themselves...

CONTENTS

INTRODUCTION

This is not a book for "businesspeople."

It's a book *about* business for all people because all of us should care deeply about business and how it is conducted.

Why? Business (a.k.a. private enterprise) is today's dominant social institution, much as the church was during the Middle Ages or the monarchy during the Renaissance. Its influence is everywhere, and it affects virtually every aspect of our lives.

As it should.

Business, as a construct, is amazing. It is responsible not only for producing most of the goods and services we need, but also for generating the income to acquire them and the free time to consume them.

That's no small feat, and it's only possible thanks to the embrace of three fundamental forces: utility, specialization, and empowerment.

"Utility" is just an economic synonym for "usefulness": that is, how well a product satisfies a customer's wants or needs. The better it can satisfy a human desire, the more valuable it is and, consequently, the more a person is willing to pay for it.

This basic concept drives all sorts of transactions in our society: most obviously commerce, but also employment (where employees exchange their skills for a paycheck and, hopefully, some personal satisfaction); investing (where individuals buy stock in the expectation of a return on their investment); and communities (where governments offer tax breaks and other incentives to companies in exchange for creating jobs and paying tax revenue).

Over time, humanity has been able to steadily increase the utility in all of these transactions. Products, jobs, investments, and communities have all been improved and, as a result, our quality of life has improved.

This progress is due, in large part, to the realization that no one is good at everything.

Some of us are better at math. Others are better at writing. Still others are better at working with computers or making grilled cheese sandwiches or whatever. That's just the way it is.

However, this diversity of talent also means each of us has an area where we can be more useful — where we are able to contribute more utility to an effort.

The best visualization of this concept is perhaps the "T-shaped" person, a recruiting metaphor first popularized in the 1990s. This suggests that the ideal employee should have two types of skills: deep expertise in one particular area (represented by the vertical leg in a capital "T"), as well as a broad basic understanding of other related areas and how everything works together (represented by the horizontal bar).

The "T-Shaped" Person

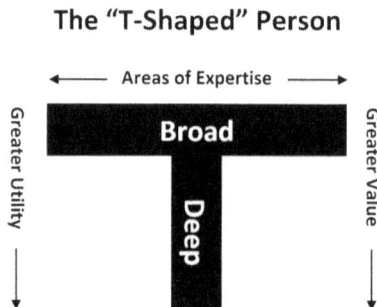

So, success for an enterprise comes from assembling a diverse team of specialists who can work together to elevate the overall effort by applying the increased utility that comes from their individual expertise. The result is a product with greater overall utility and, therefore, greater value.

It's like building a stool where the height of the legs works together to collectively elevate the seat off the floor. The arrangement is good for everyone, with each of the legs helping to support the others. In fact, without this symbiotic connection, individual legs are much more unstable and likely to just fall to the floor.

This holds true not just for teams of employees, but also for the composition of the greater enterprise. Each stakeholder, including employees, customers, investors, and the community, provides specialized utility to the effort and, without any of them, the overall endeavor will have a much more difficult time.

There's just no way around it. Unlocking the benefits of specialization requires interdependency. The only way to elevate one leg is to elevate all of them.

Of course, this type of group effort requires a significant amount of organization and coordination. Historically, this role has been the purview of a centralized clergy, royalty, or bureaucracy, where a select few make decisions for everyone: what people should believe, what they should do for a living, and what products they should produce (and purchase).

Without fail, many of these decisions are poor. People are assigned jobs for which they have no real talent. Products are of lower quality. Overall utility is restricted, and the whole system underperforms for everyone — employees, customers, investors, and communities.

And while you might think that these bad decisions are the result of malice or stupidity, it's more likely they're due to the fact that people are too diverse and our society is too large and complex to be centrally managed. It doesn't matter who's in charge. Any paradigm created by a centralized authority (even with the best of intentions) will inherently oversimplify reality, resulting in solutions that (at best) only work for a few or (at worst) don't work for anyone.

As a structural concept, private enterprise fixes this problem. Due to its decentralized, participant-driven nature, it does a better job of aligning skills as well as wants and needs because it empowers individuals to weigh in on these decisions: that is, to share where they find utility.

- Employees are empowered to choose which careers they want to pursue.
- Consumers are empowered to choose which products work best for them.
- Investors are empowered to choose who they support with their money.
- Citizens are empowered to choose what kind of community they want to live in.

Businesses respond to all of this choice by trying to create solutions that all the stakeholders will find most valuable. It's a collective navigation that ensures business is always steering toward a place where the aggregate finds the most utility.

That's not to say that business is perfect. Far from it. Business, too, isn't at its best on its own. It needs other institutional "legs" (e.g., the government) to help guide and support it.

However, by supercharging specialization with empowerment, business has created an unprecedented increase in utility, which has driven amazing progress for humanity.

Most incredibly, this progress has been sustained for generations, feeding on its own advances in technology. New technology creates the need for more and more specialization which, in turn, leads to more and more utility and more and more value.

In essence, the legs of the stool have continued to get longer, lifting everyone higher and higher.

To date, humanity hasn't discovered a better way to harness the power of working together — aligning the best people with the right roles so that everyone benefits.

Of course, progress isn't always steady. Sometimes other, larger forces, such as recession, war, or even a pandemic, can temporarily slow down the collective rise of the stool.

It was during one of these slowdowns in the 1970s that some people, including Nobel Prize-winning economist Milton Friedman, decided that business needed fixing. Specifically, they felt the dynamic was too complex, with too many competing interests, and that it could be greatly improved with some simplification.

For his part, Friedman believed that businesses should only focus on one thing: maximizing profit for shareholders. In a 1970 article in the *New York Times Magazine*,[1] he laid out his argument that such a singular focus on one type of value (money) and one stakeholder (shareholders) would remove a lot of inefficiency from the whole system.

Sure enough, as this concept of "shareholder primacy" was first getting traction, companies were able to make some easy gains by cutting the fat. But, as anyone who's ever trimmed a steak knows, if you keep cutting, pretty soon you're going to run out of fat and end up cutting meat. And that's exactly what happened.

By the 1980s, finding true inefficiencies had become harder and harder. Yet, shareholders, who had become used to their elevated status and consistent returns on investment, were demanding more.

So, under the paradigm of shareholder primacy, companies did the only thing they could: They turned the knife to the meat, extracting value from other stakeholders (including employees, customers, and communities) in order to keep paying shareholders their higher rate of return.

To put it another way, businesses started lengthening one leg of the stool at the expense of others.

This, of course, is really bad for the stool. And for business. Elevating shareholders above all other stakeholders reflects a short-sighted shift to "I-shaped" thinking, ignoring the interdependency and equilibrium that makes business so productive and beneficial in the first place.

The crazy thing is that most business leaders know this favoritism is harmful, yet they keep "maximizing shareholder value" anyway.

Indeed, a 2006 survey of corporate financial officers found that 80% would cut vital expenses such as marketing or product development in order to make quarterly earnings targets, even though they knew it would most likely hurt long-term corporate performance.[2]

Why?

Perhaps it is the simplicity of only having to please one constituency (investors) rather than having to balance multiple, competing interests.

Maybe it's that dealing with dollars and other numbers is easier than measuring more subjective criteria such as preferences and emotions.

It could also be that the bulk of executive compensation is now tied to share price rather than a salary, aligning the interests of corporate leaders with shareholders.

Or, it could be that shareholder primacy has been the "gold standard" of corporate behavior for decades now and is so deeply ingrained in our thinking that executives don't feel they even have a choice — that it's just the way things are.

Whatever the reason (or reasons), 50 years of tilting the stool of business has increasingly destabilized it, creating or exacerbating a host of problems in our society.

Favoring investors (who, by definition, have money to spare) has significantly contributed to the increase in economic inequality, where the rich have gotten richer and the poor have gotten poorer. Since 1967, the top 20% of Americans increased their share of all income from 43.6% to 51.2% (a relative increase of 17.4%). During the same time period, the bottom 20% saw their share of income drop from four percent to just 3.1% (a relative decrease of 22.5%).[3]

In fact, the top one percent of Americans today account for a staggering 18.39% of all income, a concentration not seen since the Roaring Twenties, right before the Great Depression.[4]

Share of all income earned by the top one percent of Americans. (Source: "The Chartbook of Economic Inequality," Atkinson, Hasell, Morelli, and Roser, University of Oxford, 2017)

This level of disparity inherently breeds class tension, eroding the belief that "all men are created equal" while increasing the distrust and polarization that come from an "us versus them" mentality.

Unfortunately, this toxic atmosphere only reinforces itself, spiraling us further down, and eroding the civility and cooperation on which society depends.

That's not to mention the impact that shareholder primacy has on our natural environment. This shared resource is often harvested or destroyed for the disproportionate benefit of stockholders.

Throughout this discord, business smiles reassuringly and tells all the stakeholders that they're important. It has to because it needs all of the legs to keep the stool standing. Of course, telling each of us we're equally valued while acting in a way that clearly demonstrates we're not creates cognitive dissonance and massive distrust of business, which make the stool even more unstable.

And while most of us recognize these issues and their relation to business, we tend to accept them as an unavoidable consequence of private enterprise. Like business leaders, we believe that shareholder primacy is just the way it is and there's nothing we can (or should) do about it.

But shareholder primacy hasn't always defined business. Before the 1970s, the dominant theory was called "managerialism," a belief that business leaders were "stewards or trustees charged with guiding a vital social and economic institution in the interests of a wide range of beneficiaries."[5] It not only sounds nice, but it also worked. From 1930 to 1970, managerialism oversaw the rise of the U.S. as an economic superpower, flourishing innovation, rising employee wages, and a steady stream of dividend checks for shareholders. (In fact, the S&P 500 returned a compound average annual return of 7.5% during this time frame.[6])

So maybe it's time to actually notice what we blindly accept. To question the unquestionable. And to see if there's a better way forward.

That's what this book aims to do.

It examines the entire dynamic of shareholder primacy, starting with something most of us have personally experienced: mistrust of business. Following those feelings to their source, it diagnoses who (or what) is to blame for our current situation, including some questionable assumptions that underpin today's system of private enterprise.

Next, it reviews the broader context of business, how we got here, and how the same forces that used to be beneficial have become so destructive.

Finally, it offers an alternative. A simple, straightforward approach that can stabilize the stool of business, repairing it so it once again elevates all of us, including shareholders.

The simple fact is we need business. It is the only institution with enough resources — accounting for almost 90% of U.S. Gross Domestic Product (GDP)[7] — to solve the massive societal and environmental problems we face today.

But as long as shareholder primacy reigns, we don't stand a chance. A one-legged stool *will* fall over. It's just a matter of time.

1

A LOSS OF TRUST

"Don't trust everything you see. Even salt looks like sugar."

— UNKNOWN

How good are you at predicting the future?

That's what "trust" is, really. A prediction about whether or not someone will live up to your current expectations in the future.

The prediction is actually a near-instantaneous subconscious calculation based on a long list of inputs, including the person's word choice, tone, facial expressions, body language, proximity, overall appearance, etc. It's all pretty subtle, yet most people are pretty darned good at quickly determining whether or not someone can be trusted.

Why? Experience. By the time we reach adulthood we've run the "trust" calculation thousands if not millions of times, tweaking our mental formulas, making them more and more accurate each time. And if we have history with a specific person, our predictions about them get better still, as we know that people don't act randomly. They tend to say and do things that are similar to what they've said and done before.

Interestingly, when our calculations are wrong, the way we update our "algorithm" differs depending on which way we were off. If the error leads to our disappointment (i.e., we trusted someone too much), this new, negative information has enormous weight in our trust calculation about that person moving forward (meaning it's much harder for us to trust them after they fail us).

However, if the calculation leads to the opposite, and we are "pleasantly surprised" when we were expecting the worst, this new data is not nearly as influential in the future. Which is why it's hard for us to believe that someone — be it a paroled felon or a former boyfriend/girlfriend — has truly changed.

Clearly, people do change, but thousands of years of evolution demanded that we protect ourselves in order to survive, so judgments were harsh, and second chances were few and far between.

It all comes together in the truism, "Trust takes years to make, a second to break, and forever to repair."

It's a saying that's not just true for people, but also for businesses. It's trust that allows a person to voluntarily hand over payment, expecting the company will live up to its promises. For the business, trust is the catalyst necessary to "close the deal" with a customer (and keep it closed). Without trust, why would these two parties enter into this "relationship"?

Indeed, a 2018 study by Survey Monkey found that 68% of U.S. adults say trust influences their decision "a great deal" or "a lot" when making a big purchase.[1]

This mirrors the 2016 Edelman Global Trust Barometer survey of more than 32,000 people, which found that 68% of adults are more likely to buy from companies they trust, 59% are more likely to recommend a trusted company, and 37% are willing to pay more when buying from a trusted company.[2]

Trust dominates, even when things go badly and customers walk away from a company, with 41% doing so because of an issue of trust.[3]

For businesses, trust is often encapsulated in the concept of a "brand." That is, the broader relationship someone has with a company beyond the simple goods and services it sells. And, like any relationship, the most valuable brands are built on trust. To quote Keith Weed, CMO of Unilever for 35 years, at the 2018 Cannes Lions Festival of Creativity, "Trust is everything for a brand. A brand without trust is simply a product."[4]

And a product is certainly a lot less valuable than a brand. How much less? The annual Intangible Asset Market Value Study by Chicago-based valuation firm Ocean Tomo shows that intangible assets (e.g., patents, copyrights, franchises, trademarks, and trade names) have grown to represent 84% of the market value of S&P 500 companies (up from just 17% in 1975).[5] A further correlation with Interbrand's Best Global Brands showed that a full 25% of this intangible value can be attributed solely to the brand.[6]

That means a staggering $6.4 trillion of U.S. market capitalization is entirely dependent on trust.[7]

Knowing that, you would think that companies everywhere would put a premium on building and securing such a valuable asset.

You would think.

But the sad truth is that brand trust continues its decline.

Accenture's Global Consumer Pulse survey of over 25,000 people in 33 countries discovered that a whopping 23% of customers trust companies "much less" today than they did five years ago.[8] Ouch.

Focusing just on the U.S., a study by McCann's Truth Central unit found that 42% of Americans find brands and companies less truthful today than 20 years ago.[9]

But a 2019 study by the global media and advertising agency UM takes the cake, finding that just *four percent* of internet users believe what social media influencers say (often on behalf of brands) is true.[10]

To put the situation into perspective, consider this: every year since 1973, Gallup has surveyed Americans to see how much confidence they have in major institutions, such as the military, the Supreme Court, organized religion, and corporations. Over the last three years, only an average of 20% of Americans had "a great deal" or "quite a lot" of confidence in big business, with a much larger 37% having "very little" or "none."[11]

All this mistrust isn't just an academic observation. Loss of trust is driving real-world actions that are decidedly bad for business.

Today's world is one where customers are more empowered than ever before. And a big part of that empowerment is the freedom to break up with a company if and when things go south. According to Forrester, 40% of consumers now have a high willingness and ability to shift their spending, with an additional 25% building that mindset.[12]

To quote the report, "Today's customers reward or punish companies based on a single experience — a single moment in time. This behavior was once a Millennial trademark, but it's now in play for older generations. It has become normal."[13]

All too often that punishment means simply taking their business elsewhere.

The Accenture study found that 53% of customers in mature markets switched at least one of their providers in 2017, with 41% of U.S. customers doing so because of an issue of trust.[14]

Following a bad experience, some customers take a more moderate approach to the relationship and shift away only a portion of their spending. But almost half the time (47%), they immediately stop doing business with the company altogether.[15]

Customers and companies today are not exactly paragons of marital bliss. It's more like they are in a relationship that could use some counseling.

So, when you get customers on the couch, what do they say is the reason they stop trusting brands?

The Product

According to the 2018 study conducted by Survey Monkey, the top two reasons are related to the actual product: specifically, a poor experience with the product or its inability to do what the company claimed it could were each cited 81% of the time.[16]

Seriously? Companies still haven't learned these lessons?

Giving people what they paid for is the absolute minimum in a voluntary exchange. If your product provides a sub-par experience or, worse yet, you're overstating its benefits when making the sale, you deserve to come home and find your stuff out on the lawn.

Listen, learn, and improve. Enough said.

Service

Similarly, "poor customer service experience" was also a top reason for mistrust, showing up in 78% of responses.[17] How a company interacts with customers before, during, and after a sale is an integral part of the overall customer/brand relationship. After all, customers are human beings and humans are hardwired to engage with other humans, whether it's in person, on the phone, or online. Customer service representatives are the day-to-day human face of a brand, and often the only brand representatives that customers will ever encounter. These human-to-human experiences can be positive or negative, but either way, customers project them onto the overall company.

This is not a new concept either. Marketers have known for decades that customer service is a critical part of the brand that can build or salvage customer relationships every day. Yet, many companies still fail to adequately fund, staff, or inform their customer-facing employees, nor do they empower them to make business decisions on the spot. They see customer service as voices to be micro-managed and a cost to be cut rather than an investment in customer retention. Which begins to explain why Accenture's 2017 study found that 61% of customers switched companies at least once that year due to poor service.[18]

Data Security

Data security was also a frequently cited reason for a loss of trust, with 49% of respondents selecting it.[19] We've all heard hundreds of stories of data breaches and compromised identities. But beyond these high-profile events, customers nowadays are more and more aware of how much of their data is being harvested, stored and shared, and they want to know the specifics. In fact, 92% of U.S. consumers believe it is "extremely important" for companies to safeguard their information, and 66% want companies to be more transparent about how their information is being used.[20]

This is a real change from even 10 years ago. Way back in the 2010s, people had a pretty good idea of what data they were giving to companies and what those companies were doing with it. And, except for a bit of spam and junk mail here and there, they were mostly okay with it. But today's data harvest is infinitely broader and more invisible, as is the composition of the algorithms that determine who gets what (and for how much). This lack of transparency has bred caution among consumers, which is reflected in how they allow it into their lives. For example, 72% of consumers are open to having AI tools monitor and adjust energy in their home. But that willingness drops significantly when what is monitored and adjusted is more personal: like their health (56%), their baby or children (40%), and their financial affairs (38%).[21]

Offensive Advertising

Next on the list of trust-breakers was "offensive advertising," with 46% of people listing it.[22] For better or worse, good advertising (like art) is in the eye of the beholder. For example, some people like puns and wordplay. Others (including me) can't stand them. But lately, more and more brands are crossing the line from "bad" to "offensive," where the music stops and everyone, in unison, asks, "uh, what were you thinking?"

Recent lapses in judgment are numerous, with most seeming to fit into one of a handful of unfortunate buckets:

Racism

Consider the following advertisements, starting with Nivea's "White is Purity" campaign promoting its nearly invisible deodorant. The campaign was quickly hijacked by white supremacist groups.[23]

WHITE IS PURITY

H&M's ad showing a dark-skinned child wearing a sweater emblazoned with "Coolest Monkey in the Jungle."[24]

Dove's ad for a body wash for "all types of women" that, unfortunately, seemed to imply that it could help a woman with dark skin turn into one with lighter skin.[25]

Sexism

Examples include:

McDonald's celebrating International Women's Day by turning its golden arches "M" upside down at a few locations, so it resembled a "W." Unfortunately, this stunt was overshadowed by McDonald's troubled history of allegedly tolerating sexual harassment and underpaying female employees compared to males. [26]

Protein World's "Are You Beach Body Ready?" weight loss campaign, overtly defining women by their physical appearance while body-shaming those who don't look like a stereotypical model.[27]

Huggies' "Dad Test" campaign claimed that their diapers were so good they could withstand the neglect of a baby being left alone with a father.[28]

Cultural Misappropriation

Examples of this include:

Ram Trucks' "Built to Serve" Super Bowl commercial featuring a sermon delivered by Martin Luther King, Jr., as the voiceover.[29]

Pepsi's Kendall Jenner ad, showing the celebrity diffusing tensions between authorities and street protesters by handing a can of Pepsi to a police officer. The ad was widely seen as co-opting the Black Lives Matter movement.[30]

The North Face, which decided it would be a good idea to swap out Wikipedia photos of famous outdoor destinations with similar photos prominently displaying its products (and then brag about it online).[31]

THEN WE SWITCHED THE WIKIPEDIA PHOTOS FOR OURS.

In the examples above, none of the brands in question *meant* to offend anyone. They weren't seeking publicity, thinking that "any press is good press." So, what were they thinking when they created these incredibly tone-deaf messages?

One word: "Performance." Advertising has always been a business expense, but its impact is notoriously difficult to measure (which explains the famous John Wanamaker quote, "Half the money I spend on advertising is wasted; the trouble is I don't know which half.") The plethora of digital media data available today has changed this, ensuring that advertising is measured and managed with the same expectations as any other company expenditures. That means meeting ever-escalating quantitative goals for efficiency, often with a marketer's or agency's job hanging in the balance.

That's not to say that advertising shouldn't be held accountable for performance. It should be, against both short-term and long-term goals. But pushing to meet these marks means taking more risks. And taking more risks inherently means more failures. And, because advertising lives in a *very* public space, more failures mean more people could be offended by the messages a brand is sending.

Even if the *quality* of the brand message is good, customers can easily be offended by the *quantity* of advertising they're exposed to (estimates range from 4,000 to 10,000 messages every day).[32] Many of these, of course, are found in the almost infinite real estate of the digital world, where customers (who are now spending 6.8 hours per day online[33]) have noticed more ads in more places, and find those ads to be more intrusive than they used to be.[34]

Twenty-five percent of mobile users find the amount of advertising they see "overwhelming" with another 56% finding it "more than ideal." (Oddly enough, 1% actually want more ads.)[35]

Beyond the sheer volume, frequent complaints about digital ads include them blocking desired content, auto-playing sound, slowing down the load or performance of a webpage, or being shown when they are not relevant to the customer.[36] In fact, the digital ads that U.S. internet users remember most aren't ads that are personalized or relevant or even helpful, but ads that they have seen too many times.[37]

Overall, they believe that companies are too aggressive in following them around online,[38] with 63% wishing they saw fewer targeted ads.[39] This holds especially true in the social media space, where 69% of users are either "somewhat concerned" or "very concerned" by social media companies targeting them with ads based on their data.[40]

Let's face it. Brands talk. All. The. Time. Everywhere. About their product. About themselves. About what's happening in the news. About anything and everything, even if it has nothing to do with them or the customer.

Like a talkative date who drones on and on, today's collective brand narrative has become a nonstop cacophony of chatter. And, just as they would in a conversation with a real person who won't shut up, people sooner or later find a way to excuse themselves from the table.

For customers, that means blocking or skipping these distractions.

More than a quarter of U.S. internet users block ads, up from just under 16% in 2014. And the rate is only expected to keep rising.[41]

"Pre-roll" fares far worse, with about 90% of users skipping these commercials-before-the-video either by switching to a different browser tab or hitting the "skip ad" button as soon as it's available.[42]

And speaking of video, when was the last time you watched live TV? If you still do, the chances are that you either left the room or looked at your phone/tablet when commercials came on. That's a pretty safe bet, with 87% of consumers using a second screen while watching TV.[43] If, instead, you watch something prerecorded on a DVR, there's a good chance you're one of the 86% of people who always fast-forward through the commercials.[44]

That is, of course, assuming you aren't one of the 31% of U.S. internet users who avoid TV commercials altogether by subscribing to a service such as Netflix, Hulu or Amazon Prime.[45]

Leadership Scandals

Rounding out the top reasons why people lose trust in a brand was "scandal with leadership in the company," which was selected by 36% of respondents.[46]

This is truly a "Wizard of Oz" problem. Unlike all the above elements, what the leadership of the company does is rarely an intentional part of the external, customer-facing brand. At least until Toto pulls back the curtain and we glimpse the men/women behind the brand, what decisions they're making, and what actions they're taking. At that point, we can't look away. We want to know who they are and what we're supporting when we buy from the Wizard.

How much do the executives make? How do they treat women and minorities? Which politicians do they support and what have they received in return? Are they cooking the books? Are they trading stock based on inside information? Have they cheated on their spouse? Have they bribed a university to enroll their children? Are they cutting corners on safety? What are they doing to the environment? In short, are they living the same "brand" that the company is trying to project?

There are a lot of switches and dials behind the green curtain, and customers want to look at them all, passing judgment on what they see.

———

As discussed before, regaining someone's trust doesn't happen quickly or easily. However, many brands seem to think otherwise. Either that or they just don't think there's a problem, that their customer is being a little sensitive or that, if they turn on the charm and post some fresh content, all will be forgiven.

Others (probably on advice of counsel), don't do anything, ignoring it all, hoping it will just blow over.

Some will swear on a stack of bibles that they'll do better. They will promise to better protect your privacy, stop polluting the environment, reform their hostile work environment, or whatever, depending on what the misstep was. They might even send you a form letter apology (with an enclosed coupon!), but that doesn't exactly scream sincerity, does it?

In extreme cases, a company executive may even lose their job. A scapegoat, sacrificed to appease the gods of commerce.

Yet, somehow, no matter what the response, the behaviors for many brands never seem to change.

That's because they're behaviors. And behaviors don't just happen. They materialize when beliefs react with circumstances. So, the only way to truly change behavior is to identify and address those upstream drivers.

In the customer/brand relationship, the current decline in trust coincides with two huge societal changes over the last few decades: the rise of shareholder primacy as the dominant business model (the belief) and the emergence of modern information technology (the circumstances).

Put these two forces together and you have a perfect recipe for customer mistrust.

Shareholder Primacy (The Belief)

Born in the 1970s, the concept of shareholder primacy states that business executives should only concern themselves with one constituency (shareholders) and one goal (maximizing shareholder value, or MSV). According to this model, any expense or action taken by a manager that does not benefit shareholders is inappropriate. Instead, executives should solely concern themselves with efficiency, profit, and stock price.

Even if you hadn't heard the term "shareholder primacy" before you picked up this book, you almost certainly recognize the pursuit. It has become standard business practice. This is how business leaders measure success: If it's good for shareholders, it's the right thing do to.

Focusing so much on shareholders is problematic for many reasons, as we'll see later. But one that bears mentioning now is that shareholder primacy is a *management philosophy*. That is, it is designed as guidance for the people working *inside* the corporate walls. It is not meant to be part of the *external* marketing or sales process since, by definition, it doesn't even mention the customer.

As long as this belief is isolated and contained inside the corporate walls, it could, theoretically, be beneficial to the people running the business part of the business.

But how often do things stay neatly isolated and contained?

Information Technology (The Circumstances)

It's an understatement to say that a lot has been written about the rise of information technology and its impact on our world: the way digital data, computers, fiber optics, cellular networks, the internet, search engines, social media, and artificial intelligence (among other things) have played major roles in transforming fundamental portions of our life: How we communicate, learn, work, shop, and even date have all changed radically in less than a generation.

Historically, the adoption of new technologies (and the subsequent effect they have on our lives) has happened much more slowly. Consider this: it took 76 years from the time Alexander Graham Bell made the first telephone call until landlines could be found in 50% of U.S. households.[47] The cell phone hit the same milestone in just 28 years.[48] Smartphones? Twelve years.[49] And social media reached 50% usage in just seven years.[50]

Humans have a hard time with rapid change. Evolution has taught us to look before we leap and to abandon tried-and-true at our own peril. (That's one reason why it takes, on average, 12-15 years for a new drug to go from the laboratory to the pharmacist's shelf.[51] Our lives are at stake.)

So, try as we might, we (and our institutions) are having a hard time understanding all the implications of this technological blitzkrieg — not to mention adapting to them.

Two of the biggest ramifications we struggle with are these:

1. We all have seemingly endless amounts of information at our fingertips.
2. We can all instantly communicate our thoughts around the world, virtually for free.

On the surface, these facts may sound innocuous, but they have created an unprecedented level of transparency that continues to surprise us. Everywhere we go, the walls have turned to windows and everything we do is there for the world to see.

Being self-conscious, it's only natural that we start curating our lives for this ever-present audience. We check our teeth in the mirror, walk a little taller, and consider our words and actions a bit more before we release them.

The same holds true for brands. They've updated their websites, created social media handles and hashtags, and media-trained their executives on what to say (and what not to say). Yet, despite all this customer-centric preening, brands seem to have overlooked one REALLY BIG THING.

That is, while a company may claim it's *customer-centric*, its actions show that it is actually *shareholder-centric*. These are actions we can see, thanks to the transparency created by modern information technology.

This massive contradiction creates cognitive dissonance and mistrust that is almost impossible to overcome. It's like being on a first date and noticing a wedding ring on the other person's hand.

How do you explain that?

For brands, this competing narrative is a gale-force headwind that diminishes the impact of all their marketing efforts, making it harder to gain traction at every step along the customer journey.

It's not just a brand problem. It is *the* brand problem, driving every single one of the "trust breakers" customers cited above. And until it's fixed, companies' relationships with their customers will continue to deteriorate, becoming more and more antagonistic, growing further and further apart.

So how do you fix this problem? How do you turn off this headwind? Fortunately, this headwind is self-inflicted, which means that companies can turn it off all by themselves. All they have to do is change what they believe.

As hard as this sounds (i.e., changing the dominant business model of the day), there really is no other choice. No one can put the technological genie back in the bottle. The circumstance (transparency) is here to stay.

2

WHO'S TO BLAME?

Joseph Takagi: "You want money? What kind of terrorists are you?"
Hans Gruber: (Laughing) "Who said we were terrorists?"

— *DIE HARD*, 1988

B lame is underrated.

When something goes wrong and we're injured, ripped off, pissed off, or just plain frustrated, we all want someone to be held accountable. While it may sound petty, it's not. Our entire legal system is based on the rule of law and the threat of punishment for the right person when someone breaks that law.

The key, of course, is to find the right person. Punishing the wrong person does nothing productive. It doesn't solve the problem. It hurts someone who wasn't responsible. And it weakens faith in the whole concept of justice.

The same holds true for lesser infractions that don't require police involvement or a lawsuit. To fix the problem you need to start by finding the right person.

However, when the offending person is a company, this gets a bit tricky. Yes, corporations are technically "persons" in a legal sense, but you really can't yell at one without yelling at a person who works for the company.

Usually, the person being yelled at works in some sort of customer service position — someone whose job it is to interact with the public when they have a complaint or (in rare cases) a compliment. As a call center director at DIRECTV once so wisely told me, "Customer service is 99% about recovery. By the time they call us, they're already mad." As a result, companies religiously train customer-facing personnel in how to deal with upset customers; how to listen patiently; how to document all the facts; and, most importantly, what the company can (or can't) say or do in response.

So, whether it's in person, on the phone, in email, or on social media, when you're communicating with one of these professionals, they're not being themselves. Literally. They're conduits, running the company's playbook. You may be talking with a person, but you're dealing with the company.

If you reach an impasse that isn't covered by their training, they've been taught to escalate the matter to a manager — a supervisor who has more training, experience, and responsibility. They're more empowered to determine what a company can say and do for a given situation.

Of course, these supervisors also have supervisors. Everyone has a supervisor, all the way up the chain of command until you reach the head of the company. By definition, the buck stops with the CEO. They are ultimately responsible for everything that happens at the company. (Yes, some companies have a board of directors that can remove a CEO, if necessary, but boards rarely involve themselves in day-to-day business.)

So, Let's Blame the CEO

As the singular head of an enterprise, a CEO today is an almost mythical creature, believed to be both omniscient and omnipotent. Nothing happens at a company without their knowledge and approval.

This is, of course, ludicrous. There's no way the CEO can be briefed or consulted on everything. At best, they can manage their immediate leadership team, deferring to them and the cascading hierarchy below for everything else. But, as companies have become more dominant in society, popular culture has responded by elevating these mere mortals to personalities, if not downright celebrities. Think Steve Jobs. Sir Richard Branson. Elon Musk.

When times are good, this party is great for everyone. The CEO gets their ego stroked. The corporate brand is personified. And the rest of us want to do business with the company run by such a successful, larger-than-life person.

In this respect, today's CEO provides the ultimate celebrity endorsement. And like any celebrity endorsement, it's subject to a "morals clause" (even if it's implied), where bad or questionable behavior can result in a breach of that contract, and them being jettisoned from the company.

Morals clauses appeared in the early 1920s as a way to protect a company's reputation from the unsavory exploits of its employees' personal lives. A radical idea at the time, the first application appears to have been in 1921, when Universal Studios demanded that silent movie star Roscoe "Fatty" Arbuckle sign such a contract. Universal felt compelled to take this unusual step after he was accused of the rape and manslaughter of actress Virginia Rappe, following a party hosted by Arbuckle at the St. Francis Hotel in San Francisco. While ultimately acquitted after three trials, Arbuckle's alleged actions were so widely reported that Universal feared it would be irrevocably tarnished by them. The text of the clause read:

> *"The actor (actress) agrees to conduct himself (herself) with due regard to public conventions and morals and agrees that he (she) will not do or commit anything tending to degrade him (her) in society or bring him (her) into public hatred, contempt, scorn or ridicule, or tending to shock, insult or offend the community or outrage public morals or decency, or tending to the prejudice of the Universal Film Manufacturing Company or the motion picture industry. In the event that the actor (actress) violates*

any term or provision of this paragraph, then the Universal Film Manu-
facturing Company has the right to cancel and annul this contract by
giving five (5) days' notice to the actor (actress) of its intention to do so."[1]

Fast on the heels of the Arbuckle contract, Colonel Jake Ruppert, owner of the New York Yankees, had his star player sign a similar contract in 1922 requiring him to "refrain and abstain entirely from the use of intoxicating liquors and that he shall not during the training and playing season in each year stay up later than 1 o'clock A.M. on any day without the permission and consent of the Club's manager."[2] The player in question? Babe Ruth.

Today's CEOs are rarely tripped up by drinking, drugs, sexual promiscuity, or other illegal activity in their personal lives. Sure, Elon Musk smoking a joint during a podcast in 2018 raised more than a few eyebrows and temporarily knocked nine points off Tesla's stock price.[3] And Gurbaksh Chahal was rightfully dismissed as the head of the RadiumOne online advertising network after he was charged with 45 felony counts stemming from a security video that allegedly showed him hitting and kicking his girlfriend 117 times before attempting to suffocate her in their San Francisco home.[4]

Instead, business leaders nowadays are much more likely to be taken down by how they behave at work. In 2018, a record 18% of CEOs at global public companies were replaced by their boards of directors. And, for the first time ever, the number one reason wasn't financial performance. It was "ethical lapses," an issue that has been growing in significance for the last decade.[5]

So, what's happening here? Have executives suddenly become more immoral? Of course not. The vast majority of CEOs, like the vast majority of the general population, aren't evil, hell-bent psychopaths intent on dominating the world. They don't live inside a volcano on a tropical island, laughing maniacally and petting a cat while launching nuclear-tipped missiles. They're normal folks, just like you and me, with spouses, kids, friends, mortgages, empty toilet paper rolls, and phones that don't always work.

What's changed is *transparency*. Thanks to information technology, more and more of what CEOs do at their job is visible to the public, increasing the chance that any action can trigger the next social media storm or customer boycott.

Remember that saying, "it ain't a crime if you don't get caught"? Well, increased transparency means more executives are getting caught for things they've always done: Making decisions that benefit the company over the rest of the world. Things like avoiding corporate taxes by having profit go through an overseas subsidiary, using contractors instead of employees to avoid paying for benefits, or mandating arbitration agreements in contracts so that legal disagreements remain secret.

That is their job, after all. To do what's best for the company.

For a long time, we've collectively accepted the paradox that people live two distinct and separate lives: work and personal. How many times has a heartbreaking action at work (such as a termination) been followed by the phrase, "it's not personal, it's business"? It's a rationale for the conflicting roles many people play. It rings hollow but it can help people go home and sleep at night.

But increased transparency is quickly eroding this demarcation. The public is seeing businesspeople as people and demanding that they be held accountable for their actions, even at work.

At the same time, companies aren't willing to accept worse performance. (Note that the number two reason why a record number of CEOs were fired in 2018 was "poor financial performance.") It's a conflicting duality where executives are "damned if they do and damned if they don't."

Take, for example, the story of Sir Mark Moody-Stuart, former chairman of the petroleum giant Royal Dutch Shell. While at home in rural England one day, Moody-Stuart and his wife, Judy, were surprised to look outside and see a group of about 25 protesters, some wearing masks, walking up their driveway. The protesters proceeded to climb onto the roof of their cottage and hang up a large banner that read "murderers." Another banner read "Earth First."[6]

Prepared for an altercation, the protesters got just the opposite. Moody-Stuart and his wife walked outside, introduced themselves, and asked their visitors about their beliefs and why they were protesting. The protest against the chairman of the Royal Dutch Shell turned into a rather civil two-hour conversation (including tea and coffee, served by the Moody-Stuarts.) Along the way, both sides discovered that they were all people worried about the same things: climate change, oppressive regimes, human rights, etc. And the protesters realized the problem wasn't Moody-Stuart. It was the company, Royal Dutch Shell.[7]

Former MIT professor Noam Chomsky is more dramatic, likening the distinction between a businessperson and the company they work for to the difference between a slave owner and slavery:

> *"So, slavery [...] or other forms of tyranny, are inherently monstrous, but the individuals participating in them may be the nicest guys you could imagine — benevolent, friendly, nice to their children, even nice to their slaves, caring about other people. I mean, as individuals they may be anything. In their institutional role they're monsters because the institution is monstrous. And then the same is true here."*[8]

Okay, Then Let's Blame the Company

The list of companies that have been disgraced by their monstrous behavior is as long as it is shocking. A sampling from my lifetime includes some real low points for human life, the environment, and the simple concept of telling the truth:

Bhopal Disaster — The world's deadliest industrial accident involved the release of 40 tons of highly toxic methyl isocyanate gas from a pesticide factory in central India. The plant, owned by Union Carbide (now part of Dow Chemical), had suffered from years of corporate neglect, with many safety systems completely inoperable. The overnight leak killed at least 3,787 people[9] and injured more than a half a million.[10]

Deepwater Horizon — The world's largest oil spill occurred after a deadly explosion on board an offshore oil platform in the Gulf of Mexico. Investigations found that cost-cutting, gross negligence, and reckless conduct by BP and its partners had caused the disaster, which killed 11 people and leaked a staggering 210 million gallons of oil, covering over 68,000 square miles of ocean (an area the size of Oklahoma.)[11] As of 2015, BP had already paid $54 billion (that's with a "B") for the cleanup, environmental and economic damages, and penalties.[12]

Volkswagen Emissions Scandal — The German carmaker intentionally programmed millions of its diesel cars to activate their emissions controls only during laboratory emissions testing, allowing them to pass U.S. Environmental Protection Agency (EPA) requirements. The cars, which were marketed as having new "Clean Diesel" technology, emitted up to 40 times more toxic emissions in real-world driving. Volkswagen denied the cheating for over a year, blaming it on "technical glitches," only admitting the deception when presented with indisputable evidence taken from portable emissions testing devices, which measured levels while a car was actually driving.[13]

If any of these companies were people, we would have locked them up in prison, where they couldn't hurt society anymore. Yet, all three companies remain free, alive, and kicking to this day.

It's an odd exception to the way we tend to anthropomorphize companies. We ascribe them human characteristics, describe their actions as if they were a real person, and even make them our "friends" on social media.

We do this because we humans are extremely social creatures, and our default relationship model is human-to-human. It's a lens we're comfortable with and, for the most part, applying that lens to inanimate objects seems to work for us. Have you ever named your car? A houseplant? A musical instrument? These things are important to you. So much so that they have earned quasi-human status.

Companies are well aware of this, of course, so they invest a ton of time and money into creating and expressing "brand personalities." The hope is to clearly position themselves not as a collection of hundreds or thousands of disparate employees, but as a single relatable entity you'll want to spend time and money with.

But if this institution really was an individual, would they be the kind of person you would hang out with?

In his 2005 book, *The Corporation: The Pathological Pursuit of Profit and Power*, author and filmmaker Joel Bakan asked as much of Dr. Robert D. Hare, a Canadian psychologist and creator of the Hare Psychopathy Checklist — the standard tool used by mental health professionals around the world to diagnose if someone is a psychopath.

The results of the test were simultaneously shocking and unsurprising: Modern corporations are a "close match," demonstrating many of the same behaviors as psychopaths such as Ted Bundy, Jeffrey Dahmer, and Charles Manson.

The institution (not the individuals who work there) is consistently:

- **Irresponsible** (putting its own corporate goals above everyone else)
- **Manipulative** (especially when it comes to public opinion)
- **Superficial** (always presenting themselves to the public in a way that is appealing)
- **Grandiose** (insisting they're the best or "number one")
- **Asocial and lacking in empathy** (not truly concerned with those they interact with)
- **Unable to feel remorse or accept responsibility for their own actions** (often paying fines for breaking the law, but not changing their behavior)[14]

Sound like any companies you know?

The psychopathic diagnosis is yet another disconnect in our relationships with brands. We like *so much* about them, but deep inside, we get the feeling there's something unhealthy about them, not to mention our relationships with them.

To paraphrase Albert Einstein, "you can't judge a fish by how it climbs a tree." Nor can you judge a company for not acting in a more "moral" fashion. True, corporations are "persons" in the eyes of the law. But they're not "natural persons" like you and me. So, we can't expect them to act morally, any more than we can expect a building, an organizational chart, or a contract to.[15]

As Bakan so eloquently put it, a corporation's legal construct compels them to "cause harm when the benefits of doing so outweigh the costs. Only pragmatic concern for its own interests and the laws of the land constrain the corporation's predatory instincts, and often that is not enough to stop it from destroying lives, damaging communities, and endangering the planet as a whole."[16]

Over the last few decades, the number one self-interest for corporations has been generating profit.

Profit is, of course, a simple construct: bring in more revenue than you pay in expenses. Consequently, there are two ways to increase profit: raise revenue or lower expenses.

Raising revenue is hard. It requires a company to invest significant time and money coming up with something of value before convincing a person to voluntarily pay for it.

Lowering expenses, on the other hand, is relatively quick and easy. The equation flips. The company becomes the customer, letting suppliers invest time and money creating products and courting them. As the customer, the company only has to decide what price it's willing to pay.

If the buying company is looking to make more profit, it simply negotiates a lower price with its current suppliers. (Walmart is famous for this, demanding regular cost cuts in order to "maintain the business.") The rationale shared with the supplier is often as simple as, "we don't have that in the budget" or "we need to cut costs." If the current supplier can't meet the new terms, the company will just go to a different supplier or even substitute goods or services of lessor quality — whatever it takes to reduce expenses and grow its margin.

Of course, the best way for a company to reduce expenses is to not pay anything at all for costs it incurs. Economists call these one-sided transactions "externalities" and they're the equivalent of a company eating dinner at a restaurant but skipping out before the bill arrives.

Nobel Prize-winning economist Milton Friedman defined an externality as "the effect of a transaction ... on a third party who has not consented to or played any role in the carrying out of that transaction."[17] Since someone who receives no benefit ends up paying the price, externalities are considered market failures. And companies have gotten very, very good at leveraging these failures, essentially making their costs other people's problem. (Remember that one key characteristic of psychopaths is that they are unable to accept responsibility for their own actions.)

A simple example of an externality is air pollution. A company whose production process generates large amounts of carbon monoxide or carbon dioxide must do something with these toxic gases. If there was a market for them, the company could sell them as a byproduct. Unfortunately, that's not the case, so the company has two other options: pay for someone else to dispose of it or pay nothing and release it into the atmosphere. Given the choice, most companies would not pay the additional cost and just let the gases escape into the air. In doing so, they are receiving a benefit (i.e., disposing of the unwanted gas) without paying any cost. The cost (the impact of these toxic gases on the environment and human health) is borne by everyone else on the planet.

Before the 18th century, the aggregate "cost" of combustion-related emissions was much smaller, and scientists didn't understand the impact of these pollutants on our world and our bodies. But starting with the industrial revolution, the volume of these emissions skyrocketed, as did their impact, driving the science that discovered exactly what large quantities of these chemicals can do. Hundreds of years later, the consequences of air pollution are well understood. So, it's difficult for companies to claim ignorance of this very damaging externality.

Yet, many companies persist in denying the science, even when their own scientists agree it's a problem.

As one of the largest oil and gas companies in the world, Exxon-

Mobil clearly has a vested interest in our society's continued use of fossil fuels. They employ thousands of the world's smartest and best scientists and engineers, leveraging their expertise to better understand everything about oil. In the 1970s and 1980s, this quest for knowledge included understanding the impact of burning fossil fuels on the environment. In fact, for much of those decades, Exxon was considered a pioneer in climate change research, conducting its own studies, as well as collaborating with universities to better understand how internal combustion engines were changing the planet.[18]

As early as 1977, Exxon scientists reported to company executives that there was general scientific agreement that burning fossil fuels was the most likely way mankind was influencing climate change. The significance of those temperature increases on the planet and humanity was further detailed to Exxon management in 1982, describing the "considerable adverse impact including the flooding of some coastal land masses as a result of a rise in sea level due to melting of the Antarctic ice sheet."[19] The path to this future was mapped in climate models created by Exxon scientists. These models predicted that, if fossil fuel use remained unchecked, carbon dioxide would increase to over 400 parts per million (ppm) by 2020.

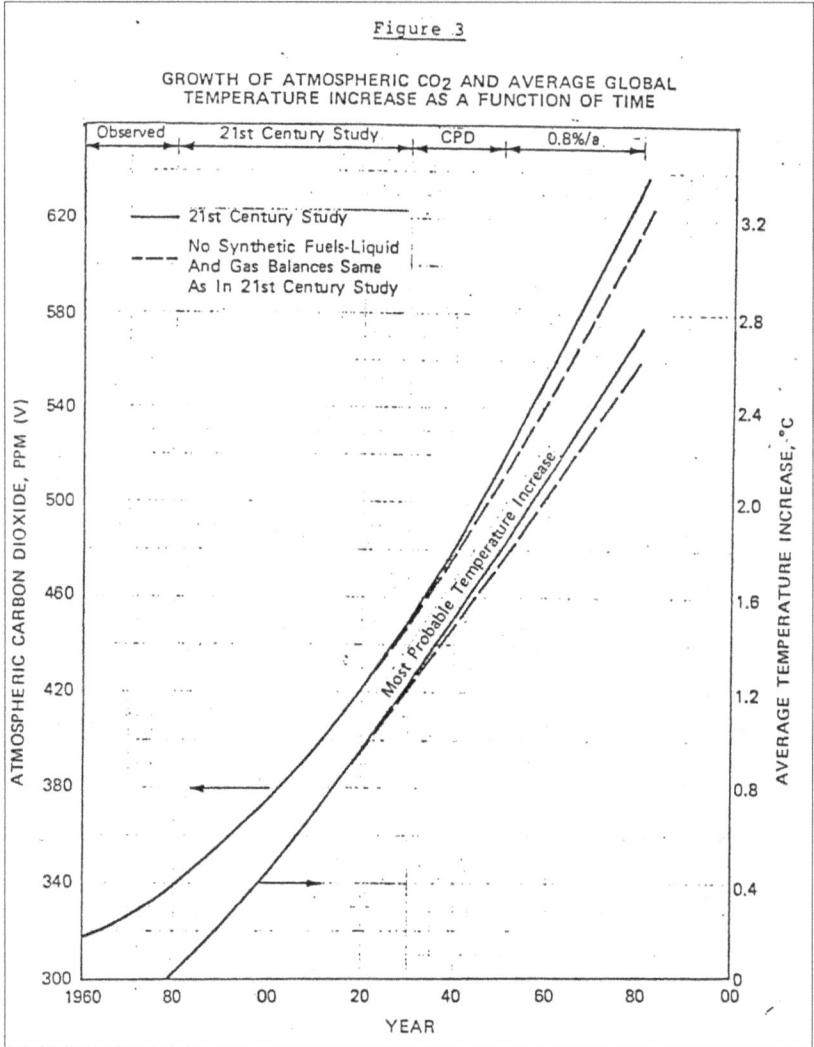

Internal Exxon climate change model from 1982.

It's worth noting that carbon dioxide measurements taken at the Mauna Loa Observatory in Hawaii first reached 400 ppm earlier than this prediction, in 2013. Measurements are now consistently above 400 ppm, a level not seen since the Miocene period, 16 million years ago.[20]

Upon learning about the catastrophic consequences of its

industry in the 1980s, what did Exxon management do? Did it adapt its business model, exploring other, cleaner sources of energy? Or did it put significant effort into discovering ways to mitigate the climate-altering effects of burning fossil fuels?

Of course not.

Seeing a threat to its existence and profitability, ExxonMobil shifted its position on climate change from "research pioneer" to publicly questioning its very existence. During the 1990s and 2000s, ExxonMobil spent millions of dollars funding lobbyists, advertising campaigns and organizations that all deliberately spread misinformation about climate change and the scientific consensus surrounding it. Along the way, the company utilized many of the same strategies, tactics, organizations, and personnel the tobacco industry used in its denials of the link between lung cancer and smoking.[21]

The target of these efforts was not just the general public, but also key government officials, who are the only ones who could impose industry-altering regulations on Exxon.

To a great degree, ExxonMobil was successful in its efforts to preserve the status quo. The public conversation shifted from how to address the threat of climate change to arguing if it was even real and if human activity was to blame. These seeds of doubt blossomed into a resistance to taking any action that might damage our economy and way of life, especially if there was any uncertainty that the problem was real.

Perhaps ExxonMobil's biggest "win" was its influence in stopping ratification of the Kyoto Protocol by the United States Senate.[22] The U.S. (which accounts for 36% of global emissions[23]) is one of only four countries (along with Andorra, Palestine, and South Sudan) not to have ratified the protocol,[24] which seeks to halt climate change and mitigate its impact on human existence.

However, as scientific evidence continues to mount that climate change is real and 97% of active climate scientists agree that human activity is significantly contributing to it,[25] ExxonMobil has had to shift its position.

In 2007, ExxonMobil finally acknowledged the risk of climate change in a filing to the SEC. Interestingly, the risk they focused on was not the risk to the planet, but the risk to their profits.[26]

Having acknowledged the concept of climate change, Exxon-Mobil is currently trying to regain the mantle of scientific leadership in the area. Its website now touts its 40 years of climate change research[27] — a claim designed to foster the idea that it understands the situation and should be trusted to address it appropriately, without any government regulations that might hurt its business. Interestingly, while it admits the threat from the use of fossil fuels is real and serious, it also publicly declares its intention to extract and sell all 25.2 billion barrels of petroleum in its reserves.[28]

But if the people and the governments of the world decide that regulation is appropriate, ExxonMobil also says it would support a carbon tax.[29] Such a tax, which is already in place in over two dozen countries around the world,[30] would finally start to internalize the externality of carbon emissions, essentially forcing fossil fuel customers to pay for the release of carbon dioxide into the atmosphere, thereby driving down demand for fossil fuels.

Indeed, the one thing companies fear is the government.

The government is the only institution left that has any real power over them. The church, once the dominant institution in the world, holds no sway. The church's promise of eternal life means nothing to an entity that frequently outlives its employees and executives. For instance, Kongō Gumi Co., Ltd., a Japanese construction company, stayed continuously in business for over 1,400 years, until it finally failed in 2006.[31]

To quote Edward Thurlow, Lord Chancellor of England in the 18th century, corporations have "no soul to be damned and no body to be kicked."[32] Which also makes it pretty hard to put one in jail. And, thanks to limited liability protection (and the fact that corporations are considered persons in their own right), the misdeeds of a company rarely result in its employees, executives or shareholders going to jail on the company's behalf. Instead, most corporate punishment involves a fine. And companies can sometimes avoid paying the fine, opting to be put on short-term probation instead.

That said, the government does hold one incredibly powerful card. It can kill a company. After all, state governments grant life to corporations when they are first chartered. So, these same state governments could revoke a corporation's charter, in essence, killing it. This card has only rarely been played, primarily against small companies that have refused to pay their taxes for multiple years.

With mortality not being a concern, companies instead tend to focus on removing impediments to their success. Key among these are the laws and regulations that seek to protect consumers, employees, shareholders, and the environment from a company's actions. The impact of these restrictions on companies is very real, forcing them to internalize (i.e., pay for) costs that would otherwise externalize onto society and the environment.[33] So companies put significant time, money, and effort into weakening or removing them altogether.

Their argument usually focuses on how regulations are "bad for business," implying they are consequently bad for consumers, employees, and other natural persons. In abstract, this is, of course, true. Heavy-handed regulations can exact a toll on the very people they're designed to protect. But unmitigated corporate power also exacts a toll — something which is rarely discussed by companies and the pro-business politicians they help to elect in an effort to dismantle government oversight from the inside.

Similarly, companies in a specific industry will often come together and try to convince regulators that, united, they can be "self-regulated" in place of governmental oversight. In this respect, they're like a group of teenagers, arguing to their parents that they don't need a chaperone at prom. One has to question if a group of them would be more responsible, or if it would just make matters worse. After all, teenagers are teenagers. And companies are companies.

Bakan sums it up nicely:

Deregulation [...] rests upon the suspect premise that corporations will respect social and environmental interests without being compelled by government to do so. No one would seriously suggest that individuals should regulate themselves, that laws against murder, assault, and theft are unnecessary because people are socially responsible. Yet oddly, we are asked to believe that corporate persons — institutional psychopaths who lack any sense of moral conviction and who have the power and motivation to cause harm and devastation in the world — should be left free to govern themselves.[34]

So, like most things in life, the key is finding the best balance. In this case, that would be the right amount of oversight that maximizes not only protection for natural persons, but also the benefits that companies provide to those same real people.

Another argument the company uses to advance its interests is the one for privatization — the notion that private industry can take over many functions handled by government (particularly those that are a natural monopoly) and do them faster, better, and cheaper. It's a very appealing pitch that serves two corporate goals: First, it expands the footprint of the private sector, giving companies another area from which to harvest profit. Second, it shrinks the overall importance of government, further weakening the one real institutional check on corporate power.

In practice, privatization has been a mixed bag. In many cases, the initial impact of free-market competition has provided increased efficiency for the general public — a positive, to be sure. But, over time, the *self-interest* of the company begins to conflict with the *public interest*. The drive for more profit can lead to price increases and/or reduced service quality — actions that are in direct conflict with the very concept of the public sector, where everyone in society, regardless of their ability to pay, is entitled to basic services that provide safety, security, and stability.

For an extreme example of what public services can look like when delivered by private enterprise, consider what firefighting was like in the 19th century — before it became a municipal responsibility. Neighborhoods were served by multiple volunteer fire societies, which competed to be the first to arrive at a fire. While the spirit of this competition initially led to faster response times (fire insurance companies would often pay a cash prize to the first fire company to start putting water on a burning building), the desire to win had gotten out of hand by the 1850s.[35]

As dramatized in the 2002 film *Gangs of New York*, fire companies utilized "plug guards" — auxiliary groups who would rush to the scene of a fire, place barrels over the fire hydrants and sit on them until their engine showed up. When multiple fire companies did arrive on the scene, it was not uncommon for them to throw rocks or physically attack each other. In 1851, two of Cincinnati's volunteer fire companies "crossed paths on the way to a fire in a planing mill, and before the fight was over ten companies were involved. Help was sent from Covington, Kentucky, across the river — not help to put out the fire, but to assist one of the volunteer companies in the fist fight. The planing mill burned to the ground."[36]

More modern examples of the failure of privatization aren't as violent but are just as scandalous. Take the City of Chicago, which privatized its parking meters via a 75-year contract starting in 2008, only to see hourly rates rise from $3/hour to $6.50/hour just five years later. This was despite the city having to pay the company for every single meter taken out of commission for construction or for public events, such as parades.[37]

Or take the State of Michigan, which canceled a private contract to provide all of its prison meals after unsanitary conditions (including maggots in the food) were discovered, not to mention the surfacing of allegations involving private employees engaging in sexual activity with prison inmates.[38]

It goes without saying that the institution of government is far from perfect. Throughout history, societies where government played an overly dominant role have suffered mightily. And I guess that's the point. A world dominated by the pursuit of profit is just as problematic as one dominated by the public interest. In reality, the best outcomes seem to come from having a check and balance between the two.

It all goes back to trust. In this case, a quote from Charles Dickens' *Nicholas Nickleby* (1839) seems appropriate: "You may trust them as far as you can see them, and no farther."

Government is, relatively speaking, fairly transparent. We pay taxes and elect officials to serve the common good and, in return, we receive a fair amount of a visibility into their actions. It's not complete but, compared to private industry, we see a huge amount of information about its process, its participants, and its outcomes in the "public record," which is accessible by anyone.

Contrast this to the private sector, which is fairly opaque. We have no choice but to believe what companies choose to share. In fact, government oversight is often the only way society has been able to find out what's really going inside corporate America. And regulations are sometimes the only recourse available to influence business actions that impact us and our world.

However, the rise of information technology over the last few decades has increased society's visibility into companies as well as provided an alternative way for the populace to express concerns over corporate behavior.

What we've seen, of course, is many brands with split personalities, where the company's charming, customer-focused words clash with its predatory, profit-obsessed actions.

So how do brands move forward? How do they reconcile these two personas? Is it even possible to reform the corporate psychopath to make it a productive member of society?

I believe it is.

But first, it's important to understand how corporations became the way they are today. Because how a person (even a legal person) was raised explains a lot about their behavior.

So, to paraphrase David Byrne in the Talking Heads' "Once in Lifetime," "well, how did we get here?"

Corporations first appeared in ancient Rome. (In fact, that's where the term comes from: "corporare" is Latin for "to combine into one body," describing how the institution allowed groups of people to come together and act as one individual.) Ancient corporations were more social than the business-oriented corporations most of us think of today and included clubs, political groups, guilds, and even religious cults. But these early corporations had some of the same benefits as modern ones. This separate "individual" could own property, sign contracts, sue and be sued, and even outlive its members. Importantly, only the government (in this case, the emperor) could bestow "life" on a corporation, which made them, in a way, instruments of the government, serving the public good.

By the 17th century, governments had expanded the use of corporations to include more externally focused efforts, including the creation and monetization of colonies. Colonization is a massive undertaking, requiring huge amounts of capital to build, supply, and staff ships that would be gone for years at time, seeking new lands to capture, new peoples to conquer, and new resources to exploit. Before 1600, these costs and risks were shouldered by royalty, who also reaped all the rewards. Indeed, this was the model used to build the dominant empires of the day (Spanish and Portuguese). To compete with these much wealthier monarchies, the English and Dutch opened up their own colonization efforts to private investment, most notably through each country's respective "East India Company," created to challenge Portugal's dominion over the spice islands (part of modern-day Indonesia).

To boost participation, the Dutch and English introduced many features associated with modern corporations. They allowed outside contributions (meaning that you didn't have to be a member of the group to invest), limited liability (so your risk was limited to the money you invested, rather than everything you owned), and the ability to buy and sell shares on a secondary market (allowing investors to buy more shares or cash out after the "initial public offering"). These steps also loosened royal control over corporations, allowing them more freedom to act how they wanted.

These new corporations were wildly successful, not just in driving financial returns for their investors, but also in helping to shift the balance of world power to England and Holland.

But these returns were not without cost. The fact that these corporations were acting, literally, on the other side of the world, allowed them to behave with impunity in the name of commerce. And I'm not just talking about the now-archaic belief that subjugating unknown peoples and cultures in far-off lands in order to access their resources is acceptable.

For example, while negotiating trading rights with the Sultan of Achin, representatives of the British East India Company were asked if they could provide a European girl for the Sultan's harem as part of the compensation. Intent on closing the deal, the representatives gladly agreed, with one of the managers even offering up his own daughter for the transaction. Only the governmental oversight of King James I stopped the girl from being handed over.[39]

The Dutch East India Company was no better, torturing and beheading 20 people (including ten employees of the rival British East India Company) on the suspicion that they had encouraged the ruling Sultan of Ternate to stop doing business with the Dutch in favor of the Spanish. The actions of the Dutch corporation greatly upset not just the English government, but also the Dutch government, which was trying to maintain an alliance with the English.[40]

Corporations continued to serve the purpose of the state for the next 200 years, with royalty (or in the case of the United States, the legislature) deciding which corporations could be chartered and which could not.

The lure of the corporate structure was so enticing to businesses by the time of the industrial revolution that, in the mid-19th century, the "royal charter" method of granting corporate status was expanded to include parliament/legislature even in monarchies,[41] meaning virtually anyone could create a corporation by applying to the government and paying a registration fee, leading to an explosion in the number of corporations doing business.

This change paralleled the shift away from monarchies as the dominant form of government across Europe. Just as people were rejecting the concept of being subservient to inherited royal rulers, they were also protesting how the benefits of corporate status were determined by the whim of a king or queen. People increasingly saw corporations as entities that deserved rights similar to theirs, including the "right to life" without royal permission.[42]

This concept, known as "Natural Entity Theory," created a monumental shift in corporations. No longer tied to royalty, they could do whatever their owners wanted them to do. In fact, before the late 19th century, corporations had to declare a very narrow and specific purpose for being when they were first chartered. Any activity outside of this purpose was prohibited. Similarly, corporate status was limited to a specific lifespan of 20, 30 or 50 years. With the emergence of Natural Entity Theory, today's corporations are both immortal and able to pursue "any lawful purpose" under their charters.

From there, corporations have only expanded on their freedoms.

In 1886, corporations achieved the same legal status as you and me. This legal "personhood" was achieved in a very odd fashion following the U.S. Supreme Court's decision in *Santa Clara County v. Southern Pacific Railroad Company*.

In this case, the railroad disputed the state's right to charge it higher property taxes than it would be subject to under federal statutes. The railroad won the case and that would have been the end of it, except the court reporter, J.C. Bancroft Davis, included a comment in the "headnote" of the decision (not part of the actual legal verdict) stating that an argument based on the Fourteenth Amendment to the U.S. Constitution had been presented during the trial. This argument, which claimed the "equal protection clause" of the amendment should apply to corporations and not just natural human beings, was not a determining factor in the case, nor was it included anywhere in the actual legal decision. But its inclusion in the headnote was seized upon by corporations, which successfully used it as a precedent to establish legal personhood over the following decades. In fact, between 1890 and 1910, corporations used this argument 288 times, whereas former slaves (for whose protection the amendment had originally been created) only cited it 19 times.[43]

In 1978's *Marshall, Secretary of Labor, et al. v. Barlow's, Inc.*, the Supreme Court held that, just like natural persons, corporations were protected from unreasonable "searches and seizures" thanks to the Fourth Amendment. Before this verdict, health and safety inspectors could just show up at a business to examine the workplace, looking for conditions that were dangerous for workers. Now, government inspectors have to give advance notice to corporations before a visit, unless they have enough evidence to secure a warrant from a judge.[44]

In 1986, corporations secured the right to free speech thanks to *Pacific Gas & Electric v. Public Utilities Commission*. In this case, the U.S. Supreme Court found that the State of California could not stop the utility from including pamphlets that promoted various political views with its monthly bills.[45]

And, of course, 2010's *Citizens United v. FEC* saw the Supreme Court remove restrictions on how much corporations could contribute to political action committees to influence the outcome of elections.[46]

Ironically, this quest for corporate-to-human equality has resulted in more than a few significant inequalities. After all, how many immortal trillionaires do you know?

As a natural person, you can do one thing corporations can't. Vote. Which is a distinction that wouldn't have lasted if Montana State Representative Steve Lavin had got his way. In 2013, he introduced a bill that would have allowed corporations that owned local property to vote in municipal elections. Fortunately, it died in committee.[47]

So, in many ways, today's companies are like teenagers. Earlier in their lives, their behavior was strictly controlled to ensure their worst, immature instincts didn't inflict too much damage. As they grew, they were given more and more freedom, rights, and privileges as they promised they would act responsibly. And we believed them, taking them at their word.

But over the last little while, something happened. The transparency of information technology has allowed us to see what these teenagers were really doing. Like a parent who finds their child's iPhone or diary, we've glimpsed a person very different from the one we thought we raised. Instead of a productive member of society who contributes to our world, we've discovered that we've raised a psychopath, one that is only concerned with itself and what it can get away with.

But let's not throw out our baby with the bathwater.

After all, our corporate creations aren't all bad. Over the last two centuries, their unique form, which allows individuals to benefit from pursuing a shared purpose, has accomplished a lot of good for humanity. Companies have helped raise life expectancy, increased the general standard of living, improved our understanding of the world, and even helped us to travel to the moon.

And, frankly, they are the only entities with the resources and capacity to solve some of the biggest challenges we face today, such as climate change, pollution, water shortages, and food insecurity. As we've seen, the private sector dwarfs the government in resources, accounting for 89% of U.S. GDP, compared to just 11% for federal, state, and local governments, combined.[48]

But over the last few decades, these resources have been applied in a very unbalanced fashion, with far too much effort being put into extracting value, rather than creating it.

To put it another way, their priorities are out of whack.

Finally, Let's Blame the Priorities

Most teenagers go through a selfish phase. Whereas previously they had behaved like relatively well-balanced children, puberty, and the need to define oneself as an individual, often knocks the pendulum too far toward immediate gratification with little concern for the bigger picture or long-term consequences.

It's the same with companies.

Before the current state of short-termism and hyper-selfishness, companies were a bit more balanced; it was called "managerialism"

or "managerial capitalism," and it started in 1932 when lawyer Adolf
A. Berle and Harvard professor Gardiner C. Means studied the way
publicly traded corporations were evolving. Specifically, Berle and
Means documented the fact that, as corporations grew and gained
more shareholders, these shareholders were less and less involved in
the running of the company. It's called "rational apathy" and it's the
very logical consequence of realizing that you own such a small frac-
tion of a company's shares, you can't have any real impact on the
company and its day-to-day operations. Instead, shareholders are
best served as passive investors, leaving the running of the company
to the directors and professional managers whose expertise is actually running a business.[49]

These professional managers were paid a fixed salary, owned relatively little stock and viewed themselves as "stewards or trustees
charged with guiding a vital social and economic institution in the
interests of a wide range of beneficiaries. Certainly, they looked out
for investors' interests, but they also looked out for the interests of
employees, customers, and the nation as well."[50] They realized that
all of these stakeholders were important to the long-term success of a
business, which is what everyone wants.

For the next half-century, managerialism was the dominant business model and it worked quite well. The period from the Great
Depression to the mid-1970s saw the U.S. rise as an economic superpower. Innovation flourished. Employee wages rose. And investors
cashed a steady stream of dividend checks. In fact, during this period,
the S&P 500 returned a compound average annual return of 7.5%.[51]
(Not bad for a "passive" investment.)

Then, in the early 1970s, the U.S. economy hit a rough spot.
Foreign competition was increasing, OPEC quadrupled the price of
oil, inflation spiked, and unemployment rose (a unique dual combination called "stagflation"). The resulting recession lasted for almost
two years and caused a downturn in the performance of the stock
market.

Eager to reverse the negative impact on investors, economist
Milton Freidman argued in a 1970 *New York Times Magazine* article

that the real problem was that business managers had too many competing priorities — a problem that could be easily solved if they put shareholders above all other stakeholders and focused solely on maximizing financial returns. Executives, he claimed, were employees of shareholders and, as such, have a "direct responsibility ... to conduct the business in accordance with their desires, which generally will be to make as much money as possible."[52]

Yes, shareholders do contribute something vital (i.e., capital) to the company. But other stakeholders are clearly necessary for success, each contributing something valuable in hopes of a favorable return on their investment. Employees contribute their time and expertise in exchange for a salary and experience. Customers contribute their money in exchange for a product that meets their needs.

So, to cherry-pick one stakeholder and say they are more important than the others is questionable to begin with.

Despite this, the concept took hold in academic circles, culminating in 1976's *Theory of the Firm*, by economist Michael Jensen and business school dean William Meckling. It expanded on the concept of "shareholder primacy," claiming that this change in priorities (from many to one) would lead to better outcomes for everyone through efficiency. Additionally, it would tie the hands of managers, prohibiting them from actions that could potentially lead to them enriching themselves instead of shareholders.[53]

In truth, managers were already prohibited from using their position to directly increase their personal wealth (via the "duty of loyalty") and thanks to federal disclosure requirements in the Securities Act of 1933 and the Securities Exchange Act of 1934, lining one's own pockets was a lot easier to see and prosecute.[54] So this "agency cost," as it was called, was more of a theoretical than real concern.

Nevertheless, Jensen and Meckling went so far as to suggest that the best way to ensure shareholder primacy was adopted was to make managers some of the largest stockholders in a company, changing their compensation from mostly salary to predominantly stock, thereby aligning the manager's personal interests with those of investors.[55]

The rest, as they say, is history.

Shareholder primacy supplanted managerialism and is now the dominant business management theory. The purpose of today's corporation is to make money, plain and simple.

That simplicity was a big reason why shareholder primacy took hold. Business is complicated. Trying to understand and balance a multitude of complex and competing priorities is difficult. Shareholder primacy simplified all of that, offering everyone a simple explanation of what was important (efficiency), as well as a single way to measure success (profit).

But business, like life, isn't that simple. The "sound bite" is always incomplete and, therefore, inaccurate. And just because you turn a blind eye toward reality doesn't mean that consequences don't start piling up — especially when you stop creating value and just extract it for shareholders.

Once you commit to the goal of maximizing shareholder value, you realize two things pretty quickly:

1. Shareholders only want value to go up, never down.
2. Shareholders want it to go up all the time.

So, while the rest of the natural world goes through seasons of growth and rest, businesses are not allowed this "luxury." This, even though key inputs, such as revenue, are not under their direct control.

Under shareholder primacy, investors are like the mafia: they must be paid, or else. So, if you can't be profitable based on revenue, you have to come up with their money somewhere else. And that means cutting expenses.

Of course, as we've seen, the problem with cutting expenses is that there is only so much fat, and you soon find yourself cutting the muscle that the company needs to stay competitive, invest in the future, and grow future revenues.

Which makes it harder to meet expectations the next time.

It's a vicious circle of short-term thinking — one that executives know is damaging. But in the world of shareholder primacy, they feel they have no choice. A 2006 survey found that 80% of corporate financial officers would "cut expenses like marketing or product development to make quarterly earnings targets, even if they knew the likely result was to hurt long-term corporate performance."[56]

This "short-termism" is reinforced by stockholders, who have become increasingly likely to trade a stock that disappoints them. Indeed, in 1960, annual share turnover for firms listed on the New York Stock Exchange was 12 percent. By 1987, this figure had grown to 73 percent. By 2010, annual turnover had reached 300%, meaning the average holding period for a share of stock is just four months.[57]

Don't feel too bad for the executives. Remember, they're some of the largest shareholders in modern corporations. Back in 1984, equity-based compensation accounted for *zero percent* of median executive compensation at S&P 500 firms. By 2001, this had risen to 66 percent.[58] As a result, these executives are all in favor of "pay for performance," even if it hurts other stakeholders or leaves a mess for their successor.

Of course, investors have always expected a return on their investment when a company is doing well, either through a dividend, paid by the company on a quarterly or annual basis, or through an increased share price (which is realized only when the shareholder sells their stock).

Of these two, only one (dividends) is an immediate cash flow issue for companies. Once a dividend is declared, checks have to be written.

Share price, on the other hand, is determined by the market, with gains paid out by the buyer to the seller. The company isn't directly involved in this transaction.

At least not usually.

But in 1982, as companies were discovering how hard it was to keep creating value without investing in the future, the Securities and Exchange Commission passed rule 10b-18, which legalized an alternative way for companies to increase the stock price: let the company directly buy back shares, taking them off the market.

Prior to this, stock buybacks (or "share repurchases") were considered market manipulation since they altered the stock price calculation, not by changing the value of the company, but simply by reducing the number of shares. (It's like cutting a pizza into fewer slices. The pizza itself didn't get any bigger, but each person's slice did.)

Buying back shares is a relatively quick and easy exercise, unlike the difficult, time-consuming task of growing a company. All it takes is cash — cash that, of course, can't be spent on research and development, business expansion, or employee compensation, making it even harder to be successful in the long term.

Nevertheless, stock buybacks have become the "belle of the ball" among public corporations. In 2018, corporations in the S&P 500 spent a record $753 billion on buybacks, up 40% from 2017 and more than triple the level of 2007. Buybacks now overshadow dividends (a mere $449 billion for those same companies in 2018), and, in that single year, stock repurchases reduced the number of shares outstanding by a full three percent.[59]

It's all part of "value extraction" where, if you have a penny, or even if you don't have it, it's your responsibility to pay it out. Indeed, many of America's largest corporations routinely distribute more than 100% of profits to shareholders, funding these payments by selling off assets, taking on debt or laying off employees.[60]

At its inception, shareholder primacy offered simplicity and the belief that focusing on profit would benefit everyone. Prices would drop, innovation would accelerate, and the world would become better — all because inefficiencies would be removed from the system.

It was a nice thought, but the constant, immediate demand for more and more profit has resulted in exactly the opposite.

Don't believe me?

Look at the pharmaceutical industry, where shareholder primacy has been taken to a whole new level, thanks to the high stakes of living and dying.

Prescription for Disaster

I think we all agree that modern medication is just one step short of magic. One tiny pill or shot can prevent, treat, or cure diseases that would have killed or crippled us just 100 years ago. Analgesics, anesthetics, antibiotics, antidepressants, antiseptics, contraceptives, insulin, statins, and vaccines are just a few of the discoveries that have made our lives both better and longer. As a society, we honor these advances and the people who made them.

Modern drug companies would like you to believe they are continuing that noble journey on behalf of the human race. PhRMA, the Pharmaceutical Research and Manufacturing Association (the trade group that represents U.S. pharmaceutical companies), declares on its website that the industry is "devoted to discovering and developing medicines that enable patients to live longer, healthier and more productive lives."[61]

But today's pharmaceutical industry bears little resemblance to the aspirational world of Edward Jenner, Louis Pasteur, and Alexander Fleming. It's frankly more at home with Cornelius Vanderbilt, John D. Rockefeller, and Andrew Carnegie. Or maybe Barry Keenan, who, in 1963, believed he was bringing Frank Sinatra's family closer together by kidnapping his son and holding him for a $240,000 ransom.[62]

Americans spend a LOT on drugs. Even though we're less than five percent of the world's population, we account for 30-40% of the global pharmaceutical market. We're taking more drugs than ever before,[63] with the average American handing over $1,162 for prescriptions in 2015 — roughly twice the amount that citizens of other industrialized countries spent.[64]

But it's not just the quantity of drugs that drives the total. Americans pay up to six times what the rest of the world pays for brand-name prescriptions. And total drug costs continue to rise, increasing by 6.3% in 2016, approximately three times the increase seen in other goods and services.[65]

So much money going to drugs translates into less money being available for other expenditures, including necessities such as groceries, utilities, or rent. Medicine means life. It's usually not seen as optional, so its cost can force people to take a second job or postpone retirement to ensure they can afford their medications.[66]

Before the 1970s, drug costs were rarely a concern for doctors or patients. But today, it's not surprising that 80% of Americans across the political spectrum list "lowering drug costs" as a top priority for lawmakers.[67]

Despite this exceptional level of spending, America isn't very healthy. Even though we spend more per capita on pharmaceuticals than any other nation, we only rank 34th in life expectancy. And U.S. life expectancy actually dropped in three out of the last four years before COVID-19, something that hadn't happened since 1910.[68]

There is one exception to this decline. One group whose health has never been better. The pharmaceutical companies. They're doing just fine, thanks for asking.

According to the U.S. Government Accountability Office, pharmaceutical and biotechnology revenue increased 45% from $534 billion in 2006 to $775 billion in 2015. During that same time frame, 67% of drug companies increased their annual profits, with some enjoying 20% higher margins in a single year. In fact, their profits over those ten years were larger than almost any other industry.[69]

Despite such obese, prolonged success, the pharmaceutical industry says there is nothing they can do about the high price of their products, or the fact that they just keep getting more expensive. They claim it's the price consumers must pay for them to continue to research and develop new medications.

It's a convenient narrative, based in fact. Yes, creating and getting approval for a new drug is a long and expensive process. But it's not the only (or largest) cost driving today's high prices.

Nine of the ten largest pharmaceutical companies spent more on sales and marketing in 2013 than they did on research and development. The largest, Johnson & Johnson, spent more than double the amount on sales and marketing ($17.5 billion versus $8.2 billion).[70]

Shareholder payments, including stock buybacks and dividends, also exceed spending on research and development. From 2006-2015, the top 18 pharmaceutical companies listed on the S&P 500 spent $516 billion on shareholder payments, compared to $465 billion on R&D. As a result, these companies paid out 99% of profits to their shareholders.[71]

This is all on top of compensation paid to pharmaceutical CEOs, who, on average, earned $44.7 million per person in 2015, 71% more than executives in other industries.[72]

In fact, spending on R&D has remained relatively flat, even as revenue and profits increased. Pharmaceutical industry revenue increased by 45% ($241 billion) from 2008 to 2014, but R&D spending only increased by 8.5% ($7 billion) during the same time frame.[73]

Money that is spent on research has increasingly focused on creating higher-margin drugs that help manage long-term conditions (ensuring a long-term customer), while largely ignoring the need for drugs that quickly cure common diseases. Case in point: in 1990, there were about 20 major companies working to create new antibiotics. Today, there are fewer than five, and the number of antibiotic compounds in development has fallen from 800 in 2014, to just 50 in 2016.[74]

This is despite the growth of drug-resistant bacteria over the last few decades, which was caused, in part, by the over-prescribing of antibiotics for both humans and livestock. In the U.S. alone, 2.8 million people every year are diagnosed with a drug-resistant infection, and at least 35,000 die from it.[75]

Yet, most large pharmaceutical companies don't consider antibiotics profitable enough to invest in developing new varieties. It's much more profitable to spend those funds on television and digital advertising, building brand name awareness among consumers, understanding they'll then go to their doctor and ask for a prescription drug by name. It's a practice that was unheard of before 1983 when Boots Pharmaceutical ran the first direct-to-consumer television commercial for its painkiller Rufen.[76] At first, the Food and Drug Administration objected, but eventually relented on the condition that the advertising included the long list of disclaimers that we're all familiar with.

Interestingly, most other countries have not followed America's lead on this issue. Only one other country, New Zealand, allows prescription drugs to be advertised directly to consumers instead of solely to doctors who have medical training and are ultimately required to write the prescription.[77]

Advertising isn't the only area in which regulations have been changed to favor the pharmaceutical industry. From 1980-1984, Congress passed, and President Ronald Reagan signed, a series of laws and executive orders that allow drug companies to use federal funds for portions of their research but still claim a monopoly patent on any drugs created from it. These taxpayer dollars represent approximately 25-30% of all pharmaceutical R&D spending and were used to help create *all* 210 drugs approved by the FDA between 2010 and 2016.[78]

Thanks to this patent protection, pharmaceutical companies can keep raising prices, with patients often having no alternative but to pay.

No drug has garnered more coverage for its price increases than the EpiPen. Designed to immediately treat life-threatening allergic reactions, the EpiPen packages about a dollar's worth of the generic drug epinephrine inside a unique, patented delivery device: a pen that automatically pierces clothing and the skin before injecting the drug into the patient. For a layperson suffering an allergic reaction, often nowhere near medical help, it is an amazing tool that can be used to stabilize them until they can get to a hospital. The estimated cost to create each pen is less than five dollars.[79]

Back in 2007, when Merck sold the EpiPen to Mylan Pharmaceuticals, the list price for an EpiPen two-pack was $93.88, creating a nice profit for whichever company owned the patent. Over the next ten years, Mylan raised the price 17 different times to $608.61, an increase of more than 500 percent.[80]

That's when, in 2017, the federal government claimed that Mylan had overcharged Medicaid $1.27 billion and wanted a refund. In response to the resulting public outrage over price-gouging, Mylan Chairman Robert Coury, who earned $97.6 million in compensation in 2016 (more than the CEOs of Disney, General Electric, and Walmart, combined) was not happy. At a board meeting, he reportedly cursed and gave two middle fingers to critics and parents of allergy sufferers.[81]

EpiPen's 500% price increase over ten years is far from the largest. Martin "Pharma Bro" Shkreli, at one time known as "the most hated man in America," raised the price of the malaria drug Daraprim from $13.50 a pill to $750 a pill in 2015 (a 5,000% increase). In 2018, Marathon Pharmaceuticals raised the price of its muscular dystrophy drug Emflaza over 6,000 percent. And, since 2000, Questcor Pharmaceuticals has increased the price of its epilepsy drug Acthar by an unbelievable 97,000 percent.[82]

A single vial now costs $39,000.[83]

Such massive increases are necessary to keep increasing profits and shareholder payments. Sure, they occasionally cause some public outrage, but the pharmaceutical industry has learned to deflate this anger through a little sleight of hand. When confronted about the high price of a drug, they change the topic to the co-pay, which is what patients pay out of pocket for a prescription.

That's exactly what Jeff Aronin, chairman and CEO of Marathon Pharmaceuticals, did when the *Chicago Tribune* asked him to defend the $89,000 per-year price tag for Emflaza. Claiming the drug was "affordable," he pointed out that if the drug is covered by the patient's health insurance, they would "pay a standard co-pay of typically $20 or less per prescription."[84]

Outrage dissipated. At least until you ask, "Who pays the rest?"

Certainly, Marathon isn't willing to settle for just $240 (assuming 12 prescriptions filled per year). Its CFO, Babar Ghias, publicly said as much, claiming that the company expected revenue of about $54,000 for each year's worth of the drug it sells (after the rebates and assistance it provides to uninsured and underinsured patients).[85]

(This is despite the fact that Marathon didn't develop the drug, which is available overseas for about $1,200 per year.)

So, who's paying the other $53,760?

Your health insurance company. And because they, too, are trying to maximize profits, the only way they can cover the increased cost is to increase your monthly premium and/or increase your deductible.

So, in the end, we all pay when pharmaceutical companies increase their prices. It's just a function of shareholder primacy's focus on short-term value extraction. All that money has to come from somewhere.

Of course, at some point, the impact of all this extraction becomes apparent. Much like a sinkhole that appears after too much groundwater has been extracted, after four decades of prioritizing shareholders, the effects are becoming clear.

———

NOT SURPRISINGLY, favoring shareholders over all other stakeholders has benefited investors. That was the whole point, after all.

Since June 1982, the Dow Jones Industrial Average has increased 15-fold (from 2,147 to over 34,000). The S&P 500 has increased 14-fold (from 289.92 to over 4,200). And the NASDAQ has increased 30-fold (from 440.30 to over 13,000). So, in aggregate, shareholder primacy has accomplished its goal of increasing the wealth of stockholders.

But not everyone owns stock. In fact, less than 50% of Americans own any stock at all, with only 35% owning $10,000 or more.[86] The vast majority of stock (89%) is owned by the richest ten percent of the country,[87] with over 40% concentrated in the richest one percent of Americans (those with an average net worth of at least $26.4 million and an average annual income of $2.3 million).[88] So, from the get-go, shareholder primacy was destined to disproportionately benefit the wealthiest among us.

But this bias hasn't just been limited to dividends and share price increases. The same holds true when you look at non-stock income (i.e., wages).

Between 1948 and 1973 (during the era of managerialism), productivity increased by 97%, meaning that the average worker produced almost twice as much per hour in 1973 as they did in 1948. Similarly, the average non-supervisory worker's compensation increased by 91% during that same period.[89]

From 1973-2013 (during the era of shareholder primacy), productivity continued to increase, improving by another 74% over those 40 years. But during this time frame, workers saw a greatly reduced benefit, with wages increasing by only nine percent.[90]

This gap between productivity and worker compensation allowed companies to reduce their "wage bill" and increase profitability — an accomplishment that was rewarded by increasing the wage of the top one percent of earners (that is, management) by 138% during the same time.[91]

Indeed, if wage growth for everyone had remained linked to productivity, the federal minimum wage (made by the poorest Americans) in 2014 would have been over $18/hour, providing them with 154% more to spend than the current $7.25/hour. Instead, CEOs now routinely make 300 times what the average worker makes, in contrast to 1978, when the average CEO only made 30 times the typical worker's pay.[92]

In 2018, Bob Iger, the chairman and CEO of Disney, earned $66 million in compensation, a staggering 1,424 times the $46,127 median salary for a Disney employee. Upon learning this, Abigail Disney, the multimillionaire granddaughter of Disney co-founder Roy Disney, exclaimed, "There's a point at which there's just too much going around the top of the system." She added that Iger's compensation was having a "corrosive effect on society," echoing a previous comment that "if your CEO salary is at the 700, 600, 500 times your median workers' pay, there is nobody on Earth ... Jesus Christ himself isn't worth 500 times his median workers' pay."[93]

This difference in compensation is called "income inequality," the tendency for income to be concentrated into a group (usually the wealthy) rather than being equally distributed among the population.

To be clear, unequal income itself is not a problem. In fact, research by Yale psychologists Christina Starmans, Mark Sheskin, and Paul Bloom found most people believe that some individuals *should* make more money than others — that effort, ability (and even luck) *should* drive better outcomes.[94] This preference is seen as beneficial, encouraging members of society to be productive.

What people do have a problem with is unfairness — specifically, unfairness in the system that determines the outcomes. People believe the playing field should be level for everyone and not skewed toward or against a particular group. In this respect, shareholder primacy is inherently unfair, giving the wealthy an advantage not enjoyed by any other group.

One tool our society uses to combat extreme income inequality is taxes. Tax proceeds not only pay for programs that benefit everyone (such as highways and national defense) but also serve as a mechanism to transfer financial resources to help improve the health, welfare, and education of people in disadvantaged socioeconomic classes.

When it comes to income taxes, rates are, generally speaking, higher for those who make more money and less for those who don't. Current federal tax brackets start at ten percent and go all the way up to 37% (for individuals making over $523,601 a year in income.) There are thousands of ways to reduce your taxes. You can take deductions, make charitable donations, or open an FSA for medical expenses, just to name a few.

But one of the simplest ways to significantly lower your taxes is to make your money from stock instead of a salary.

U.S. tax law treats capital gains (the proceeds you earn by selling stock for more than you paid for it) very differently than regular income (i.e., salary and wages.) Here's an example:

Let's say there are two people who both earn $300,000 in one year. The only difference is that one person earns money from a salary, while the other earns it by selling stock that they've held for more than year.

The person who earned their money from a salary will pay

$105,000 (35%) in federal taxes, where the stock seller will only pay $45,000 because the long-term capital gains rate is just 15%.

For older Americans, who often no longer earn a salary and, instead, pay their bills with the proceeds from retirement investments, this bias makes sense, helping them stretch out their funds to live a longer, better retirement without as much need for public assistance. But as we've seen, stocks aren't just the revenue source of retirees. Intergenerational inheritances and shareholder primacy have changed how the wealthiest Americans make their money.

Back in 1996, the richest one percent of Americans made 34% of their money from salary and wages, with 49% coming from investments. By 2006 (only ten years later), this had shifted to just 26% from salary and wages, and 57% coming from investments.[95]

When you compare this to the bottom 80% of Americans who, in 2006, earned 82% of their money from salary and wages, and just three percent from investments,[96] it's clearly the super-rich who now most benefit from this tax policy.

And at least one of them thinks it's a crime.

In a 2011 editorial for *The New York Times,* titled "Stop Coddling The Super-Rich," Warren Buffett, the billionaire CEO of investment giant Berkshire Hathaway, noted that, while he paid almost $7 million in federal taxes that year, it amounted to an effective tax rate of just 17.4% on his nearly $40 million of income, most of which had been earned through investments. In comparison, the staff in his office, which primarily made their money through salary, paid an average effective rate of 36 percent.[97]

"Unfortunately" for Buffet, he still benefits from this tax component of shareholder primacy. Even more so, because Congress and then-President Donald Trump expanded this preference by reducing the tax rate for corporations in 2017.

And while this change was sold on the promise of stimulating economic growth as well as providing sizable tax cuts for individuals, the Congressional Research Service found in May 2019 that it had done neither. GDP remained "level with pre-tax cut projections"[98] and "individual income taxes as a percentage of personal income fell slightly from 9.6% to 9.2%."[99]

However, the same report found that "the estimated average corporate tax rate fell from 23.4% to 12.1%."[100]

At the *Wall Street Journal*'s CEO conference held before the tax cut was approved, former Trump economic adviser Gary Cohn asked the gathered executives, "If the tax-reform bill goes through, do you plan to increase your company's capital investment? Show of hands." After very few hands went up, Cohen asked, "Why aren't the other hands up?"[101]

The answer, according to the CNBC Fed survey from early 2018, was that "corporations were planning to shunt money to shareholders, rather than putting it into research, mergers and acquisitions, equipment upgrades, training programs, or workers' salaries."[102]

What a surprise.

Note that the report by the Congressional Research Service did find that some companies paid workers a bonus after the tax cuts went into effect. These bonuses totaled $4.4 billion, which sounds like a lot. But it only represents two to three percent of the value of the tax savings. And with U.S. employment of 157 million, this equals just $28 per worker.[103]

That's a shame because people who make less money tend to spend most (if not all) of their income, putting it back into the economy. Conversely, those with higher incomes can't or don't spend it all, instead putting significant portions in stocks, bonds, and other investments. This wealth (i.e., accumulated income), provides a financial cushion of resources that can be used for large purchases, unexpected emergencies, or to not work at all (instead, earning money by loaning out your money).

And over the last 30 years, this "wealth inequality" has increased to levels even greater than income inequality.

According to a study by the Federal Reserve Board, in 1989, the top ten percent of Americans represented 61% of household net worth. By 2018, that had grown to 70% of the country's $100 trillion in wealth.[104] (A subset of that group, the top one percent, increased its holdings from 24% to 31%.)[105]

During the same time frame, the bottom 50% of Americans (the poorest half of our country) lost most of their net worth, dropping from four percent to just one percent of U.S. household wealth. Importantly, roughly half of this group's assets are their homes,[106] which are nowhere near as liquid as other types of investments. So, the level of available financial resources is much smaller.

All this economic inequality has led to the middle class getting smaller and smaller. Almost 70% of Baby Boomers were part of the middle class (those earning between 75% and 200% of median national income) when they were in their 20s. That number dropped to 64% for Gen X, and only 60% for Millennials. Currently, just over 50% of Americans are defined as middle class, much lower than the 61% in other developed countries.[107]

The middle class represents upward mobility — the ability to rise from the socioeconomic class into which you were born into one that offers a better quality of life. Think of it as climbing a ladder, with more money and other resources necessary to get you from rung to rung.

Before shareholder primacy, economic opportunities were more widely available, so it wasn't unreasonable for just about anyone to believe they could improve their position or that their children could be better off than they were. Climbing the ladder wasn't easy, but many people were able to work hard, make smart long-term choices, and move up.

However, as economic inequality has risen, upward mobility has become more difficult. For the average American, stagnant income and higher prices have increased the use of credit to maintain a standard of living. Reduced disposable income also means there's less money available to invest in things that lead to upward mobility (such as education), to invest for retirement, or to help future generations.

As a result, it's gotten harder to reach the next rung.

And thanks to the strong tendency of children in the U.S. to inherit their parents' economic advantages or disadvantages (an effect called "intergenerational income elasticity"), today's momentum toward greater economic inequality will continue for decades, all on its own. Based on this "coasting," Alan Krueger, former chairman of the White House Council of Economic Advisers, predicts that upward mobility is expected to be 25% harder for the next generation.[108]

To put it another way, the rungs on the ladder will grow farther apart.

Restricted social mobility isn't the only consequence of rising economic inequality. A wide range of research has shown it erodes the very foundations of society, causing negative impacts virtually everywhere you look:[109]

> **Higher under economic inequality:** child conflict, drug use, homicide, incarceration, mental illness, obesity, political instability, teenage births, and terrorism.
> **Lower under economic inequality:** community and civic involvement, economic growth, educational performance, fellowship, goodwill, happiness, life expectancy, mutual sympathy, satisfaction, social cohesion, social connectedness, trust among strangers, women's status, and even the number of patents issued.

Perhaps most importantly, economic inequality is a very real threat to democracy. As the wealthy gain more influence over politics and government (greatly enabled by the *Citizens United* decision), they have a greater ability to set the agenda and alter policy to reflect their priorities, transforming our democracy into a plutocracy (a society ruled by the wealthy).

To quote Nobel-Prize-winning economist Angus Deaton in his 2013 book *The Great Escape: Health, Wealth, and the Origins of Inequality*:

> *The very wealthy have little need for state-provided education or health care... They have even less reason to support health insurance for every-*

one, or to worry about the low quality of public schools that plagues much of the country. They will oppose any regulation of banks that restricts profits, even if it helps those who cannot cover their mortgages or protects the public against predatory lending, deceptive advertising, or even a repetition of the financial crash. To worry about these consequences of extreme inequality has nothing to do with being envious of the rich and everything to do with the fear that rapidly growing top incomes are a threat to the wellbeing of everyone else.[110]

To put it another way, as economic inequality increases, so does political inequality, which is likely to skew legislative, executive, and judicial outcomes, and potentially transform rights (things many people believe should have nothing to do with wealth, such as health care or education) into privileges (which are only available to those who can afford them).

Over the last few years, there's been a lot of discussion about the existence of a "Deep State." This supposed shadow government, composed of entrenched bureaucrats, secretly controls the country in defiance of democracy, instead catering to a global elite.

It's an entertaining conspiracy theory but also an effective red herring, distracting people from the true "Deep Corp" of shareholder primacy, which is accomplishing the same thing on behalf of corporations and the wealthy — except it's doing it with elected officials and in plain sight.

Torches, Pitchforks, and Guillotines

History has shown that when people are disenfranchised or discriminated against, they eventually revolt against the dominant institution of the day. This used to be the church, and then the government.

But today's dominant institution is the corporation. So, if the practice of favoring shareholders continues to create socio-economic insecurity and alienation, it's business that will feel the wrath of the "precariat"[111] — Nobel Prize-winning British economist Guy Standing's name for those who live a precarious, unpredictable existence despite a world full of privilege.

In some respects, this is class warfare. But simply attacking the rich won't solve the problem because today's economic inequality isn't the cause. It's the *effect* of the rules that we've been playing by since the 1970s.

The mechanism that needs repair is shareholder primacy, the selfish teenage phase of today's corporations — corporations that we, the people, gave life to with the expectation that they would use their immense power, privilege, and resources to benefit all The People, not just a favored few.

As their parents, it's up to us to stage an intervention. To change this behavior and restore trust before it's too late.

Remember that corporations are legally persons, albeit artificial ones. Over the last 150 years, they've gained more and more rights, just as a teenager gains the right to drive, to vote, and to drink alcohol. But once they become emancipated, our authority over them is gone.

For the corporate person, adulthood is just around the corner. We continue to give it more and more responsibility. Currently, we're handing over the keys to artificial intelligence, allowing corporations to decide what a "good outcome" is before releasing algorithms that relentlessly pursue how to get there.

Anyone who's ever read Mary Shelley's *Frankenstein,* or watched the movies *Blade Runner* or *The Terminator,* knows that creating and releasing artificial life is fraught with the risks of hubris.

For a sneak peek of what that might look like, consider China's social credit system. Started in 2014, it's a "technology-enabled, surveillance-based nationwide program designed to nudge citizens toward better behavior."[112]

In essence, the Chinese government assigns everyone a score, much like a credit score. But instead of being based on your financial history, it's based on how you behave, with the Chinese government deciding what's good and bad.

"Bad" behavior runs the gamut from rebellious infractions (criticizing the government or supporting religion) to the more mundane (jaywalking and playing music too loudly.) "Good" behavior includes giving to charity or taking your parents to the doctor.

Punishments are significant, including bans on leaving the country, hiring for high-visibility jobs, or acceptance of children to private schools. It can also result in slower internet connections and public shaming via a searchable blacklist at creditchina.gov.cn.

Even though the program is still in its early stages, it has resulted in nearly 11 million Chinese citizens who can no longer fly on planes and four million who are barred from trains.[113]

According to the Chinese government, the ultimate goal is to "allow the trustworthy to roam everywhere under heaven while making it hard for the discredited to take a single step."[114]

Others prefer to call it "authoritarianism, gamified."[115]

Meanwhile, here in America, corporations are already starting to unilaterally decide who's good and who's bad, exacting punishment outside of the legal system:

- Life insurance companies operating in the State of New York now base premiums, in part, on a person's social media posts, deciding if certain publicized activities make someone a higher risk.[116]
- Bar and restaurant owners use PatronScan software to maintain a list of customers who they consider to be troublemakers. This list is shared with every other PatronScan subscriber in the U.S., the U.K., and Canada, effectively banning a person from thousands of establishments for up to five years.[117]
- Airbnb reserves the right to ban users for life, for any reason, without disclosing what that reason is or allowing for appeal.[118]

And just like in China, there's no way for people to change these policies through a democratic process. Only shareholders have the chance to elect corporate leadership, and those votes are concentrated among a relative few.

As bad as that future sounds, it's not inevitable. There's still time to re-educate our corporate "child" so it helps humanity, rather than victimizes it.

I don't say that to be altruistic. Remember, 100% of customers (and other stakeholders) are human beings. So, if companies can provide more value for human beings, those human beings will pay for that value. That will help the company succeed in the long term thanks to a sustainable, respectful, revenue-generating relationship, instead of a predatory, acquisitive mindset.

And I'm not the only one who thinks so.

On August 19, 2019, the Business Roundtable (a nonprofit association composed exclusively of CEOs from major U.S. companies) announced that it was officially updating its stance on what the purpose of business is.

For decades, this influential group had stated that "the principal objective of a business enterprise [was] to generate economic returns to its owners."[119]

But moving forward, they announced they would be moving away from shareholder primacy, instead putting the interests of employees, customers, suppliers, and communities on par with shareholders, committing "to deliver value to all of them, for the future success of our companies, our communities and our country."[120]

The statement was signed by 183 CEOs, including the heads of Amazon, Apple, Bank of America, ExxonMobil, GM, P&G and Walmart.

It was a landmark, hope-inspiring declaration. But changing the world's largest institution will take more than words. It will take time and focus, arguments and understanding, sacrifice and success. But more than anything, it will take *alignment* so we're all heading in the same direction.

And that starts by changing one simple belief.

3

THE 50-YEAR-OLD FALLACY

"And a step backward, after making a wrong turn, is a step in the
right direction."

— KURT VONNEGUT, *PLAYER PIANO*

F ull disclosure: I'm fortunate enough to be a shareholder. I
own some stock directly as well as through mutual funds as
part of my retirement savings. So, I'm speaking from
personal experience when I say this:

There's a certain arrogance to shareholders.

We don't actually work for the companies in which we own stock.
We don't give up our nights and weekends to ensure projects stay on
track. We don't come up with new products that will ensure future
success. We don't necessarily even buy the companies' products,
generating revenue.

All we do is loan them our money. Just like putting it into a
savings account at a neighborhood bank.

Yet, while today's typical bank savings accounts pay just 0.06%
APR,[1] as shareholders, we demand at least *100 times* that in return.

(Oh and, by the way, if that return isn't consistent, we're dumping the stock.)

It's a rather entitled perspective for someone who doesn't actually contribute any of their personal time and talent to the enterprise.

Kinda makes you wonder, "Who the hell do we think we are?"

Well, since the 1970s, the answer has been the "principal." That is, the person who hires someone else (called the "agent") to act on their behalf, doing things the principal can't or doesn't want to do.

The 1970s is, of course, when the shareholder primacy movement started. But it's also when economists and political scientists were defining the relationship between principals and their agents and, most relevantly, the so-called "principal-agent problem," which is when the agent acts in a way that isn't in the principal's best interest.[2]

First identified by Stephen Ross and Barry Mitnick at the University of Pennsylvania,[3] the principal-agent problem arises from two underlying causes:

First, the principal and agent are different people, performing different roles, with inherently different interests. As such, the two parties will sometimes want different outcomes.

Second, as the person doing the work, the agent has access to more information than the principal, which makes it difficult for the principal to determine whether the agent is always acting in the principal's best interest or if they're pursuing their own interest instead.

Ross likened the problem to the agent trying to buy an ice cream cone for the principal without knowing what the principal prefers.[4] The agent, who is at the ice cream parlor, can see all the available flavors, while the principal cannot. So, when the agent shows up at the principal's office with Rocky Road, the principal doesn't know if the agent thought it was the best available flavor for the principal or if the agent merely picked it because it's the agent's favorite flavor, or because it was cheaper.

The solution to the principal-agency problem is seen as twofold: better information about what the principal wants and incentives to ensure the agent is putting the principal's interests first.[5]

So, when the shareholder primacy movement was born in the

1970s, this emerging principal-agent theory was used as justification.[6] Shareholders declared themselves as the principals and corporate leaders as their agents, who they had hired to run their companies.

As we've seen, these newly minted principals quickly clarified that the primary purpose of business was to pay them. Additionally, shareholders instituted stock-based incentives to ensure corporate leadership was aligned with shareholder interests.

To put it another way, shareholders solved the ice cream cone problem by proclaiming that ice cream parlors should only focus on one flavor of ice cream — the one that shareholders liked (let's call it vanilla). Furthermore, they mandated that corporate executives should only eat vanilla if they wanted to keep their jobs.

It was one heck of a power play, laying the foundation for how business has been run for the last 40 years.

There's only one problem.

Shareholders aren't the principals.

"Wait," you might say. "Shareholders own the company. Why aren't they the principals?"

Yeah. About that.

As much as it challenges what most of us currently take for granted, shareholders don't actually own the corporation. They own *shares* in a corporation, which is very different from owning the corporation itself.

Yes, I know that sounds pedantic. But it's actually quite relevant. Bear with me.

Back in 2012, Vanderbilt Law professor Margaret Blair examined this distinction,[7] rigorously documenting reasons why shareholders can't be considered principals or even "owners."

First and foremost, corporations are legal entities, entirely separate from their founders, directors, employees or even shareholders. Indeed, when a corporation is formed, its founders give up certain rights in order to receive the significant benefits that come from incorporating.

This separation reinforces the idea that corporations are distinct legal persons — not just an extension of natural persons such as you and me. (Remember that legal personhood was granted to corporations in 1886 with the outcome of *Santa Clara County v. Southern Pacific Railroad Company.*) As a result, shareholders (or anyone else for that matter) can't "own" a corporation. To do so would be a violation of the Thirteenth Amendment to the U.S. Constitution that prohibits slavery.

Legally, corporations own themselves.

What shareholders do own is a "share" of the distributed profits of a corporation, as well as having very limited voting rights when it comes to things such as electing a board of directors, sale of the company, or a stock split.[8] Think of this "share" as a contract they own, the same as an employee "owns" a pension claim, or bondholder "owns" a corporate bond.

But shareholders have nothing even close to the *carte blanche* that a true "owner" has over their property.

Shareholders have no direct control over the day-to-day operations of "their" company, nor can they dictate the activities of "agents" such as the CEO. Any attempts to do so must go through the board of directors.

And while a true owner is legally responsible for the damage caused by something they own, shareholders enjoy limited liability protection, so they're not held responsible for actions the corporation takes that cause harm.

Lastly, by definition, an agent is employed by the principal. But, as we all know, corporate executives aren't employed by shareholders. They're employed by the corporation and, legally, must answer to it and its board of directors.

So not only does the corporation own itself, it's also the principal, employing executives and other employees as agents to serve *its* interests.

Without "ownership" and without "principal" status, the premise for shareholder primacy evaporates, leaving no reason for shareholders to be elevated above the corporation or for shareholders to be treated any differently than other stakeholders.

Indeed, picking *any* one stakeholder and declaring it to be the only one that matters is both illegitimate and impractical. Just like you can't start removing legs from a multi-legged stool and expect it to stand up, let alone be stable.

In the same way, business is designed in a way that works best with all of its stakeholder "legs" attached and firmly on the ground.

As a result of these missteps, we've spent the last 40 years focused on the wrong problem. The primary concern isn't the "principal-agent problem" (i.e., how to get one person what they want). It's what's called the "team production problem" (i.e., how to get people to work together).

First identified by economists Armen Alchain and Harold Demsetz in 1972,[9] the "team production problem" recognizes that when individuals work together to create something, it's often difficult to determine each party's specific contribution to the value of the final product — which, in turn, makes pricing products or determining compensation challenging.

This uncertainty doesn't exist just because it's hard to measure a person's contribution in a complex, interactive environment, but also because of the synergistic nature of teamwork. Teamwork can improve the quality and, therefore, the overall value of the final product, so that it is worth more than the sum of the participants' individual contributions.

In fact, it's this magical multiplying power of teamwork that often draws us to participate in joint enterprises. We, as individuals, know that our work product is improved when we collaborate with others, especially when they specialize in areas where we do not. These other team members not only contribute their own expertise, but they also challenge our preconceptions, offer alternatives, and provide support.

Importantly, team production theory suggests that *everyone* on the team feels this way. For a company, that means it's not just shareholders who hope to benefit from joining the enterprise. All stakeholders do, including employees, customers, suppliers, and the community.

As such, all stakeholders should realize that eliciting support and cooperation from *all* parties is important to the success of the joint enterprise which, of course, leads to success for the individual.

Just as with the "principal-agent problem," the key to solving the "team production problem" is alignment. All stakeholders need to have clear information on what purpose they're serving plus an incentive to reach that goal.

But, unlike the "principal-agent problem" the "team production problem" brings one other need. Since all stakeholders are equal in their importance, no one stakeholder is "in charge." No one is the boss, with the authority to mediate and resolve disputes that are bound to occur when different perspectives come together.

In the shareholder primacy model, the shareholder was the principal and, as such, had the last say on all disputes and decisions, with an eye toward whatever would make the most money. But, as we've seen, shareholders can't be the principal because the corporation is its own principal.

So, from a practical standpoint, how does a corporation express its interests, make decisions, and resolve disputes? After all, the corporation isn't a "natural person," only a legal one, so it can't walk into a room, listen to situation, and voice a decision.

This role must be played by one or more actual human beings. An agent who objectively represents the corporate principal's interest without a conflict of interest.

That's a pretty tall order since every single stakeholder has a built-in conflict of interest.

So, who can be that agent?

In their 1999 paper, "A Team Production Theory of Corporate Law," Blair and her co-author, Cornell law professor Lynn Stout, proposed that the board of directors already fits the bill, able to act as a "mitigating hierarchy" to all parties involved.

Corporate law views a board of directors "as more than mere 'agents,'" the authors note. "Rather, they are a unique form of fiduciary who more closely resemble trustees and whose duties are imbued with a similar moral weight. Trustees are expected to serve their beneficiaries' interests unswervingly and to settle conflicts between beneficiaries with competing interests fairly and impartially."[10]

Furthermore, existing corporate law "encourages directors to serve their firms' interests by severely limiting their abilities to serve their own."[11] Specifically, directors "can bring home their agreed upon (and publicly reported) compensation, which may be quite substantial, but beyond this compensation they cannot use their corporate positions to expropriate assets or returns that belong to the firm."[12]

Of course, today's boards of directors are often populated with individuals who own a significant amount of stock in the corporation, which inherently taints their ability to act as a fiduciary. But shareholder status is not a legal requirement for being a director, so removing this conflict is not an insurmountable challenge as the corporation assumes its proper role as its own principal.

Examples of this type of "selfless" board of directors are all around us in the form of nonprofit organizations. Directors at nonprofits not only don't receive any compensation for their service, but they also often have to *pay* to be on the board. Indeed, directors at nonprofit organizations are frequently drawn to these positions as a way to help society and are willing to pay for that privilege.

Once seated, these directors focus not on extracting value for shareholders (since there are none), but rather on stewarding the enterprise toward fulfilling its defined (nonfinancial) purpose.

This "non-distribution constraint," as it was called by Yale law professor Henry Hansmann, sends a powerful signal to all stakeholders.[13] Since there's no way for these directors to financially benefit from their own actions, they are often considered beyond reproach and are trusted to objectively guide the organization.

Similarly, a for-profit corporation with a board composed of non-shareholders could also benefit from this same elevated level of trust, even if the board received some other non-share-based compensation. All stakeholders could look to them to provide clarity and objectively mediate disputes, as everyone pursues the corporation's defined purpose.

So, what is the purpose of a corporation?

Well, Milton Friedman would say (and did say) that the purpose of a corporation is to "make as much money as possible" for its share-holders.[14] Many people share this belief, or at least believe that U.S. law requires companies to focus on maximizing shareholder value.

But this, too, is a myth.[15]

On the contrary, corporate law and the courts give directors broad discretion on how their companies are run and what goals they pursue. This legal doctrine is called the "business judgment rule," which states that as long as the board of directors doesn't use its power to enrich itself, courts won't second-guess their decisions about what is best for the company, even when those decisions seem to harm shareholder value.[16]

This means that shareholder primacy isn't the law. It's a choice. And, as such, managers can choose a purpose other than "maximizing profit."

Profit, after all, isn't really a purpose. It's a *result* that comes from being successful in a given pursuit.

To quote Henry Ford, "Business must be run at a profit, else it will die. But when anyone tries to run a business solely for profit, then also the business must die, for it no longer has a reason for existence."

Corporate purpose used to be clearly defined from the moment of corporate birth in the company's charter, granted by royalty or the legislature. This legally enforced focus left no doubt concerning what interest was being served by everyone involved.

For example, when the Union Pacific Railroad was chartered in the Pacific Railway Act of 1862, the corporation's purpose was specifically defined:

...the said corporation is hereby authorized and empowered to layout, locate, construct, furnish, maintain, and enjoy a continuous railroad and telegraph, with the appurtenances, from a point on the one hundredth meridian of longitude west from Greenwich, between the south margin of the valley of the Republican River and the north margin of the valley of

the Platte River, in the Territory of Nebraska, to the western boundary of Nevada Territory, upon the route and terms hereinafter provided, and is hereby vested with all the powers, privileges, and immunities necessary to carry into effect the purposes of this act as herein set forth.[17]

There was discretion, but no leeway. It was, quite literally, illegal for Union Pacific to set up operations outside the defined area, join the transoceanic shipping trade, or start selling textiles, even if they thought they could make a profit from any of those activities.

As a result, everyone involved in the enterprise — employees, suppliers, shareholders — knew exactly what the goal was and how to measure success.

Of course, limitations, while providing clarity, can also be restrictive. Over time, companies that were chartered with a specific purpose found themselves unable to take advantage of changes in technology and society. So, in the late 19th century, New Jersey (in 1896) and Delaware (in 1899) adopted more permissive "enabling" incorporation laws as a way of attracting more businesses (and tax revenue) to their states.[18] These laws removed much of the specificity from corporate charters, allowing companies to be chartered for "any lawful purpose," a phrase that is commonly used in articles of incorporation today.

As beneficial as this change was in allowing corporations to pursue opportunities that would help them remain competitive, it did remove inherent focus, increasing confusion around exactly why a joint venture existed, what the objective was, and how everyone would know when they got there.

For example, hundreds of disparate corporations, including AIG, Carter's, Caterpillar, Chevron, Dunkin Donuts, FedEx, John Deere, Motorola, Northrop Grumman, PayPal, Pitney Bowes, and YogaWorks all share the exact same corporate purpose, "to engage in any lawful act or activity for which corporations may be organized under the General Corporation Law of Delaware."

So, as long as it's legal in Delaware, it's on-strategy. Not a lot of focus there.

In the absence of a legally chartered (and enforced) purpose, many companies have tried filling this void with a mission statement to provide focus and engage employees. These documents are often lofty and well-intentioned, describing how the company cares about the bigger picture. But, unfortunately, once created, mission statements are rarely utilized as the constant compass they are designed to be. Instead, they are frequently set aside as short-term profit pressures conflict with long-term aspirations.

This is not a failure of vision. It's a failure of alignment with the world of shareholder primacy.

But in a world where the board of directors is no longer subservient to shareholders, extracting value based solely on the shareholder definition of success, the corporation can right itself and pursue a broader purpose. One that the corporation was specifically created for.

To benefit people.

Real, flesh-and-blood, natural human beings like you and me. All of them — not just a privileged few.

To be clear, I'm not talking about a charitable pursuit. I'm talking about a for-profit company being financially successful by focusing on creating and delivering value to human beings, regardless of what stakeholder group they belong to.

After all, humanity is the common thread that ties all stakeholders together, so it only makes sense to base corporate purpose on satisfying human needs.

Let's start with customers.

Customers are the sole source of revenue for any company. So, while they're not the only stakeholder that matters, they are "first among equals," because they are fundamental to the entire concept of trade.

This status was more eloquently expressed by management consultant Peter Drucker in his 1954 book *The Practice of Management*:

> *If we want to know what a business is, we have to start with its purpose. And the purpose must lie outside the business itself. In fact, it*

must lie in society, since a business enterprise is an organ of society. There is only one valid definition of business purpose: **to create a customer** ... *The customer is a foundation of a business and keeps it in existence. The customer alone gives employment. And it is to supply the customer that society entrusts wealth-producing resources to the business enterprise.*[19]

As human beings, customers have a long list of diverse needs, which provides an almost limitless number of opportunities for companies to create something that satisfies those needs in exchange for compensation.

Of course, to satisfy those needs, a company must create something that customers value. And that takes employees to do the work, suppliers to provide materials, and even shareholders to provide the necessary capital to help the company grow. Building the stool of satisfaction requires all of the legs (i.e., all of the stakeholder groups).

And since all of these necessary stakeholder groups are also entirely composed of human beings, their needs, too, can't be distilled down to just one simplistic element. Just as customers want more than to buy things, employees want more than a paycheck, suppliers want more than a sale, communities want more than tax revenue, and shareholders want more than a return on their investment.

In fact, even members of the same stakeholder group may have wildly different needs. A 25-year-old shareholder contributing to their 401(k) has very different investment goals than a 65-year-old facing the need for steady income in retirement. Yet, they are both "shareholders."

To make matters more challenging, it's rare that a person only fits into one stakeholder group. More often, they are "universal owners," playing multiple roles in society and, as such, they have conflicting needs that can't be satisfied by focusing on just one aspect.

As a result, while focusing on one stakeholder role may yield a payoff in that facet of their life, it may cost them dearly in other aspects that are just as important to them.

Lynn Stout illustrated this in describing the 2010 *Deepwater Horizon* disaster, the largest maritime oil spill in history:

> Consider someone who owns not only BP stock, but also holds BP bonds; owns shares in other oil companies; owns a beach home on the Florida Panhandle; has a job in the Gulf tourism industry; and values his own human capital, including his good physical health and social connections in a thriving coastal community. By skimping on safety corners, BP may have given this investor several years of above-average share performance. But by causing an enormous oil spill in the Gulf, BP's risk-taking imposed much greater "external costs" on the investor's other interests. As a result of the Deepwater Horizon disaster, the U.S. government imposed a moratorium on exploratory drilling in the Gulf that idled not only BP's operations but those of other oil companies as well. The spill hurt the value of BP bonds, which were downgraded in the disaster's wake. The value of beach-front property in the Gulf declined, and its tourism and fishing industries suffered. The Gulf ecosystem was harmed, and its ability to provide healthy seafood and safe recreation degraded.[20]

People are complicated so they require a more sophisticated value proposition than reductive solutions dominated by finance.

Fortunately, as Stout points out, corporate executives are also human and have the "capacity to balance, albeit imperfectly, competing interests and responsibilities."[21]

And isn't that the job corporate boards and leaders should be focused on? Isn't that what they should be paid for?

To adjust *all* the legs the stool was designed with, so it is as sturdy as possible?

4

THE UPSIDE OF PROGRESS

"If you think you have it tough, read history books."

— BILL MAHER

There are times in my life when I would have given every penny I had in exchange for something. These moments, almost exclusively, involved the health of people or animals I love, when all the money in the world still wouldn't make a difference. Desperation, like shopping for groceries while hungry, tends to open up your wallet.

On the flip side, there are other times when you couldn't have paid me enough money to do something. These were situations where there was extreme moral clarity and I was compelled to, in the words of Spike Lee, "Do the right thing."

In between these extremes is a near infinite spectrum of things that I'm willing to pay (or be paid) for as a way of satisfying my (or someone else's) needs. Such is the transactional nature of life.

Of course, one man's trash is another man's treasure, so my needs certainly aren't universal. Indeed, it's difficult to definitively say what everyone in the world needs. But that's not to say that people haven't tried to at least classify human needs so we can understand them a bit better.

For most of us, the phrase "human needs" brings to mind Maslow's Hierarchy of Needs. It states that human needs can be classified into five distinct categories which motivate us sequentially. That is, we need to satisfy needs in one category before we can move on to the next.[1]

Arranged in a pyramid most of us remember from high school, the five types of needs are (in order):

1. Physiological needs (food, water, sleep, shelter, sex)
2. Safety needs (personal, emotional, financial, health and well-being, safety against accidents and illness)
3. Social belonging (friendships, intimacy, family)
4. Self-esteem (ego/status needs, such as prestige, feelings of accomplishment)
5. Self-actualization (self-fulfillment needs, such as mate acquisition, parenting, utilizing abilities and talents, pursing a goal, seeking happiness).

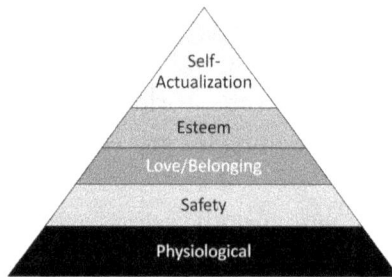

The pyramidical structure of Maslow's Hierarchy of Needs.

According to its creator, American psychologist Abraham Maslow, the goal is to reach the top of the pyramid and become a fully self-actualized individual.

This theory, originally published in *Psychological Review* in 1943, continues to strongly resonate in popular culture, in part, because it offers an easy-to-understand construct that explains human nature in a way "that most humans immediately recognize in themselves and others."[2]

That said, the pyramid most of us accept as gospel has a few cracks. Most notably, the sequential nature of its progression — the way we must satisfy lower needs before we can move onto higher motivations.

Somehow this just doesn't ring true.

Anyone who's been out to dinner with family or friends knows that being hungry (level 1) doesn't stop us from enjoying the social belonging (level 3) that comes from the conversation.

Similarly, it seems outlandish for governments to ignore "higher" needs until such time that every single person has food and shelter.

This disparity was one reason why University of Illinois psychologists Ed Diener and Louis Tay decided to put Maslow's theory to the test and see if it matched reality. Between 2005 and 2010, they worked with the Gallup Organization to conduct a truly worldwide poll on well-being. Whereas Maslow's theory was based largely on the lives of successful Americans, Diener and Tay instead surveyed 60,865 participants from 123 countries around the world, asking them about their needs and feelings.[3]

What they found was that, while human needs similar to Maslow's are universal and can't be substituted for one another, there is no need to obtain them in a certain sequence.

"Although the most basic needs might get the most attention when you don't have them," said Diener, "you don't need to fulfill them in order to get benefits [from the others]."[4]

This sets up a more dynamic model of needs, replacing the rigid sequential pyramid with more fluid waves of intensity, based on someone's circumstance.

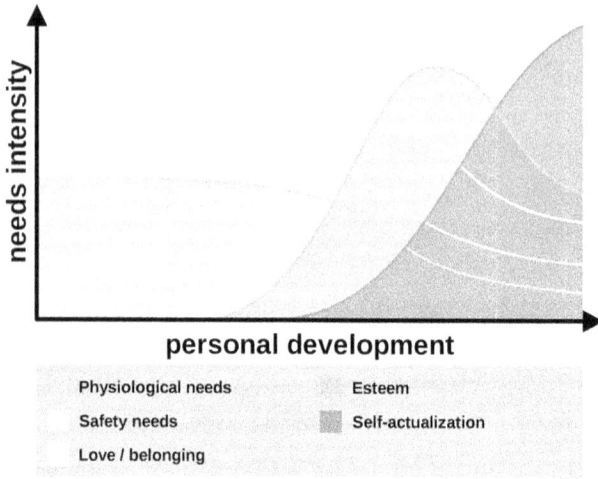

Figure axis labels: needs intensity (vertical), personal development (horizontal)

Legend:
Physiological needs   Esteem
Safety needs   Self-actualization
Love / belonging

Dynamic version of Maslow's hierarchy of needs (Referring to Krech, D./Crutchfield, R. S./Ballachey, E. L. (1962), Individual in society, Tokyo etc. 1962, S. 77. Graphic by Philipp Guttmann [CC BY-SA 4.0.])

"All the needs are important all the time," Diener continued. "Our leaders need to think about them from the outset, otherwise they will have no reason to address social and community needs until food and shelter are available to all."[5]

Unfortunately, our society's current focus on money, finance, and all things quantifiable inherently hamstrings efforts to broaden how it satisfies non-basic needs. After all, while it's quite easy to exchange dollars for things such as food, clothing, and shelter, money is an exceedingly poor currency when it comes to satisfying higher needs such as love, self-esteem, and fulfillment. These are much more dependent on "softer" and "qualitative" interpersonal relationships.

Broadening our society's mindset beyond basic needs also means overcoming thousands of years of sheer momentum. After all, for most of human history, we've had a hard enough time just feeding ourselves, putting clothes on our backs, and keeping a roof over our heads.

But we've made a lot of progress in the "basic needs" department over the last few centuries.

Food

Before the 18th century, agriculture had remained relatively unchanged since humans traded hunting and gathering for farming. Individuals practiced "subsistence farming," whereby a family was able to produce just enough food to feed themselves with maybe a little left over to barter or sell to others. If they were lucky, they wouldn't experience a catastrophic crop failure from pests, disease, floods, or drought. Famines and malnutrition were not uncommon.

However, starting around 1700, a series of inventions began to geometrically improve agricultural productivity. First was Jethro Tull's seed drill (heavily influenced by seed drills that had existed in China for centuries) which could drill holes, plant seeds, and cover them, three rows at time. Prior to this, seeds were thrown by hand, allowing them to be eaten by birds or blown away by the wind. It's estimated that this one machine increased crop yields fivefold.[6]

In the 1730s, Charles "Turnip" Townsend introduced the Dutch four-crop rotation method to England. This practice, where fields were cyclically planted with barley, wheat, turnips and then clover, naturally put nutrients back into the soil, rather than depleting them by planting the same crop season after season or allowing a field to remain fallow every few years. Additionally, the turnips and clover could be fed to livestock over the winter, so farmers didn't have to slaughter them as they had done before due to a lack of feed.[7]

The grain cradle, introduced in the early 1800s, and Cyrus McCormick's horse-drawn reaper increased the efficiency of harvesting, which had previously been done with a handheld scythe. Instead of one worker only being able to harvest a quarter of an acre per day in the 1790s, by 1890, two men and two horses could cut, rake, and bind 20 acres of wheat per day.[8]

The 20th century saw even larger gains in agricultural output, thanks to the invention and widespread use of gasoline-powered tractors, artificial fertilizers, high-yield plant varieties, herbicides, and pesticides. The largest increases occurred during the "Green Revolution" of the 1950s and 1960s during which crop yields for soybeans tripled and yields for corn, wheat and rice increased between four- and fivefold.[9]

And while we've learned that some of these practices come with significant downsides (including loss of biodiversity, increased carbon emissions, and a growth in the obesity rate), they have also allowed us to increase food production faster than population growth, even though the global population has increased 15-fold since 1700.[10]

Of course, that doesn't mean we've eliminated hunger or food insecurity, which are caused not just by the volume of food produced, but also by availability and affordability.

But increases in agricultural productivity have allowed us, as a species, to move off the farm so we can do other things — to solve other problems.

In fact, in 1870, almost 50% of employed persons worked in agriculture, with each farmer only able to supply five people with farm products.[11] By 2019, just 1.36% of the U.S. population worked in agriculture,[12] yet each person was able to supply food for nearly 129 others.[13]

Similarly, the amount of money we spend on food has drastically decreased. In 1900, the average U.S. family spent 43% of its budget just on food.[14] Today, that's dropped to 12%.[15]

Clothing

A similar pattern is seen in the production of textiles and clothing, much of which was painstakingly created locally and by hand for most of human history.

Mechanization started in 1589, with the invention of the stocking frame, which was, essentially, an automatic knitting machine, mimicking the movement of human hands knitting. But it wasn't until the 18th century that the production of clothing was truly revolutionized by the widespread invention and adoption of machines.

John Kay's flying shuttle (1733) increased the speed of fabric production by automatically throwing (and catching) a spool of thread back and forth across the loom. This essentially doubled production efficiency since a broadcloth loom could now be run by one worker instead of two, which was the case prior to its invention.[16]

Of course, twice the weavers required twice the thread. And since it had already taken eight human spinners to supply each weaver before the flying shuttle, the full benefits of mechanized weaving couldn't be realized until some form of mechanized spinning could be invented. And it was in 1764, when James Hargreaves created the spinning jenny, a machine capable of creating eight or more spools of thread at a time (although this quickly grew to 120 spools).[17]

Continuing upstream, the capacity for more spools of thread led to the need for dramatically more wool, silk or cotton (which had come into vogue around this time). As a plant, cotton was more easily scalable than animal-sourced fibers, but with one significant problem. Cotton bolls, where the cotton threads come from, also contain seeds that had to be removed by hand, which limited production.

Enter Eli Whitney who, in 1793, invented a mechanized cotton gin, which could clean the seeds from 60 pounds of cotton in one day — an astronomical rate compared to the previous one-pound-per-day rate using a hand-cranked roller gin.[18]

The 19th century saw even more improvements in apparel manufacturing productivity, including the application of steam power (replacing water, horse, or man power), the factory system's division of labor, the use of punch cards to "program" the Jacquard loom, and, of course, the sewing machine. Before its invention, an experienced seamstress required 14 hours to make a man's shirt and ten hours to make a woman's dress. With the advent of the sewing machine in the mid-1800s, these dropped to 75 minutes and one hour, respectively — a tenfold improvement.[19]

Artificial fibers, such as rayon, nylon, polyester, and spandex were introduced in the 20th century, offering even cheaper materials with which to make our clothes.

Also in the 20th century, globalization and improved transportation infrastructure (including transoceanic container ships) provided a way to dramatically reduce the labor costs associated with textiles and clothing production by shifting the work overseas where wages and standards of living were much lower than in the U.S. While Americans benefited from lower clothing prices, the constant downward pressure on expenses has created many opportunities for exploitation in countries where workers' rights, health and safety are not as tightly regulated as in the U.S.

Today, almost no one makes their own clothes at home, choosing instead to purchase relatively affordable and readily available clothing made by others, in an almost infinite variety of materials, colors and styles.

These technological improvements have also reduced the amount the average U.S. family spends on clothing, dropping from 14% of all expenditures in 1900[20] to just 2.3% today.[21]

Housing

Once humans stopped living in caves and started building their own dwellings, several factors influenced their choice of construction materials.

Stone was the most durable, but it was also difficult to acquire, manipulate and assemble, making it too expensive and time-intensive for most homes.

Wood, on the other hand, was much easier to harvest, shape and assemble, first into tepees or simple huts and, later, into more resilient, permanent log cabins.

Over time, construction techniques evolved, improving both the durability and sophistication of timber-based structures. But these benefits were not cheap. Civilization's expansion was depleting old-growth forest, making large logs scarcer. And the ability to precisely cut and join heavy beams required skilled, expensive labor.

It wasn't until the late 18th century that technological advances started to make quality housing available to the masses.

First was the invention of the circular saw in 1777.[22] Its ability to keep the teeth in constant motion made it much more efficient than a "back-and-forth" or "up-and-down" reciprocating saw that lost all momentum at the end of a stroke. Powered by wind or water instead of human hands, this "always moving" tool dramatically increased the volume of timber that a sawmill could process, making precut lumber much more available and affordable.

Second was the development of machines in 1794 that could quickly and efficiently cut nails from sheets of wrought iron.[23] Prior to this, each nail had been shaped, one at a time, by a blacksmith, a practice dating back as far as 3400 B.C.E, in ancient Egypt.[24] Hand-wrought nails were so expensive that some people would burn down their houses when moving to extract the nails for future use. The practice was so widespread in Colonial America that Virginia passed a law against it in 1644.[25]

By the 1830s, the availability and affordability of nails and standard-sized, precut lumber (such as the 2x4) allowed for the widespread adoption of "balloon framing"[26] as the dominant house construction technique. This type of framing (like its modern cousin "platform framing") quickly creates a sturdy skeleton without the need for large logs or the highly skilled labor required for timber framing, making housing more affordable and available.

Around the same time, there were two significant advances in the large-scale production of steel. Oddly, both of them had to do with air.

In 1828, Scottish engineer James Beaumont Neilson realized that the furnaces used to smelt iron ore could be made much more efficient by injecting preheated air into the combustion chamber instead of using room-temperature air. Furthermore, the heat needed to warm the air could be extracted from the furnace exhaust itself. This closed-loop improvement not only cut fuel consumption by almost two-thirds, but it also allowed furnaces to burn hotter, increasing their output by two-thirds, even while using less fuel.[27]

Then, in 1856, English inventor Henry Bessemer patented a process[28] for blowing high-pressure air directly into molten iron, "burning off" excess carbon and other impurities, leaving behind much higher-strength steel (which is, essentially, iron with the right amount of carbon — anywhere between 0.05-2%, by weight).[29] Using the Bessemer process, foundries could convert three to five tons of iron ore into steel in about 20 minutes, an amount that had previously taken a day or more to produce,[30] an improvement that finally made steel affordable enough for structural use, including high-rise housing in urban areas.

Other developments added comfort and convenience to these sturdy, yet affordable structures, including mass-produced window glass (1834),[31] gas lighting (1843),[32] water and sewage systems (1850s),[33] electric light bulbs (1879),[34] electrical delivery grids (1882),[35] and air conditioning (1914).[36]

The 20th century built on these basics, refining building codes to improve fire safety as well as structural resilience to earthquakes, hurricanes, blizzards, and other environmental forces. At the same time, the introduction of home appliances such as electric refrigerators, ranges, toasters, washing machines, and dishwashers transformed the interior of our homes.

THANKS to all of the advances of the last few centuries, our lives have changed dramatically. No longer need we spend every waking moment and every dollar we earn on survival, constantly wondering whether or not we'll be able to secure enough food, clothing and shelter for ourselves and our families.

In fact, it's this extra time and money that are the greatest dividends we've received from technology.

Back in 1900, the average American family spent 80% of its budget on the basics of food, clothing, and shelter.[37] Today, that number is just 49%,[38] meaning we have more "discretionary income" than ever.

Similarly, the average American's work week has dropped by more than a third since 1870, from 62 hours to 40.25 hours in 2000.[39] Time dedicated to household chores such as preparing meals, laundry and cleaning has also declined from 58 hours per week in 1900 to just 15.5 hours in 2015,[40] thanks in part to the introduction of home appliances in the early 20th century. As a result, we've found ourselves with more time to pursue other interests and solve other problems.

To a certain extent, that's what we've done. We've used the twin dividends of time and money to satisfy needs that are "higher up" on Maslow's pyramid.

Here are a couple of examples:

Health and Well-Being

Significant investments in science and medicine over the last 200 years have improved not just the quality, but the length of our lives.

A very incomplete list of these advances includes:

- Vaccinations (1798)
- Anesthesia (1804)
- Pasteurization (1864)
- X-rays (1895)
- Electrocardiograph (1901)
- Blood transfusion (1906)
- Antibiotics (penicillin) (1928)
- Chemotherapy (1942)
- Organ transplantation (1954)
- Pacemaker (1958)
- Artificial heart (1963)
- Cochlear implant (1969)
- Antiviral drugs (1979)
- Artificial skin (1981)
- DNA sequencing (1985)
- Gene therapy (1990)
- Cloning (1996)
- Stem cell therapy (1998)
- Human genome mapped (2003)
- Artificial eye (2007)
- Organ regrowth (2013)

The payoffs from these investments have been significant. Child mortality (the percentage of children who die before their fifth birthday) has plummeted from 43% in 1820 to four percent today,[41] while overall U.S. life expectancy has doubled from 39.4 years in 1880 to 78.9 years in 2019.[42]

Social Belonging

Before the 19th century, the two primary modes of travel were walking and riding a horse (or other pack animal.) However, starting in the 19th century, advances in transportation made it faster and easier to visit friends and family:

- Steam train (1804)
- Internal combustion engine / automobile (1807)
- Bicycle (1885)
- Airplane (1890)
- Jet engine (1939)
- High-speed rail (1964)

These inventions have hugely increased the distance someone can travel in a day, from about ten miles (on foot, with luggage) to 13,422 miles, the current commercial record, set by a Boeing 777 in 2015, which flew nonstop from Hong Kong to London.[43]

And thanks to the advent of liquid-fueled rockets (1926) and artificial satellites (1957), the U.S. was able to introduce the Global Positioning System in 1989, making it much easier for us to know where we are and how to get to our destination.

Of course, staying in touch doesn't mean you have to travel. While not as robust as in-person communication, remote communication technologies have transformed the way we stay connected:

- Mass-produced paper (1799)
- Telegraph (1816)
- Fountain pen (1827)

- Telephone (1876)
- Ballpoint pen (1888)
- Radio (1895)
- Television (1909)
- Transistors (1947)
- Personal computer (1957)
- Email (1965)
- Internet (1973)
- World Wide Web (1989)
- Text messaging/SMS (1992)
- Facebook (2004)
- iPhone (2007)

CHANGE IS GOOD. Problems get solved. Life gets better.

However, an inherent aspect of change in our world is that the *rate* of change is not constant but increasing. And it's not increasing linearly (1,2,3,4,5,6…) but exponentially (1,2,4,8,16,32…).

That's an important difference.

At the beginning, linear growth and exponential growth look very similar. The inputs are small and so are the differences. But as time moves on, the impact of doubling versus adding becomes incredibly obvious, with a steep "hockey stick" curve seemingly coming out of nowhere.

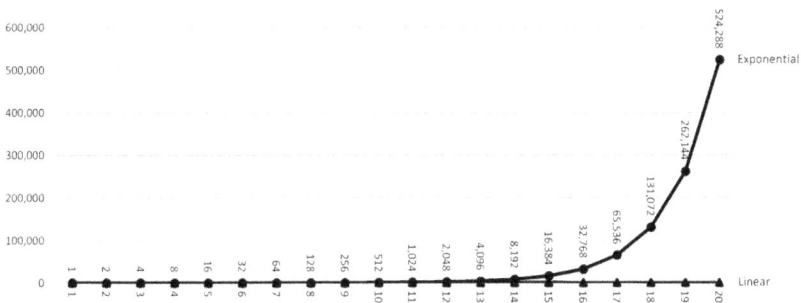

Twenty cycles of linear vs. exponential growth.

If that sounds like the pace of "new" in your life over the last decade, that's the power of exponential growth.

We've already seen an example of accelerating change back in Chapter 1, when we looked at how new technologies have been adopted faster and faster over the last couple of centuries. But, arguably, the most famous example of exponential change in our lives is Moore's Law. Named for Gordon Moore, the co-founder of Fairchild Semiconductor and former CEO of Intel, Moore's law predicted way back in 1965 that the number of transistors that could be placed on an integrated circuit would double every two years,[44] representing a doubling of computer power every two years, for the next decade.

Moore was right, but not just for a decade. Moore's law has continued to reflect reality for over 50 years, meaning we can process more and more information faster and faster.

This exponential growth in "processing power" isn't just a function of modern computers. Inventor and futurist Ray Kurzweil analyzed the price and quality of computing machines since 1900 and found, essentially, that Moore's Law is accurate going all the way back to 1900, even as we moved from mechanical calculators to relays to vacuum tubes to transistors to modern integrated circuits.[45]

The product of all this accelerating processing power has been an explosion in the amount of information that the human race has accumulated. This effect, called the "Knowledge Doubling Curve," was identified by futurist Buckminster Fuller in his 1981 book, *Critical Path*, where he observed that what we "know" has increased exponentially.[46] In his estimation, it took 1,500 years for the number of things we knew in the year one C.E. to double. However, the next doubling of knowledge only took 250 years (until 1750), and then just 150 years (to 1900). By 1945, the time had dropped to 25 years. Today, knowledge is doubling every 13 months.[47] And, according to IBM, with the advent of the Internet of Things (IoT), it will soon double every 11 hours.[48]

Simply put, the world is not only changing faster, but it's also getting bigger, more sophisticated, and more complicated. (As an example, compare your understanding of how the components of a bicycle work versus those of a jet airplane.)

To make matters even worse, all this change causes some of the information we used to consider valuable to become irrelevant. So, even as we try to learn new things, we also have to determine which knowledge is obsolete and should be abandoned and/or replaced.

For example, just 20 years ago, if you wanted to drive to a destination you'd never been to before, you had to know how to read (and refold) a map. Plotting the route to your destination was up to you. Today, most of us don't own a single road map and instead find it much more important to understand the latest Google Maps interface changes (not to mention why it wants me to make so many left-hand turns at busy intersections without traffic lights).

The one exception to all this accelerating change is, well, *us*.

We, and our processors/brains, haven't changed that much in thousands of years. And I don't expect evolution will suddenly kick-start itself to match Moore's law.

In the end, we are linear beings. So, at some point, we just won't be able to keep up with exponential change.

Futurist and author Alvin Toffler coined a term for this feeling of "too much change in too short a period of time" in his 1970 bestseller: *Future Shock*.[49]

As individuals, this means we tend to give up. Unable to grasp the "big picture," we instead focus on "our picture" — the stuff that affects us directly and immediately.

And, for the most part, "our picture" means time and money.

5

THE CATASTROPHE OF EFFICIENCY

"Efficiency is the foundation for survival. Effectiveness is the foundation for success."

— JOHN C. MAXWELL

When I was starting my career, I learned a saying pretty quickly: "Faster. Better. Cheaper. Pick two."

It's true. If you want something faster and better, you're going to pay through the nose. Similarly, if you want something amazing and cheap, it's going to take a while. And if you want it quickly and inexpensive, it's probably not going to be that good.

You just can't have all three. The mechanics of "value" don't allow for it.

"Faster" and "cheaper" are downward forces. We don't want to pay more in time or money than we absolutely have to. "Better," on the other hand, is an upward force. We always want the best possible "thing" in exchange for our time and money.

The exchange of time and money for quality is, of course, how we measure "value."

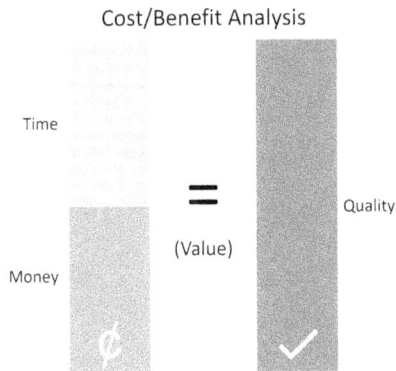

Cost/Benefit Analysis

If I receive more quality than I paid for with my time and money, it's a "bargain."

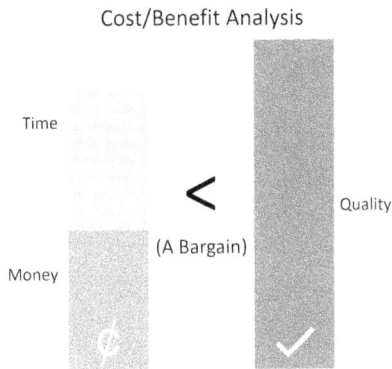

Cost/Benefit Analysis

On the other hand, if I pay more in time and/or money than I get in quality, it's a considered a "rip-off."

Cost/Benefit Analysis

Time

>

(A Rip-Off)

Money

Quality

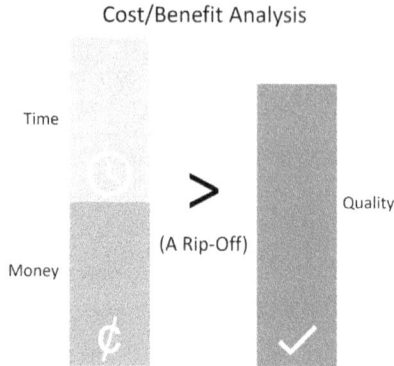

But here's the thing: It's a heck of a lot easier to measure "faster" and "cheaper" than it is to measure "better." That's because "faster" and "cheaper" are easy to quantify, using the inherently numeric measures of time and money, respectively.

The same can't be said for "better." What defines it is often qualitative, ill-defined, and subjective. Sure, we have a pretty good idea of the immediate, direct benefits of a purchase to us personally. But beyond that, we have a hard time understanding indirect impacts on us or any impacts on others.

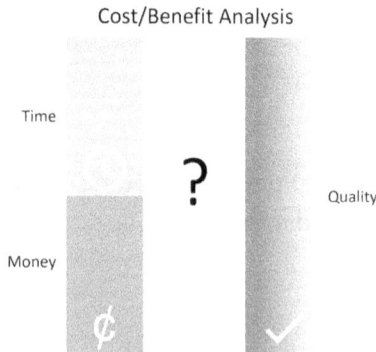

Cost/Benefit Analysis

Time

?

Money

Quality

And, as we've seen, the increasing speed and complexity of our world is making it harder and harder to see beyond "our picture." So, we increasingly guess, assume, or just ignore what lies "out there" when making decisions, assuming companies and the government have it all "handled."

But, also as we've seen, businesses seeking to maximize shareholder value have little motivation to spend more time and money "handling" the big picture either. If customers don't include indirect impacts in their calculus, then why should they? So, unless the government mandates that they do something, businesses prefer to write off the unknown as an externality.

Of course, this doesn't mean the unseen or unmeasured consequences and impacts don't happen. They absolutely do. We have just turned a blind eye to them, out of ignorance or convenience, until they get too big to avoid.

To put it another way, this world of increasingly imperfect information means we are caring less about overall *effectiveness* (how well something works) and more about *efficiency* (how much it costs.)

It's a myopic quest for "more for less" that is already impacting us and, in some cases, giving up progress we've worked so hard to achieve.

Food

There are many benefits to eating, including the pleasure we receive from the taste, feeling satiated when we're done, and the social interactions that can be shared over a meal. But the primary purpose of food is to keep us alive — to provide the calories and nutrients our bodies need to function and stay healthy.

So, efforts to make food more available and affordable (i.e., "faster" and "cheaper") are certainly well-intentioned. However, somewhere along the way, how we define the "better" part of the equation became corrupted, favoring calories over nutrition.

Perhaps it's because calories aren't as perishable as nutrients and are better able to survive the processing and transportation technologies that have driven the efficiency gains in food production.

Perhaps it's because the energy boost one gets from calories affects us immediately, whereas the impact (or absence) of vitamins and minerals is more subtle and long term.

However it happened, the last few decades have seen high-calorie/low-nutrition foods become cheaper and cheaper, while lower-calorie/high-nutrition foods have become more expensive.

Between 1978 and 2020, the cost of fresh fruit increased by 38% more than overall consumer prices, and the price of fresh vegetables increased by 34% more (even when adjusting for inflation). By comparison, the price of butter decreased by 4%, beer by 8%, and sodas by 31%, compared to overall consumer prices.[1]

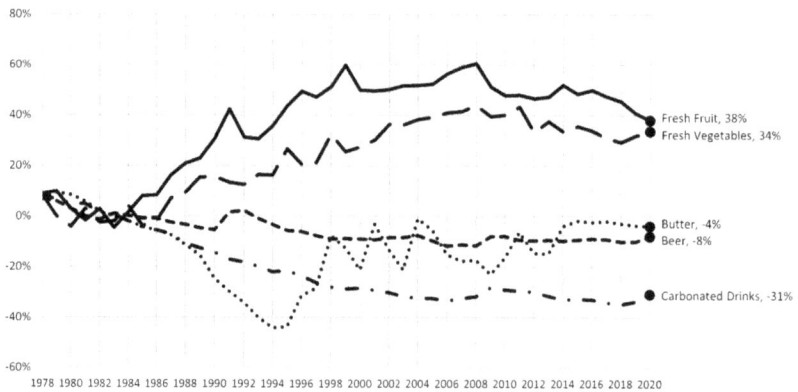

Annual change in U.S. food prices compared to all consumer prices (1978-2020)
(Source: U.S. Bureau of Labor Statistics, Consumer Price Index, U.S. City Average,
Adjusted for inflation)

According to a study by Adam Drewnowski, director of the Center for Public Health Nutrition at the University of Washington, the combined impact of this divergence is staggering. Satisfying a 2,000-calories-per-day diet with only high-calorie/low-nutrition foods would cost just $3.52, while choosing lower-calorie/nutrient-dense foods would increase the price tenfold, to $36.32 per day.[2]

High-calorie/low-nutrition foods tend to be highly processed and ready-to-eat, saving the eater preparation time in addition to money. So, is it any wonder that today's "more for less" shopper chooses to spend their dollar on 1,200 calories of potato chips instead of 250 calories of vegetables or 170 calories of fresh fruit?[3]

That assumes, of course, they have a choice.

According to data from the U.S. Department of Agriculture, almost 29.7 million Americans (9.7% of the population) live in a "food desert."[4] Defined as an area where residents live more than one mile from a supermarket (in urban or suburban areas) or more than 10 miles from a supermarket (in rural areas), these blank spots are created when supermarkets decide they can't make enough profit and close their doors.

Especially for individuals who don't have access to a car, this distance is a further disincentive to eating fresh, nutritious food. Instead, they are often forced to consume the less healthy, highly processed foods found in convenience stores and fast-food restaurants that are often much closer to home, especially in low-income or African American neighborhoods.[5]

Overall, our planet has no shortage of fresh, nutritious food. We just seem to have a hard time getting it to where it's needed, further driving the manufacture and consumption of processed food, which lasts longer and can travel farther.

Despite this, we still waste an enormous amount of food. The United Nations estimated in 2011 that we throw away a full one-third of food produced for human consumption.[6] It's lost throughout the supply chain, from the agricultural stage all the way down to final household consumption, averaging 527 calories per person, per day.[7]

That amount of food waste gets larger in more affluent countries, driven by an increase in waste at the end consumption stage. And, you guessed it, the U.S. generates more food waste than any other country in the world, throwing away over 1,500 calories per person, per day.[8]

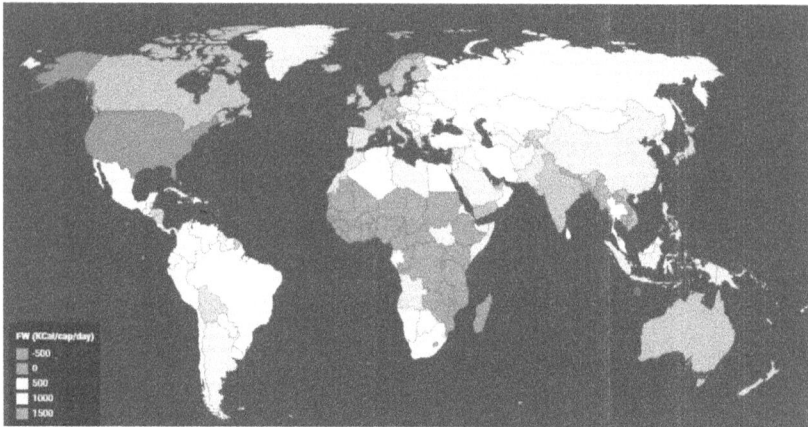

Existing comparable literature	Region/country of focus	Consumer FW estimate from literature: Kcal/day/cap (year)	Comparable affluence based estimates of FW from current work Kcal/day/cap (year)
Kummu et al. 2012[27]	World	214 (2005–2007)	326 (2005)
	World	510 (2010)	526 (2005)
			727 (2011)
Hic et al. 2016 [10]	USA	1050 (2010)	1572 (2011)
	China	620 (2010)	329 (2011)
	India	210 (2010)	121 (2011)
Hall et al. 2009 [3]	USA	1400 (2003)	1482 (2005)
Buzby et al. 2014 [28]	USA	1249 (2010)	1572 (2011)

Source: Compilation using estimates from the recent studies and current work

https://doi.org/10.1371/journal.pone.0228369.t003

Food waste by country (Source: Verma MvdB, de Vreede L, Achterbosch T, and Rutten MM, "Consumers discard a lot more food than widely believed," PLoS ONE 15(2), February 12, 2020.)

Even those of us with easy access to grocery stores stocked with fresh, healthy food we can afford frequently choose to save time and effort and let someone else do the cooking. Back in the mid-1960s, Americans spent just one-third of their food dollars eating out. By 2014, that number had grown to a full 50 percent.[9]

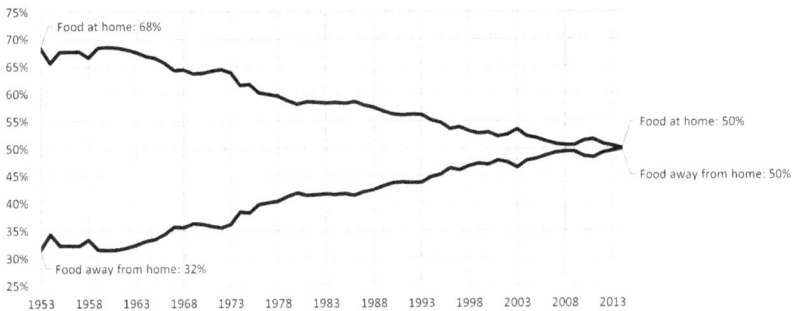

Percentage of food expenditures spent on eating out versus eating at home (Source: USDA, Economic Research Service, previously published Food Expenditures, 2016.)

And while this shift to restaurant dining certainly saves us food preparation time, it also leads us to eat more unhealthily.

According to Ruopeng An, professor at the University of Illinois, just the act of eating out adds an average of almost 200 calories and 10 grams of total fat to our daily intake.[10]

If you eat at a fast-food restaurant, it also adds 10 milligrams of cholesterol, 3.49 grams of saturated fat, and 300 milligrams of sodium. And while you might think that "full-service" restaurants are better, they're actually worse in many respects, adding 58 milligrams of cholesterol, 2.46 grams of saturated fat, and 412 milligrams of sodium to a diner's daily diet.[11]

When you put together all this processed and prepared food, the totals really start to add up, with the average American now eating 2,568 calories per day, compared to just 2,109 just 40 years ago.[12] That difference (459 more calories) is the same as adding a double cheeseburger to your diet, every day. Our current diet has also increased our consumption of sodium, saturated fats, and sugar,[13] while less than one in ten adolescents and adults eat enough fruit and vegetables.[14]

So, while the food we eat has definitively gotten cheaper and faster, has it gotten better? Or even stayed the same? Given that the primary purpose of food is to keep our bodies healthy, I'd argue that it hasn't and that it's actually gotten worse.

According to the Centers for Disease Control, 73% of U.S. adults are now overweight, including 43% who are considered obese, a designation that also applies to a significant percentage of our children: 21% of 12- to 19-year-olds, 20% of 6- to 11-year-olds, and 13% of 2- to 5-year-olds.[15]

All this extra weight (not to mention all that extra sodium, saturated fat, and sugar) puts a significant percentage of our population at a higher risk of serious, chronic illnesses, including heart disease, cancer, and diabetes, whose prevalence has increased from less than one percent of U.S. population in 1953, to 7.4% (23.35 million Americans) by 2017.[16]

Due, in part, to these increases, life expectancy in the U.S. *declined* from 2015-2018 — the first time that's happened in modern history. (It finally ticked back up in 2019, but only by four extra days to 78.86 years.[17])

The same cannot be said of other high-income, developed nations. Individuals living in Australia, Britain, Canada, France, Germany, the Netherlands, New Zealand, Norway, Sweden, and Switzerland enjoy at least 2.5 years more life than those living in the U.S.[18]

Americans started falling behind in 1989, with life expectancy becoming stagnant around 2010, even while all these countries have continued to increase.

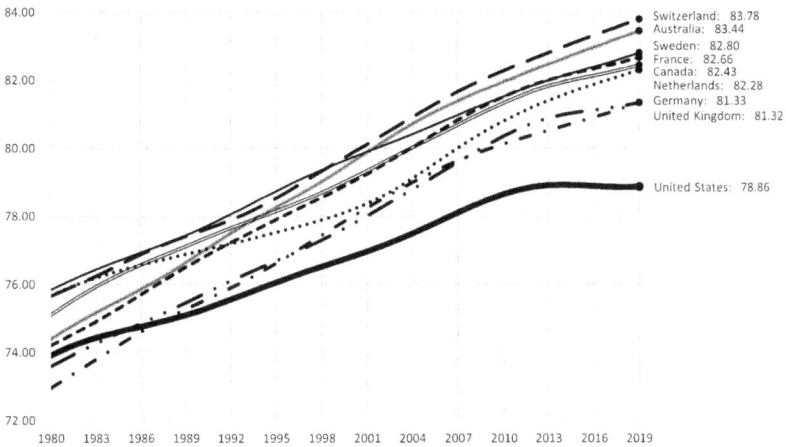

Average life expectancy by country (1980-2019) (Sources: Our World in Data, Riley (2005), Clio Infra (2015), and UN Population Division (2019.)

This is despite the fact that the U.S. now spends nearly twice as much per capita on health care ($8,715 vs. $4,608) as these other countries.[19]

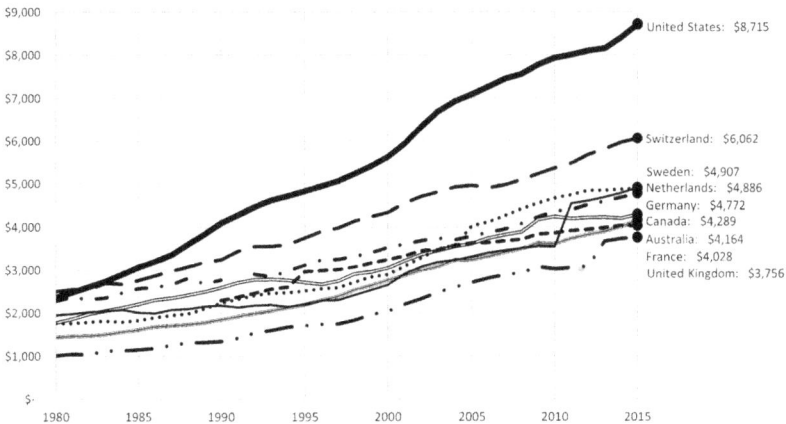

Per capita health spending by country (Sources: Our World in Data, Organisation for Economic Co-operation and Development (OECD) Statistics)

Clothing

Calories aren't the only thing we've been super-sizing. We've also been growing the size of our wardrobes. Don't believe me? Go check out the clothes closet in your bedroom.

Do you have one? Even a small one?

Congratulations, you have something most people in 1830 didn't have. Why? Well, they really didn't need a whole room (even a small one) to put their clothing in. Most Americans at the time only owned about three outfits: one for everyday wear, one for church, and perhaps another one (or parts of one) for seasonal changes.[20] Storage for this meager wardrobe was usually a hook on the wall or perhaps a chest or chest of drawers.[21]

Of course, if you were wealthier, you could afford to hire a seamstress to make more clothes, and maybe even a freestanding armoire in which to keep them.

However, as we've seen, technological advances in the manufacture of textiles and clothing in the late 19th century made clothing cheaper and more accessible to everyone. And the built-in clothes closet soon followed.

The first modern "reach-in" closets were introduced in 1880 as part of the luxurious Dakota apartment building in New York City.[22] These closets are tiny by today's standards (only about 24 inches deep)[23] but they did provide wealthy individuals with a built-in place to keep their growing collections of clothes and shoes.

Similarly, wire coat hangers were patented in 1903,[24] providing a cheaper alternative to wooden hangers on which people could hang all the new clothes they were buying.

By 1930, the average American woman's wardrobe had tripled in size compared to 1830, being composed of nine outfits.[25] This increase allowed for more variety and self-expression, as well as making it easier to launder clothes on a regular basis.

Wardrobes continued to grow after World War II, leading to the introduction of small "walk-in" closets in the 1950s.[26] These closets offered hang bars and/or shelves on two or three of the interior walls, allowing for even more clothes storage.

Today, the average American woman owns 30 outfits, enough to wear something completely different every day of the month.[27]

Keep in mind, that's an average. So, while many people own fewer than 30 outfits, others own more, leading to the introduction of "boutique" closets that can hold hundreds of garments. These closets are more like small rooms, easily measuring over 100 square feet in size and frequently containing seating, a storage island, or both. [28]

Lurking in these cavernous closets (or even smaller ones), are a substantial number of items that rarely see the light of day. A 2018 survey found that 28% of Americans own at least 15 garments that have never been worn or have gone untouched for over a year. And six percent own nine or more pieces that still have price tags on them.[29]

All in all, we spend an average of eight hours per month deciding what to wear, adding up to almost 100 hours per year inside our closets.[30]

Despite all this time, and all these options, 61% of Americans admit that they regularly or sometimes find themselves struggling to find something to wear. On average, we experience this "wardrobe panic" 36 times per year.[31]

So, what do we do when we can't decide what to wear? We buy more clothes, of course.

Currently, Americans buy nearly 20 billion garments every year. That's an average of 70 pieces per person (more than one item per week),[32] up from 40 pieces in 1990.[33] And while we're buying 75% more clothing than just 30 years ago, that's only half the story. We're also spending 38% *less* for it.[34]

These two factors ("more" for "less") compound to create a remarkable result: Today, we get almost three times as many garments for our clothing dollar as we did in 1990.

It's only possible thanks to the advent of what's called "fast fashion" — a segment of the clothing industry that focuses on constantly delivering new designs (often inspired by high fashion designers) to consumers at an affordable price. Fast fashion brands include Forever 21, Gap, H&M, UNIQLO, and Zara (which is often credited as the first company to focus on speed and low price).

How fast is fast fashion? When Zara opened its first New York store in 1990, they bragged that it only took 15 days for a garment to go from a designer's brain to being sold on the racks.[35]

This speed allows brands to introduce new clothing lines much more frequently. Whereas many high fashion brands release collections twice a year (spring/summer and fall/winter), H&M offers 12 to 16 per year. And Zara releases 24, meaning there's something new to buy (and another reason to visit their stores) every two to three weeks.[36]

The paradigm of fast fashion creates a never-ending series of seemingly perfect shopping moments: constantly refreshed styles at affordable prices. But while these shopping moments *seem* perfect, it's often because we're only looking at the moment itself, and how little money we're paying for something we want. We rarely take indirect or external costs into our calculations.

So that "bargain" might be costing you more than you think.

It starts with the simple fact that, with lots of clothing in our closets (and more purchased all the time), we don't wear each piece of clothing as much as we used to. This is called "clothing utilization" — the average number of times a garment is worn before it ceases to be used. And, worldwide, it has decreased by 36% compared to just 15 years ago,[37] with some garments now only being worn seven or eight times before being discarded.[38] The U.S. is particularly bad about this, wearing clothes for around a quarter of the number of times compared to the global average.[39]

So, while it's true that you're paying less for a garment, you're also getting less "usage" from it, making the price more equivalent to the utility you receive. It's like a disposable plate. You pay a lot less for one than for a ceramic plate, but you also use it a lot less, so the lower price matches the level of usage. Not to mention the level of quality.

The same is true of fast fashion, which often uses lower-quality materials and construction to maintain a low price point. The fact that these garments start to fall apart more quickly is justified by the fact the companies know they won't be worn more than a few times.

This is, of course, a self-reinforcing concept. If a garment is of lesser quality and starts to fall apart quickly, we customers aren't willing to pay as much for it, leading us further down the spiral of price and quality to where we are now: the era of disposable clothing.

It's true. A 2009 study published in the *International Journal of Consumer Studies* found that when we pay more for clothing, we tend to hold onto it (even if we don't wear it), as we are unwilling to throw away the investment we've made in higher-quality fabrics and crafts-manship. But if clothing is cheap, we are much more likely to just toss it in the garbage.[40]

According to the EPA Office of Solid Waste, Americans throw away almost 13 million tons of clothing and footwear every year. That's almost 80 pounds per person.[41]

The vast majority of it (70%) ends up in landfills,[42] accounting for approximately 6.3% of all municipal waste. In cities such as New York and Chicago, the percentage is even higher at ten percent of every-thing being buried in the ground.[43] Another 17% (2.2 million tons) is burned to create energy,[44] with the unfortunate side effect of sending millions of tons of CO_2 and other greenhouse gases into the atmosphere.

That leaves just 13% (1.7 million tons) of clothing that is recycled.[45] Unfortunately, the bulk of what is recycled doesn't end up as new clothing. Rather, most of it is "cascaded" into other industries and used in lower-value applications such as insulation, wiping cloths and mattress stuffing.[46]

But the end of a garment's life isn't the only time clothing has an impact on the environment. Its footprint can be measured all the way along the production and use path, starting with fiber production.

Clothing fiber is split into two categories based on the resources used to create it: man-made and natural. Man-made fibers account for about 70% of the market, totaling 60.4 million tons produced in 2014.[47]

The most popular man-made fiber by far is polyester, a synthetic made from petroleum. Incredibly inexpensive, the 46.1 million tons produced in 2014[48] required approximately 95 million barrels of oil for raw materials and production, the energy equivalent of seven trillion kilowatt-hours of electricity.[49]

That's 76.55 kilowatt-hours of energy to produce one pound of polyester — the same amount of electricity the average American home uses in 2.5 days. For one pound of polyester.[50]

The second most popular man-made fiber is viscose, a cellulose-based rayon made from wood pulp. In 2014, 5.2 million tons of it were produced,[51] requiring slightly less energy per pound (61.24 kilowatt-hours) than polyester. Still, that was over 636 billion kilowatt-hours.[52]

By contrast, natural fibers (such as cotton and wool) require much less energy to produce. The most popular natural fiber (cotton) requires just a third of the energy (26.95 kilowatt-hours per pound) that polyester requires, when it is grown conventionally. And when cotton is grown organically, that drops even more to just 8.57 kilowatt-hours per pound produced. For comparison at the other end of the spectrum, the most energy-efficient textile fiber is organic hemp, which requires just 1.22 kilowatt-hours per pound produced[53] — the equivalent of less than an hour of household electricity.[54]

Of course, cotton isn't without its problems. What it saves in energy use, it loses in other areas. Cotton farming is responsible for 24% of insecticide usage, plus 11% of pesticide usage, despite occupying only three percent of the world's arable land.[55]

Cotton is also a thirsty plant. It's estimated that each cotton plant requires ten gallons of water to achieve its maximum yield.[56] And that maximum yield isn't really all that much. One pound of cotton lint (what cotton thread is made from) requires the output of over 100 cotton plants.[57] And considering that a single pair of blue jeans requires about 24 ounces of cotton,[58] that new pair of pants represents the use of over 1,500 gallons of water — just to grow the cotton it's made of.

If that sounds like a lot of water, you're right. It's over 37 bathtubs filled to the top. Or enough water for a person to drink eight cups a day for eight and a half years. And that doesn't even include the water to dye the fabric. The world uses 1.3 trillion gallons of water every year — just for dyeing fabric. That's enough to fill two million Olympic-sized swimming pools.[59]

In fact, the fashion industry is the second-largest user of water, worldwide[60] (93 billion cubic meters annually[61]), and produces 20% of global water pollution.[62] Over 8,000 chemicals are used in the fashion business, many of which are highly toxic.[63]

Examples include chlorinate solvents such as nonylphenol ethoxylates (NPE), used to prepare fabric before dyeing. After use, NPE degrades into nonylphenol (NP), a toxic hormone disruptor and known bioaccumulative. Since 2005, products that contain more than 0.1% NPE or NP can't be sold in the E.U.[64]

Sixty to eighty percent of fabric colorants used are azo dyes,[65] many of which are toxic, including a class known as phthalates. Examples include diethylhexyl phthalate (DEHP), benzyl butyl phthalate (BBP), and dibutyl phthalate (DBP), which have all been shown to be toxic to the reproductive system. Other phthalates, such as diisononyl phthalate (DINP) and diisodecyl phthalate (DIPP) have had effects on the liver and kidney in high doses.[66]

And while you'd expect the worst exposure to these chemicals to be found in third-world garment factories and the surrounding neighborhoods, we, the end users, are not immune. A 2012 study examined 141 articles of clothing from 20 global fashion brands, such as Armani, Levi's, and Zara. What it found was that 63% of the 110 garments tested for NPE still contained measurable amounts of the chemical, with 20% of the garments registered at least 100 ppm and 11% registering over 1,000 ppm. Even worse, 100% of the 31 garments tested for phthalate showed measurable residue, with the image printed on one shirt containing 37.6% phthalate by weight.[67]

If you ever wondered why you're supposed to wash new clothes before you wear them, that's why.

However, washing clothes isn't an entirely innocent activity. If the garments are made of synthetic fibers, such as polyester, washing them releases microfibers into the water supply, which then end up in rivers, lakes, and oceans.

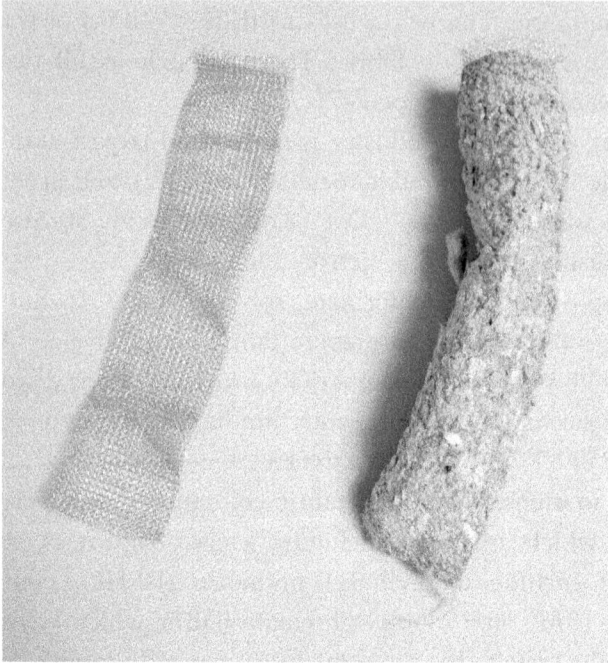

*Two washing machine "lint snares," one brand new, the other
after three months of average use.*

A 2017 report by the International Union for Conservation of
Nature (IUCN) estimated that 500,000 tons of microfibers are
released into the oceans this way every year — the equivalent of 50
billion plastic bottles. In fact, it's believed the 35% of all microplastics
in the ocean came from washing synthetic textiles.[68]

And then, of course, there are greenhouse gases.

Any industry that produces 100 billion items per year[69] will have
a significant output, and the clothing industry is no exception,
exceeding 1.2 billion tons of CO_2 every year, more than all
international airline flights and maritime shipping combined.[70]

These emissions come from a variety of sources ranging from
the output of wood-fired boilers in Phnom Penh's garment factories
(which burn through 2.3 million cubic feet of wood every month,
much of which has been cleared from old-growth forests)[71] to the
intentional incineration of unsold, yet perfectly usable merchan-

dise by brands such as Burberry (which torched $38 million worth just two months after announcing that it was committed to reducing its environmental footprint) and H&M (which, in 2017, burned 19 tons of "obsolete" clothing in a commercial waste-to-energy facility).[72]

No matter how you look at it, the impact of the fashion industry is massive.

Many of us have donated clothes to organizations such as Goodwill, the Salvation Army, or other local charities. Some of us have even shopped at their thrift stores, buying "gently used" clothing for an affordable price.

This secondary clothing market is truly a "feel-good" idea, knowing we're helping others with our castoffs while also reducing the amount of clothing that ends up in the landfill. The problem is the volume of clothing. Even though most of us don't donate clothes, and those that do only donate some, the system is still overwhelmed with more donated clothes than there are people to buy them. (After all, why buy a used t-shirt when a brand-new one is just five bucks?)

As a result, most charities only keep the best ten percent of contributions to sell in their stores. The other 90% are sold by the pound to textile recycling firms.[73] And while this does provide the charity with more revenue, it doesn't solve the problem of all those extra used clothes. It merely kicks it down the road to the recycler.

The recycler steers the worst three-quarters of what they buy into cleaning cloths and other industrial items. But the best 25% is bundled and transported overseas to developing nations, mainly in East Africa, where they are sold at prices so low that locals can afford them. For example, a pair of jeans can be sold for seven dollars.[74]

This, too, is a great idea, allowing the market forces to extract additional value from items that might otherwise be dumped in a landfill. However, this system, too, is swamped by the volume of clothing we don't want.

In 2015, East African countries imported $151 million worth of used clothes and shoes, mostly from the United States and Europe[75] where clothing utilization is lowest. This was so much inexpensive

clothing that it flooded the local economy, making it impossible for
the African textile industry to compete.

The situation got so bad that, in 2016, the members of the East
African Community (EAC), including Burundi, Kenya, Rwanda,
Tanzania, and Uganda, announced they would ban the importation
of all secondhand clothing and leather by 2019[76] in an effort to save
the local textile industry and preserve jobs.

In America, there are very few textile jobs left. In 1960, 95% of the
clothing we bought was made in the U.S. By 2013, that had dropped to
just three percent, largely due to the use of inexpensive overseas
labor and aggressive bidding practices, pitting hundreds of factories
against each other for even a small share of the work.

For example, in 2003, Gap utilized more than 1,200 different factories in 42 countries to create its clothing. In Bangladesh, one of the
countries Gap used for manufacturing, the average worker earns just
1/38th as much as their counterpart in the U.S.[77]

To be clear, Bangladesh is such a poor country that garment
factory jobs are considered well paid. They account for almost five
million jobs and 80% of the nation's export revenue.[78] But that
doesn't mean that factory owners, nor the fashion brands who hire
them, are willing to pay any more than is absolutely necessary to
secure workers or the final product. Someone is always willing to
work for less, creating strong economic pressure to reduce costs not
just through lower wages, but also by cutting corners on worker
safety and environmental protections.

Overseas garment production inherently lends itself to poor
working conditions, including long hours, repetitive tasks, quotas,
and exposure to toxic chemicals.[79] But since these dangers are all
"hidden" from consumers, they are often ignored in favor of saving
money.

But sometimes, these hidden costs suddenly become visible, as
was the case on April 24, 2013. That's the day the Rana Plaza, an eight-
story commercial building outside of Dhaka, Bangladesh, collapsed,
killing 1,134 garment workers.

It was a disaster that was completely avoidable. The day before, loud bangs were heard throughout the structure, and cracks had appeared in the walls and support columns. After inspecting the building, a local engineer declared it unsafe, and everyone had been evacuated.[80]

However, later that day, the building owner, Sohel Rana, stated that the cracks were only superficial, that the building wasn't compromised, and that the multiple garment factories that occupied the building (creating clothing for brands such as Benneton, Mango, and Walmart) could resume business as usual. Factory managers ordered employees back to work the next day, threatening those who didn't return with the loss of their jobs.[81]

On the day of the collapse, over 3,100 workers were in the building as the day began.[82] Shortly before 9 a.m., there was a power outage and backup diesel generators on the roof were activated so that work could continue. The vibrations from these generators (which weighed several tons each) were transmitted through the building, which had not been designed for industrial use to begin with and, in fact, had originally only been four stories tall.[83]

Soon thereafter, the structure crumpled, floor after floor, crushing those who couldn't escape.

In the aftermath, there was plenty of blame to go around. Over a dozen people were charged with building code violations stemming from the doubling of the building's height without a permit and without strengthening the lower walls and foundation — all cost-cutting measures. [84]

More importantly, 42 people, including Rana (who made a run for the Indian border after the catastrophe), were charged with murder[85] for sending people into a building they knew was unsafe, solely because they didn't want to fall behind on orders.[86]

Of course, the short deadlines that drove this type of pressure reach up the ladder all the way up to the brands who had hired the factories in the first place. So, it wasn't surprising that they were also seen as part of the problem.

In May 2013, a coalition of garment worker unions and NGOs created the Accord on Fire and Building Safety in Bangladesh (the

"Accord").[87] This voluntary, but legally binding agreement between factory owners, fashion brands, and labor unions was designed to significantly improve safety conditions in Bangladesh's garment industry.

The terms required independent inspections of all facilities, public disclosure of findings and action plans, democratically elected worker safety committees, and the empowerment of workers to refuse to work in unsafe conditions. But most importantly, the Accord included a requirement that brands pay factories enough so that there were sufficient funds available to actually fix working environments and keep them safe.

Driven by the magnitude of the Rana Plaza disaster and the accompanying negative publicity, the Accord was soon signed by over 200 fashion companies from around the world, including Benneton, H&M, Mango, Marks & Spencer, and PVH (the parent company of Calvin Klein and Tommy Hilfiger).[88]

Conspicuously absent from the list of signatories were major U.S. retailers such as Walmart, Gap, Macy's, Sears/Kmart, JCPenney, VF Corp (parent of The North Face, Wrangler Jeans, and Vans), Target, Kohl's, Carter's, Nordstrom, and Foot Locker.[89]

Citing liability concerns, many American brands instead signed an alternate statement that was less stringent. This agreement, the Alliance for Bangladesh Worker Safety, was widely criticized for being vague, allowing companies to leave the agreement any time they wanted, and failing to include any legally binding requirements to actually pay for safety improvements.[90]

DESPITE SOME U.S. BRANDS' lack of participation, the Accord has been highly successful. Facing the threat of being cut off by western buyers, thousands of factory owners have invested in fire doors, sprinkler systems, electrical upgrades, and stronger foundations — repairing more than 97,000 issues identified by Accord inspections.[91]

While the Accord doesn't cover all factories, workers, or brands, the overall improvement is undeniable. In the years before the Rana Plaza disaster, an average of 71 workers died every year, due to fires or building collapses. Since the Accord went into effect, that number has dropped to 17.[92]

And last time I checked, the cost of clothing hasn't skyrocketed from these life-saving changes or from the slightly higher prices brands pay the factories. Imagine that.

OTHER COSTS of our clothing addiction aren't hidden at all. Unless you regard them as hiding in plain sight. Take, for example, the amount of time we spend shopping for all those clothes we buy.

Some estimates show that we make over 60 trips a year to shop for clothes, shoes, and accessories, racking up over 180 hours looking for our purchases.[93] That's more than a year and a half of our lives, just shopping for clothes.

In the end, there's just no way around it. Clothing has enormous costs beyond the monetary price you pay at checkout. Today's focus on fast fashion has only exacerbated the situation, as companies trade "faster" and "cheaper" for increased resource consumption, environmental damage, and worker endangerment — consequences that all of us agree to whenever we purchase something to wear.

Sure, those impacts vary based on the methods and materials used (polyester versus cotton, for example). But you really can't make an argument that one is better than the rest. Because, given the volume of clothing that we consume, the impact is huge no matter what we choose.

Housing

As we saw in the last chapter, technological advances starting in the 18th century have made all three of the basic needs (food, clothing, and housing) much more affordable and accessible.

We've also seen how these gains in efficiency have allowed the average household to spend much less of their budget on these necessities. The share of the budget spent on food has declined from 43% in 1900 to 13% today. For clothing, it has fallen from 14% in 1900 to just three percent today.

But not housing.

The percentage of the average household budget spent on housing has actually gone *up*, from 23.3% in 1900[94] to 34.9% today,[95] despite the efficiencies gained in building materials and construction technology.

A look at home prices confirms it. We're paying more for housing now than we used to. In fact, between 1950 and 2000, the median home value more than tripled, even when accounting for inflation.[96]

How is this possible?

Let's start with the size of the house. In 1950, the average American home contained two bedrooms, one bathroom, and measured just 983 square feet. By 2004, the median new home had grown to four bedrooms, three (or more) bathrooms and measured 2,349 square feet.[97] (Never mind the fact that the average American household shrunk from 3.37 to 2.57 members during the same time frame.[98])

So, while we're paying more for housing, we're getting more for our money.

A lot more.

Master bedrooms the size of small apartments. *En suite* bathrooms with Jacuzzi tubs, rainfall showers, multiple toilets, and chandeliers. Game rooms. Home gyms. Home theaters. Man caves. She sheds. And, of course, the aforementioned "boutique" closets.

You'd think that would be enough space. Yet, at a time when garages are full of everything but cars, Americans turn to self-storage. It's estimated that almost one out of ten households rents a storage unit, paying an average of $89 per month, just to hold stuff. All told, there are 1.9 billion square feet of self-storage space in America, enough for every man, woman, and child to have 5.9 square feet to themselves.[99]

But ballooning home sizes don't fully explain the rise in housing costs. The price of land has also gone up. In fact, between 1975 and 2015, the price of land for an average home increased nearly four-fold, from $19,776 to $97,138 (measured in 2015 dollars.) [100]

As the saying goes, "God only created so much land." So, the supply is, essentially, static. But the same can't be said about demand. The U.S. population has grown by more than 50% since 1975,[101] contributing to higher and higher land prices,[102] especially in urban areas that were popular to begin with.

Yet there's more at play here than just simple supply and demand. There's also financialization — when housing is seen as a commodity or investment, instead of shelter and security.

For most of the 20th century, credit to buy a home was usually secured from a single, local lender, such as a bank or savings and loan. Similarly, rental housing was owned by individuals who lived in the community where the building was located.

But housing deregulation and the introduction of mortgage-backed securities (MBS) in the 1970s and 1980s changed that,[103] allowing anyone (even people living in other countries) to invest their money in bonds, with the proceeds going to fund home mortgages or purchase rental housing.

Designed to increase the amount of money available for housing, these changes succeeded in this respect but, in the process, they fundamentally altered the goal of home finance. No longer was a mortgage or an apartment building about helping a neighbor succeed in a shared community. Overnight, they became detached investments, judged solely on their financial performance.

After all, investors in these bonds have no idea whose mortgages or apartments they own. In fact, they own only tiny fractions of thousands of anonymous mortgages and rental properties, bundled together to spread the risk before being traded on the secondary market. So, when it comes to decisions such as evictions and foreclosures, information about the people living in the house or the impact on the community is absent.

The same holds true with the development of property. Commercially owned real estate is usually focused on the quickest, largest return on investment, not meeting the needs (and budgets) of the community. As a result, it's not uncommon for affordable housing (designed to be lived in) to be replaced by luxury housing (which is designed to be sold for a profit).

Indeed, a significant portion of investor-owned homes are intentionally left vacant, making them easier to sell. For example, a 2015 study found that one-fifth of investor-owned units (82,000) in Melbourne, Australia, were empty. And in the affluent London boroughs of Chelsea and Kensington, the number of vacant units increased by 40% between 2013 and 2014.[104]

This is the perverse nature of financialized housing: Luxury homes sit vacant while over a half a million Americans are homeless on any given night.[105] And everyone who can afford a home pays more for a place to rest their head.

Financialized housing was also a prime cause of the Great Recession of 2007-2009. Reduced government regulation and oversight allowed lenders to issue ever-larger mortgages to increasingly unqualified borrowers — all in search of more profit. Of course, when the housing bubble burst, it was U.S. taxpayers who bailed out many of the banks in question, since these institutions were deemed "too big to fail." The cost? $498 billion.[106]

———

GAINS IN EFFICIENCY have undeniably improved the ways we satisfy basic physiological needs such as those for food, clothing, and housing. But, at some point, we came to expect that these gains would continue (or even accelerate) forever.

However, all systems reach a point of diminishing returns and, as we've seen, reductions in price are now achieved not just through technological advancements, but also by shedding costs through externalities and/or compromising the effectiveness of the product.

For the most part, we don't seem to notice or just don't care what saves us time and money. We've got it in our heads that "more for less" will solve all of our problems.

Sometimes, we even try to satisfy higher-level needs with lower-level solutions. Who among us hasn't tried to console ourselves by eating most of a container of ice cream? To boost our self-esteem by buying some new clothes? Or escape loneliness by binge-watching the latest show from the solitude of our home?

But, obviously, these lower-level solutions aren't effective answers to higher-level needs, at least not in the long run. Yet, we continue to embrace these simple pleasures again and again, increasing the "dosage" from time to time, hoping that more is the answer.

Why wouldn't we? These low-level solutions are faster and cheaper than higher-level solutions, such as education, exercise, community involvement, and the arts.

And we're all about faster and cheaper.

Higher-level solutions require more investment of time and money because they work better at solving higher-level needs. To put it another way, you're paying for effectiveness.

Although, interestingly, if simple pleasures weren't so cheap, higher-level solutions would actually be more affordable, thanks to a quirk of economics called "Baumol's cost disease."

Back in the 1960s, economists William J. Baumol and William G. Bowen were curious as to why the wages of classical musicians continued to rise, even though the performing arts industry really hadn't benefited from any gains in productivity over the years. After all, they observed, it still takes the same number of musicians to play a Haydn trio (three) as it did when Haydn first composed it in the late 18th century.[107]

This seemed to fly in the face of classic economics, in which gains in productivity are a prime driver of higher wages for workers as well as lower prices for consumers.

Take, for example, the software industry which, like most technical industries, has seen massive gains in worker productivity over the years. As a result, consumer prices have plummeted (down 67% between 2001 and 2020),[108] while wages have risen dramatically (up 74%) during the same time period.[109] In fact, software is consistently one of the highest-paying industries in the country, with an annual average wage of over $182,000.[110]

But other industries, particularly services (as opposed to goods), have still seen significant wage increases over the decades, even without corresponding gains in productivity.

For example, look at college education. Wages for college and university workers increased by 91% between 2001 and 2020,[111] while student/faculty ratios remained largely the same (16-to-1)[112] during this time frame.

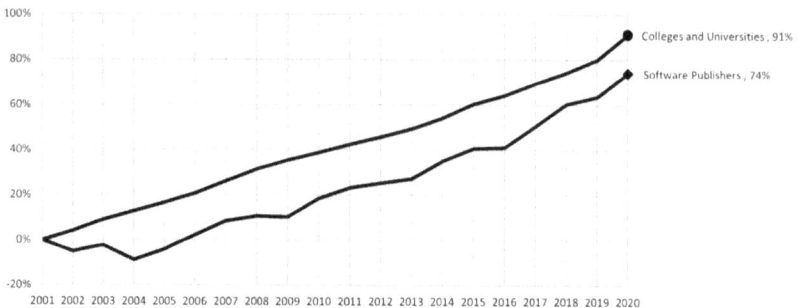

Percentage change in average annual wage since 2001 (Source: Bureau of Labor Statistics.)

What's driving the wage increases in the absence of productivity gains?

Baumol and Bowen established it was competition. Specifically, the competitive wages being paid by other industries.

Yes, musicians love to play music and university professors love to conduct research and teach. But they also want to make a decent living. So, to stop musicians, teachers, and other service sector employees from leaving (to become software developers, for example), managers have to pay more to retain them.

So, productivity increases in one industry indirectly drive higher wages in other industries.

And since these service sector industries can't make up the necessary margin through productivity gains, they raise the extra money for increased wages the only way they can. They raise prices.

That's one reason why the cost of college tuition increased by 152% between 2001 and 2020[113] (the same period over which the price of software dropped by 67%).[114]

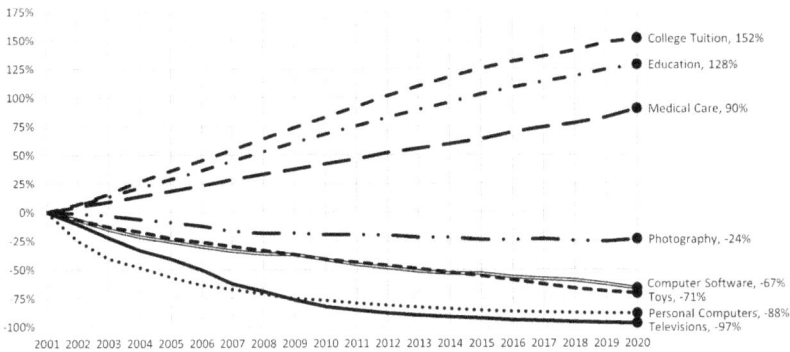

175%
150% ● College Tuition, 152%
125% ● Education, 128%
100%
75% ● Medical Care, 90%
50%
25%
0%
-25% ● Photography, -24%
-50%
-75% Computer Software, -67%
 Toys, -71%
-100% Personal Computers, -88%
 Televisions, -97%

2001 2002 2003 2004 2005 2006 2007 2008 2009 2010 2011 2012 2013 2014 2015 2016 2017 2018 2019 2020

Change in Consumer Price Index since 2001, by Industry (Source: Bureau of Labor Statistics.)

This odd side effect encourages us to further favor faster and cheaper lower-level solutions over more expensive and time-consuming higher-level solutions — even for our higher-level needs. That, in turn, only increases the disparity, accelerating the downward spiral of both cost and effectiveness.

It's hard to stop. After all, the twin dividends of efficiency (time and money) are powerful forces, having transformed large portions of the world over the last few centuries.

But somewhere along the way, Americans developed a stronger taste for one of these dividends (money) over the other (time), compared to other highly developed countries. And we've been trading time for money ever since.

Back in 1950, employed Americans worked an average of 1,989.24 hours per year (about 38.25 hours per week.) This was the shortest work week among a large group of industrialized countries, including Australia, Austria, Belgium, Brazil, Canada, France, Germany, Ireland, Italy, Japan, Netherlands, Spain, Switzerland, and the United Kingdom. Workers in these 14 nations averaged 2,158.98 hours per year (41.52 hours per week.) Most notably, Germans logged 2,427.43 hours per year (46.68 hours per week.)[115]

By 2017, the situation had completely flipped. Americans were working more hours per year (1,757.23 (or 33.79 hours per week)) than any of these 14 countries, which averaged 1,624.71 hours per year (or just 31.24 hours per week.))

And Germany, which had the longest work year/week back in 1950, enjoyed the shortest, with the average worker putting in just 1,353.89 hours per year (or 26.04 hours per week).

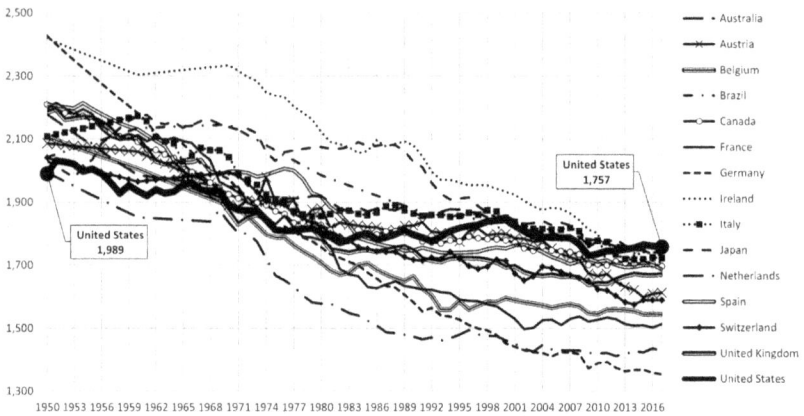

Annual hours worked, by country, 1950-2017 (Sources: Our World in Data, Feenstra, Robert C., Robert Inklaar and Marcel P. Timmer (2015), "The Next Generation of the Penn World Table" American Economic Review, 105(10), 3150-3182, available for download at www.ggdc.net/pwt. PWT v9.1.)

Sure, the average working American saw their work week decrease by 4.5 hours (an 11.7% reduction.) That's certainly an improvement and something to be thankful for. But workers in these other countries saw their work week decline by 10.3 hours (a reduction of nearly 25%) during the same time frame. And it's not like life in any of these countries could be considered backward, third-world, or in any way meager. These are some of the richest countries on our planet.

Residents of these countries just decided that they wanted a more balanced distribution of their efficiency dividends. They chose more time off *and* a better standard of living, rather than a heavier focus on monetary benefits.

It's simply a matter of priorities.

For many Americans, work is more than a necessity. It's how they define themselves and how they measure their life's worth. To these people, the concept of working less is at least misguided, if not downright heretical.

Oddly, a lot of these people don't even need to work. They are wealthy enough that they could easily afford more downtime. But, instead, they have chosen to elevate the Protestant work ethic to a quasi-religious status and devote themselves to what *The Atlantic's* Derek Thompson calls "workism."[116]

Thompson theorizes that the rise of workism sprung, in part, from the decline of traditional faith in America. Lacking the church, temple, or mosque at the center of daily life, people sought out new places to find community, new activities to give their lives meaning, and new things in which to believe.

Our jobs were an obvious choice. Work consumes a large part of our lives and provides for many of our necessities, so it wasn't long before the office became the new "house of worship."

This elevation was supported not just by our bosses, but also by our government, with neoliberal policies and programs that fully support the concept of more work. Unlike most advanced nations, the U.S. fails to guarantee paid leave for new parents, expects people to gain access to health care through their employer, and even requires welfare recipients to work in order to get food stamps.

In fact, the U.S. is the only developed country that doesn't legally require paid time off. All 35 other countries in the Organization for Economic Cooperation and Development mandate at least ten days of paid vacation, with most offering more than 20. (And that's on top of paid holidays, of which the United States requires zero.)[117]

That leaves it up to employers to decide when to offer paid time off and, if so, how much. Currently, only 77% of American workers receive any paid time off, averaging ten days of vacation and six paid holidays.[118]

But that doesn't mean people actually take those days off. A 2018 survey by the U.S. Travel Association found that 55% of Americans failed to use all their paid time off that year, wasting a whopping 768 million days (27.2% of what they had earned).[119]

After all, the culture of workism frowns upon vacations, personal days, or even sick days, which are not legally required for hourly workers who put in less than 30 hours per week.

If you're fortunate enough to be on salary, you're probably eligible to earn paid time off. But, in exchange, you're also probably *ineligible* for overtime pay, and working an average of five hours more per week than if you were paid hourly.[120] So your reward for success is actually more work. Congratulations!

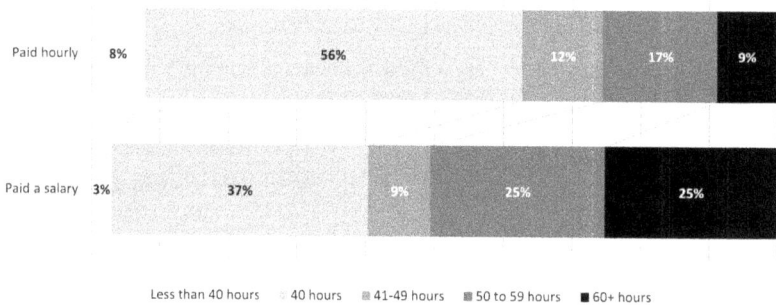

Paid hourly	8%	56%	12%	17%	9%
Paid a salary	3%	37%	9%	25%	25%

Less than 40 hours   40 hours   41-49 hours   50 to 59 hours   60+ hours

Percent of full-time employees by length of average work week (Source: Gallup, The "40-Hour" Workweek Is Actually Longer -- by Seven Hours.)

Today's youth are so indoctrinated in workism that a 2019 survey by the Pew Research Center found that 95% of teens believed that "having a job or career they enjoy" was either a "very important" or "extremely important" goal as an adult. In fact, this was their number one reported goal, easily beating out "helping others who are in need" (81%), "getting married" (47%), or "having children" (39%).[121]

Thompson notes that these are quite different priorities than our grandparents and great grandparents had expected for us, quoting economist John Maynard Keynes' 1930 essay, "Economic Possibilities for Our Grandchildren."

Keynes argued that, despite the setbacks of the Great Depression, society would continue to invent and create new ways to improve the world. And, thanks to these advances, the work week would have shrunk to just under 15 hours by the 21st century. Along the way, mankind would finally be released from its "traditional purpose" of survival and, instead, allowed to focus on "how to occupy our leisure."[122]

Clearly, we've chosen a different path. One that's efficient (if only in the narrowest terms), but not especially effective in the aggregate.

It's also one that we might want to reconsider. Fortunately, we still have a choice.

6

UNDERSTANDING SATISFACTION

"Any fool can be happy. What I'm interested in is satisfaction."

— CHARLIE TROTTER, AWARD-WINNING CHEF
AND RESTAURATEUR

I n the spring of 1968, Abraham Maslow must have been excited.

Not because the snow was disappearing from the sidewalks of Brandeis University where he taught. But because, 25 years after his "hierarchy of needs" had first been published, the world finally seemed to be embracing a broader view of humanity and its values.

The counterculture of the 1960s was in full swing and established thinking was under attack from all sides. Civil rights. The war in Vietnam. Environmentalism. Feminism. The sexual revolution. Music. Arts. Fashion.

It seemed as though everything was up for debate.

Maslow believed this spirit could even carry over into the world of business, suggesting that "classic economic theory, based as it is on an inadequate theory of human motivation, could be revolutionized by accepting the reality of higher human needs, including the impulse to self-actualization and the love for the highest values."[1]

But as we all know, that didn't happen.

Somewhere along the way, the rebellion of the '60s gave way to the narcissism of the '70s. And Baby Boomers, who had been so determined to transform society, gradually became more and more focused on themselves. By 1976, the transformation to self-indulgence was complete, and author Tom Wolfe christened them "the 'me' generation."[2]

Now, after almost 50 years of this generation being in the driver's seat, we've seen what happens when "me" culture fully develops. Yes, it has benefited us in some ways (particularly when it comes to satisfying our most basic needs), but it's clear that "Gordon Gekko" selfishness hasn't solved all our problems.

So here we are again. In a time of change.

A time, much like the 1960s, when people are questioning the establishment, elevating the value of human life, and looking for a better way for society to serve us and satisfy our needs.

Fortunately, we've learned a lot since the 1960s. That knowledge can better inform the decisions we make today so that, hopefully, the solutions we come up with this time will work better than the ones from last time.

But more important than anything we've learned is something we seem to have forgotten.

The concept of "enlightened self-interest."

That is, the realization that the best way to further your own interests is to also serve the interests of others.

It's an idea that recognizes the complexity of our society and the fact that our satisfaction only rarely depends solely on ourselves. Instead, everything is intertwined, so the best way to work towards our own success is to work towards making the whole system successful.

Most of us have heard of the concept, sometimes referred to as "doing well by doing good." It goes back a long time and is often attributed (like many things) to Benjamin Franklin.

But our understanding of it today is rather abstract and academic. To most of us, it's merely a "feel-good" philosophy that can't exist here and now.

That wasn't always the case. The idea used to be one of America's fundamental mores — a shared, internalized belief that helped to define our country, our culture, and our society.

This trait so impressed French diplomat Alexis de Tocqueville during a visit to America in 1831, that he described it as one of the keys to America's success in *Democracy in America*, his definitive book on early American democracy, published in two volumes between 1835 and 1840.

Tocqueville, along with his lifelong friend Gustave de Beaumont, traveled to America under the pretext of studying America's prison system, which at the time was considered to be among the best in the world.[3] In reality, they used their nine-month visit to study the broader United States in the hope of helping their own fledging French democracy to become more successful.

What they found was that, while the U.S. Constitution was a vital structural component, America's democracy truly succeeded because this structure was animated by certain unwritten norms that were common among the populace.

One of these was enlightened self-interest or, as Tocqueville called it, "self-interest rightly understood."

> *The inhabitants of the United States almost always manage to combine their own advantage with that of their fellow citizens ... they show with complacency how an enlightened regard for themselves constantly prompts them to assist one another and inclines them willingly to sacrifice a portion of their time and property to the welfare of the state.*[4]

In other words, early Americans didn't just talk about a democracy, they *acted* like one, knowing it was up to each and every one of them to actively build and maintain their new collective society.

Think of the motto for Alexandre Dumas' *Three Musketeers*: "All for one, one for all."

Enlightened self-interest isn't altruism. It's not doing something for others while expecting nothing in return. It's a half-step between selfishness and altruism. Call it being "indirectly selfish." Because focusing on the group of which you're a part ends up benefiting you.

Enlightened self-interest isn't an extreme exercise. Nor is it socialism or communism where everything is bound up in the state and what the state decides is best.

It's the collective impact of small decisions made by individuals. To quote Tocqueville, "the principle of self-interest rightly understood produces no great acts of self-sacrifice, but it suggests daily small acts of self-denial."[5]

One of those "small acts of self-denial" is delayed gratification, where you defer immediate gains in favor of longer-term interests.

To be specific, when you choose to not pursue everything you want, you're also choosing to not interfere with others' pursuit of self-interest, often involving limited resources and potentially greater need than yours. Your deference then builds a positive relationship with other members of your group, who can return the favor down the road when there's something you truly need.

This prioritization of personal needs and acknowledgment of community also have the side benefits of de-escalating competition, reducing conflict, and minimizing other stressful consequences that come from myopic selfishness.

Which are also things members of the group usually want.

Interestingly, the ability to delay gratification is associated with greater success in life, including better academic performance, social competence, self-assuredness, self-worth, and the ability to cope with stress,[6] not to mention being less likely to have drug problems, get divorced, or be overweight.[7] And some studies have shown that current generations are actually better at delaying gratification than previous ones.[8]

Unfortunately, human beings can have a hard time delaying rewards, especially as that delay gets further and further away.

For example, we may be willing to give up $5 now in exchange for $100 in an hour, but if we won't get the $100 for a day, a week, a month, or a year, the proposition quickly loses interest. Unable to determine if our future selves will value the $100 as much as we value the $5 right now, we end up discounting the value of the future payoff.

Behavioral economists call this "hyperbolic discounting"[9] because we reduce the future value estimate quite steeply as the potential delay is introduced but as the delay lengthens, additional discounting flattens. So, the value of waiting a month for that $100 is discounted significantly over just an hour's delay, but our estimated future value of that $100 would be about the same whether the wait would be a year or thirteen months.

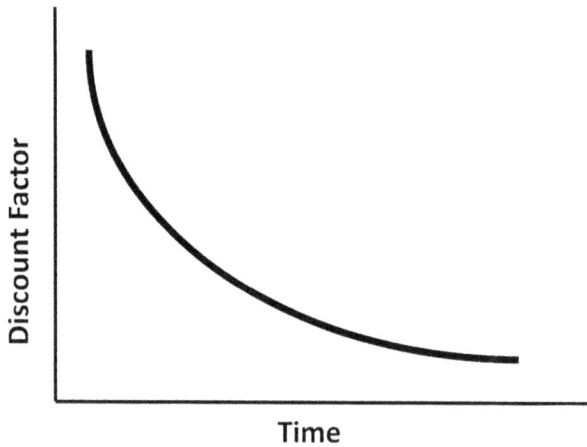

Hyperbolic Discounting

As a result, our "now" selves' impulse is to take the $5 *now*. And while that may be just fine in the moment, over time, those impatient choices catch up with our "future" selves, making it harder to get what we want down the road.

Such is the "tyranny of small decisions," a phrase coined in 1966 by the American economist Alfred E. Kahn[10] to describe how small, seemingly insignificant decisions can cumulatively result in a large and significant outcome, which is often undesired.

Kahn was inspired to study the problem when passenger rail

service to and from Ithaca, New York, was ended in 1961.[11] At the time, trains were the only reliable way to get in and out of Ithaca, especially in the winter (when the city gets over five feet of snow and average temperatures are below freezing).

However, during fairer weather, bus and airline companies would often lure away rail passengers with cheaper or faster service, depriving the train of much-needed revenue to maintain operations.

After a while, the collective financial impact of these individual travel decisions caused the railroad to discontinue service, leaving people with no reliable way to travel to and from Ithaca during the winter months.

Kahn classified this as a market failure because, even though both parties (passengers and the railroad) were making rational decisions, they were making them with different time perspectives.

Passengers were making decisions looking at only the very short term — one trip at a time. The railroad, on the other hand, was making one major, long-term decision: could they sustain train service to Ithaca?

If passengers had, instead, realized the long-term consequences of their short-term actions, they might have behaved differently to preserve the rail service to and from Ithaca — something that would have been in their own self-interest in the wintertime.

Another example of the "tyranny of small decisions" is what's known as the "tragedy of the commons."

A hypothetical example published in 1832 by British economist William Forster Lloyd,[12] it describes how herders, who are allowed to use public land (known as the "commons") as a pasture for their cattle, will each let their own cows eat as much free grass as they want, which satisfies each herder's short-term, rational self-interest.

However, because the commons is a shared, limited resource, all of these individual decisions will quickly lead to the commons becoming overgrazed, reducing its longer-term value to everyone.

As in Ithaca, the herders of the commons weren't acting maliciously. They just didn't have enough information to understand the broader consequences of their actions.

Most modern economic theory tends to assume that everyone has "perfect" information. In reality, that's rarely the case. No one has access to all the information. Instead, different people have access to different pieces of information — different pieces of the overall puzzle.

This "information asymmetry" allows individuals to take advantage of what they know, but keep it hidden from others, either consciously or based on feasibility.

Furthermore, individuals can choose not to gain *new* information that might be relevant to themselves or others. Again, this "ignorance" can be willful or merely pragmatic.

After all, there's a *lot* of information out there. And, as we've seen, it's increasing at an exponential rate, doubling as quickly as every 11 hours.[13]

Of course, the bulk of this information isn't especially useful to any one individual at any given time.

Take, for example, all the terabytes of data flying around the Internet of Things (IoT), updating corporate databases with minuscule and esoteric information about a zillion different things: like when my clothes washer finishes a spin cycle, what the soil temperature is in the corner of an Iowa cornfield, or when a FedEx truck crosses the Seri Wawasan Bridge in Putrajaya, Malaysia. Yes, each of these nuggets is important to someone, somewhere, but the rest of us can probably ignore it.

Probably.

Given the intertwined, complex nature of our world, it's hard to know for sure what's important and what's just noise.

Fortunately, while the last 50 years has created a lot more information, it's also created a lot more information processing power.

In 2011, two researchers estimated that all the computers in the world in 2007 could have collectively processed 6.4 quintillion instructions per second.[14] (That's "6.4" followed by 17 zeroes, by the way.)

To make that number a little easier to comprehend, it's about the same amount of processing power as one human brain.

And since then, thanks to Moore's law and exponential growth, computing power has continued to grow while its cost has continued to shrink.

Back in 2001, inventor and futurist Ray Kurzweil created a forecast of what our computing future might look like.[15] He estimated that by 2023, we'd be able to buy one human brain's worth of processing power for about $1,000. By 2037, he predicted that same computer would cost just one penny.

By 2049, his calculations showed that computing capabilities would have accelerated to the point where you could buy the processing power equal to the entire human race (200 septillion instructions per second [a "2" followed by 26 zeroes]) for $1,000, with that price dropping to just one cent by 2059.

This accelerated growth in information processing power coincides with its accelerated miniaturization to the nanoscale (measured in billionths of a meter).

To Kurzweil, the realization of nanotechnology paves the way for us to exceed the hard limits of our biological intelligence (i.e., our skulls can only hold so much brain) by augmenting it with nonbiological intelligence.

Specifically, he shared a compelling vision for how, in the not-too-distant future, we could affordably and exponentially increase our brains' abilities by introducing into our bodies millions of nanobot computers, connected to our own neurons and linked to each other via a local area network.[16]

Now, the idea of tiny "brain extenders" inside your body may sound like the coolest thing ever. Or it may horrify you to no end.

Either way, such augmentation may be the only way for us to evolve fast enough to deal with the coming "singularity" — the inevitable point where exponential growth in information technology changes our world so quickly that it exceeds our ability to understand it and adapt to it.

Fortunately (or unfortunately), we're not there yet. Similarly, nano-computers like the ones Kurzweil described aren't quite a reality.

That doesn't mean we can't start using extra computing power right now to better understand the broader consequences of our actions. We'll just need to access those computers remotely, rather than having them inside our bodies.

We already do this in lots of areas. Take, for example, weather forecasting.

Predicting future outcomes of such a large and complex system as the Earth's weather is only possible if we run huge amounts of data through sophisticated mathematical models. This requires a significant amount of computing power, such as NOAA's Weather and Climate Operational Supercomputing System (WCOSS), a 40-foot-long twin array of servers rated at 8.4 petaflops[17] (that's the ability to complete 8,400,000,000,000,000 calculations every second).

Clearly, we each don't need our own supercomputer to know our local weather forecast. Accessing the outcome of all these calculations is as simple is refreshing an app, switching on the local news, or reading an old-fashioned newspaper.

So, why not use the same idea to peer over the horizon into the indirect or unintended consequences of decisions we're about to make?

Machine learning, an integral part of artificial intelligence, is exceptionally good at unearthing this type of complex "cause and effect," using processing speed to quickly examine millions or billions of historic data points to see which actions were more or less likely to lead to a particular outcome.

All you need to do is define what outcome you want.

Of course, that's the trick.

Supercomputers are still quite expensive (costing hundreds of millions of dollars), so only governments and large businesses can truly afford them. Which, of course, means that many AI/machine learning efforts are focused on outcomes that benefit "un-natural persons" such as corporations.

As we've seen, these outcomes are overwhelmingly short term and financial, so as to better satisfy the perceived needs of their primary constituency, shareholders.

But, as we've also seen, shareholders aren't just shareholders, interested solely in today's share price. Shareholders are multifaceted "natural" human beings, playing many other stakeholder roles (e.g., customer, employee, neighbor, etc.), so they are interested in many other things.

So, companies would do well to utilize some of that supercomputer processing power to solve for the best ways to satisfy the broad needs of *all* of these stakeholder roles.

Which takes us back to human needs.

Which takes us back to Abraham Maslow.

His "hierarchy of needs" was truly groundbreaking in helping us understand ourselves and what motivates us.

But, as we have seen, this familiar pyramid has some flaws: most notably, its use of a hierarchical progression, which implies that lower-level needs (like food, clothing, or shelter) *must* be satisfied before you can satisfy higher-level needs (like self-esteem and self-actualization).

And, from a practical standpoint, Maslow's hierarchy of needs provides little guidance on how to *satisfy* our needs, especially higher-level ones.

To be clear, this isn't Maslow's fault. His was an academic theory, focused on classification, not resolution. But this does limit its application to everyday life.

For example, you can't go to the store and buy a can of "self-actualization." Nor can you instruct a supercomputer to solve this problem for you.

In short, the "hierarchy of needs" needs some refinement.

Unfortunately, we can't look to Maslow to provide that refinement. He died of a heart attack while jogging on June 8, 1970 — just three months before Milton Friedman sparked the shareholder primacy movement with his editorial in *The New York Times Magazine*.

To advance our understanding of human needs — and how to satisfy them — we had to wait 16 years.

And travel to Chile.

That's where an economist named Manfred Max-Neef was trying
to figure out a better way for struggling Latin American countries to
become more fully developed.

The standard way, sometimes called the "Washington Consensus," due to its promotion by Washington-based institutions such as
the International Monetary Fund (IMF), World Bank, and the U.S.
Department of Treasury,[18] allowed developing countries to borrow
money, but only if they made significant changes to their economies.

Specifically, these "reform packages" required countries to adopt
sweeping neoliberal, market-based policies including privatization of
state enterprises, liberalization of foreign trade policies, and the
reduction of government regulations.

In essence, they were required to create a much more favorable
environment for companies, including international corporations,
which were consequently gifted with new markets for their products,
as well as new sources of cheap labor and natural resources.

Meanwhile, the average citizens of these countries, who were
often poor, saw only limited improvements to their lives and a growth
in income inequality.[19]

Max-Neef believed there had to be a better way. A way for
economic development to benefit everyone.

After all, he was a self-described practitioner of "barefoot
economics," believing that economists couldn't just theorize about
what works from the comfort of their offices but had to get out and
get their feet in the mud where so many people stood every day.

The name stemmed from an experience he had early in his
career, high in the jungles of the Peruvian Sierra:

> It was an ugly day. It had been raining all the time. And I was standing in
> the slum. And across [from] me, another guy also standing in the mud —
> not in the slum, in the mud. And, well, we looked at each other, and this
> was a short guy, thin, hungry, jobless, five kids, a wife, and a grand-
> mother. And I was the fine economist from Berkeley, teaching in Berkeley,
> having taught in Berkeley and so on. And we were looking at each other,
> and then suddenly I realized that I had nothing coherent to say to that

man in those circumstances, that my whole language as an economist, you know, was absolutely useless. Should I tell him that he should be happy because the GDP had grown five percent or something? Everything was absurd.[20]

It was this "every person" mindset that drove Max-Neef to seek an alternative way for developing countries to improve conditions for *all* of their citizens. One where the economy served the people, rather than the people serving the economy.

He realized that the problems in Latin America were extremely complex and were probably shared by other cultures around the world. So, to help him on his quest, he enlisted professionals from a wide variety of disciplines, including anthropology, geography, journalism, law, philosophy, political science, psychiatry, sociology, and technology, and invited them from a variety of countries such as Bolivia, Brazil, Canada, Columbia, Mexico, Sweden, and Uruguay.[21]

What they came up with is called "Human Scale Development,"[22] an approach that starts with the realization that development should be about people, not things.

As a result, traditional metrics that measure the growth of things (such as a country's Gross National Product, productivity, or foreign trade balance) aren't appropriate indicators of success.[23]

Instead, more "human" metrics (such as those related to quality of life) are much more appropriate because they directly measure the impact of an effort on the lives of the general populace. Consequently, defining a universal set of fundamental human needs was integral to their efforts.

Not surprisingly, Max-Neef's "Fundamental Human Needs" has some similarities to Maslow's "Hierarchy of Needs." But it also has significant differences.

Whereas Maslow had hierarchical levels that had to be satisfied in order to reach fulfillment, Max-Neef presents complementary desires that can be pursued simultaneously.

More importantly, Max-Neef draws the distinction that needs are different from the things that satisfy them.[24] This seemingly obvious insight makes Max-Neef's Fundamental Human Needs a much more actionable matrix, rather than just a one-dimensional list.

Specifically, Max-Neef lists on one axis nine axiological needs (things that human beings value): subsistence, protection, affection, understanding, participation, idleness, creation, identity, and freedom.

On the other axis, he lists four existential needs (types of needs that are inherent to human existence): being, having, doing, and interacting.

This creates a matrix of 9 x 4, with satisfiers located at each of the 36 intersections.

Existential needs

Axiological needs

	Being	Having	Doing	Interacting
Subsistence				
Protection				
Affection				
Understanding				
Participation		Satisfiers		
Idleness				
Creation				
Identity				
Freedom				

As a very simple example, the intersection of "subsistence" and "having" could be food, because having food helps to satisfy the need for subsistence.

Existential needs

Axiological needs

	Being	Having	Doing	Interacting
Subsistence		Food		
Protection				
Affection				
Understanding				
Participation				
Idleness				
Creation				
Identity				
Freedom				

Similarly, a game of basketball could be at the intersection of "idleness" and "doing," because playing basketball is an activity that satisfies the need to relax and not work (in other words, to be idle).

		Existential needs			
		Being	Having	Doing	Interacting
Axiological needs	Subsistence				
	Protection				
	Affection				
	Understanding				
	Participation				
	Idleness			Basketball	
	Creation				
	Identity				
	Freedom				

Multiple existential intersections (that is, utilizing several cells in the same row) create greater potential for satisfaction.

For example, the need for "understanding" can probably be satisfied by reading a book. But, add in "having" a teacher and "interacting" on a college campus and you significantly increase the chances of understanding the subject you're studying.

		Existential needs			
		Being	Having	Doing	Interacting
Axiological needs	Subsistence				
	Protection				
	Affection				
	Understanding		Teacher	Reading	College Campus
	Participation				
	Idleness				
	Creation				
	Identity				
	Freedom				

In addition, Max-Neef points out that human needs are rarely isolated, so a satisfier for one axiological need (one specific row) often contributes to the fulfillment of other axiological needs (other rows).

For instance, when a mother breastfeeds her child, it primarily satisfies the baby's need for "subsistence." But, at the same time, it contributes to a sense of "protection," the need for "affection," and development of an "identity" as defined by the relationship between mother and child.

These synergistic benefits are what make breastfeeding such a valuable practice.

		Existential needs			
		Being	Having	Doing	Interacting
Axiological needs	Subsistence			Breast-feeding	
	Protection			Breast-feeding	
	Affection			Breast-feeding	
	Understanding				
	Participation				
	Idleness				
	Creation				
	Identity			Breast-feeding	
	Freedom				

For a more commercial illustration of a synergistic satisfier, consider your smartphone.

Say you're sitting on your couch and decide you're hungry. Your smartphone can help you order food (subsistence), without leaving the safety of your home (protection).

While you're waiting on your delivery, you can always play a game (idleness) or check out your feeds for the latest news (understanding).

When your food does arrive, of course you're going to take a few artful photos of it (creation) and post them on social media (participation). Then, while you eat, you'll be pleased to get emojis and compliments on your food photos (affection), which reinforce the image of yourself (identity) you're trying so hard to curate.

Is it any wonder that smartphones are so ubiquitous, even when the average one costs over $600[25] (not including data plans, apps, and other enhancements)?

Of course not. Because smartphones help us satisfy so many needs.

It's also an example of how companies can be hugely successful when they align their products (aka satisfiers) with human needs.

After all, while human needs may be finite and structured, the potential number of satisfiers are limitless. And we consumers will gladly pay for things that satisfy our needs.

Even if they don't actually satisfy them.

Wait. What?

In his work, Max-Neef points out that some satisfiers aren't real. They only pretend to satisfy a need or else they create other problems along the way.

In the smartphone example, the only needs that were truly satisfied were the needs for subsistence (the food), idleness (the game you played on your phone), creation (the photos you took), and protection (your desire to stay at home).

But that last need, protection, arguably went too far. Even with no real threat to your safety, it caused you to substitute what Max-Neef called "pseudo-satisfiers" for real ones.

Instead of you going out into the world to be social, only your virtual self went outside. As a result, you, as a human being, didn't truly interact with other people and didn't truly have certain needs satisfied. Your participation via proxy significantly diminished the social "bandwidth" of your experience in several ways:

- It curtailed your "understanding" by algorithmically limiting the content you see in your news feed to what will reinforce what you already believe, rather than challenging you with conflicting thoughts.
- It restricted your "participation" in society by limiting what and how much you're allowed to contribute (a photo and a few words) as well as who sees it.
- Similarly, the "affection" you received (i.e., emojis and text) was nowhere near as nourishing as the facial expressions and warm embrace that an in-person visit can yield.
- And the only "identity" that got enhanced was your virtual one.

In the end, these pseudo-satisfiers probably left you feeling pretty unsatisfied. But, rather than recognizing the shortcomings of our devices and trying something different, we tend to believe that we just need more of the same. So, we pick up our smartphones and try it all again.

And again.

And again.

Understanding the structure of human needs gives us the vocabulary to describe (and hopefully solve) this problem, but how do we recognize it in the first place?

There's a clue in the sentence above that says, "these pseudo-satisfiers probably left you feeling pretty unsatisfied."

Feelings.

Our feelings are much more than an emotional companion in our lives. They're a rich, built-in diagnostics system to help us get what we need. Broadly speaking, our feelings and emotions can help us in three ways:

1. They can help us determine what we need at any given moment in time.
2. They can let us know if a satisfier has worked (i.e., the desire goes away, leaving us feeling "satisfied") or if it hasn't worked (with the pangs of desire still growling at us).
3. If the satisfier didn't work, they can help inform a "course correction" so we can try a different satisfier that might work better.

But our feelings can only help us if we understand them beyond a cursory, binary acknowledgment of whether we "liked" or "disliked" something.

Our emotions are multidimensional and nuanced. Paying attention to this detail provides a wealth of feedback that can better inform our decisions and choices, leading to a better quality of life.

This ability to recognize emotions (in ourselves and others) and use that information to guide thinking and behavior is called "emotional intelligence," a term popularized by science journalist Daniel Goleman in his 1995 best seller, *Emotional Intelligence: Why It Can Matter More Than IQ.*

You've probably heard of emotional intelligence (sometimes referred to as EI or EQ) before. That's not surprising. At the time of this writing there are over 9,000 books about the subject. Not to mention thousands, if not tens of thousands, of consultants who are willing to help you, or your company, develop your emotional intelligence.

All those resources are probably a good thing because, unfortunately, only about a third of us can accurately identify our emotions as they're happening.[26]

That's understandable. Emotions are fleeting by nature. Sometimes they present as something clear as day: easy to recognize, name, and understand. Other times, they're vague and subtle, evaporating before we can put our finger on them.

But just because we can't identify an emotion doesn't mean it's not impacting us and influencing our thinking every minute of every day. At those times, we're just flying blind, buffeted by unseen emotional turbulence.

Which is probably why so many of us claim to be unhappy.

According to the *2019 World Happiness Report*, produced as part of the United Nations' Sustainable Development Solutions Network initiative, the United States is the 19th-happiest country in the world, scoring 6.892 out of 10.[27]

While that may sound good considering there were 156 countries in the index, it also represents the third year in a row we dropped in the rankings, down from 13th place in 2016, when our score was 7.104 out of 10.[28]

This decline happened despite consistent improvements in key U.S. financial measures such as GDP, unemployment, and inflation during the same time period.[29]

So, it seems that money can buy happiness, but only to a point.

Having money gives you the luxury to not worry about the basics of life: food, clothing, and shelter. Satisfiers for these urgent needs are quite transactional, so having money is critical. Without enough money to satisfy these subsistence needs, life is miserable, or even imperiled.

But once these immediate needs are satisfied, money's role is diminished to that of a supporting resource. After all, needs such as affection, participation, and identity require something money can't buy: other people.

While money can certainly help facilitate experiences that lead to interpersonal relationships, being rich is no guarantee against loneliness.

At this point you might be wondering, "So, how much money do I need?"

Such a question isn't surprising given how financially focused our society is. However, it's actually a great question because, if you know how much money you actually need to facilitate happiness, then you'll know the finite point at which you can stop working and start living.

That's quite different than the never-ending quest for "more" that so many of us are involved in today — constantly, mindlessly working just to keep adding to our bank accounts, never knowing how much is enough.

As it turns out, once you reach this point of enough (what scientists call the "satiation point"), making more money won't make you any happier and, in fact, will make you *less* happy.

That's based on a 2019 review of 1.7 million responses from the Gallup World Poll by psychologists from Purdue and the University of Virginia.

What they found was that, for the whole world, the satiation point is between $60,000 and $95,000 of annual income.[30] (The range is based on three different types of satiation: $60,000 to maximize short-term positive feelings, $75,000 to minimize short-term negative feelings, and $95,000 to optimize longer-term feelings about your overall life.)

Of course, differences in culture and the cost of living mean that these numbers vary by region. For North America, the satiation point is between \$65,000 and \$105,000,[31] again, depending on whether you're talking about income's effect on positive emotions, negative emotions, or overall life evaluation.

Any more than that won't make you happier and will probably make you less happy.

Extrapolating from that, you can assume that even these numbers will go up or down depending on where in North America you live.

And, no, you might not, personally, make that much money. But the important thing to recognize is that the amount of annual income associated with happiness isn't massive. It's not a billion dollars, a million dollars, or even in the mid-six-figures. It's something that is probably attainable for almost everyone if income distribution were more equitable.

So, if you're one of the "lucky" ones who makes six (or more) figures and you're not especially happy, maybe it's a sign that income inequality isn't just hurting poorer people. It's hurting you, too.

To be clear, when I talk about being "happy," I'm not talking about the short-term positive feeling that releases dopamine into your bloodstream and makes you smile for a second or two. You might call that emotion "joy" or "delight."

The happiness I'm talking about is a long-term feeling of peace, contentment, or well-being. It's a feeling that doesn't always come quickly or from just doing what we like or know we'll enjoy.

It comes from being curious and taking risks.

That's what Colorado State psychologists Todd Kashdan and Michael Steger found in a 2007 study: People who frequently felt curious also experienced the most satisfaction in their lives.[32]

This is in spite of the fact that curiosity is inherently an anxious state. After all, when you're curious, you're exploring something new, something unknown. And that comes with a certain amount of risk.

But if you accept that risk, and are able to be uncomfortable for a while, your curiosity can often lead to the satisfaction that comes from successfully navigating a new experience, even if that experience requires putting short-term happiness on hold.

When I was a teenager, I went to Boy Scout summer camp every year. Nothing fancy, just camping out in the woods of Georgia or North Carolina for a week, doing all that stuff you do at summer camp: arts and crafts, archery, nature walks. It was all very accessible, familiar, and easy.

After a while, I got bored. I mean, how many leather lanyards can you make? So, I decided to push myself and sign up for the "mile swim."

I wasn't a competitive swimmer by any stretch of the imagination, but several of my friends had completed the mile swim the year before and it seemed like a cool thing to be able to say that you had done. Then again, a mile sounded like a very long way.

Hmm.

Oh well, nothing ventured, nothing gained. So, on with the swim trunks and into the water.

Sure enough, it sucked. It was definitely not a "pleasurable experience." The water in question was a lake in North Carolina which, even in summer, was a startling 63 degrees. And, since it was a lake, the water wasn't exactly crystal-clear.

Nevertheless, the handful of other guys who had signed up and I just started swimming (if for no other reason than to warm up). Slowly, but steadily, we swam four laps around the lake, following a couple of adults in a rowboat who were there for safety.

After an hour, we climbed out of the lake and staggered down the dock, leaving a weaving trail of wet footprints on the wood planks. When I got back to our campsite, I collapsed onto my cot, exhausted.

But I was also proud. I had swum a mile. Five-thousand, two-hundred, and eighty feet. In a lake. It was an oddly rewarding bit of displeasure and a perfect illustration of how doing what's not easy can be immensely satisfying. (Certainly, it was more rewarding than if I had merely paid someone else to swim a mile.)

It was one of many times I have invested in myself, trading short-term happiness for long-term satisfaction. Other, personal examples include a 150-mile canoe trek, quitting my job to go back to grad school, and deciding to raise children.

Not to mention the countless, smaller risks I take every day to satisfy my curiosity, whether it's trying a new cuisine, saying hi to a new neighbor, or even driving a new route on the way home from work.

That's not to say life has to be all about curiosity, risk, and uncertainty. There's absolutely a place for the tried-and-true, your "regular," and the fast-and-easy. (Don't even think about messing with my morning coffee. Seriously.)

But our current society seems much more focused on reinforcing our routines, rather than rewarding our curiosities.

Our heavy dependence on computer technology brings with it the myriad of algorithms that allow our devices to actually do what they do. These algorithms, especially those for social media and news feeds, are also designed to keep us online longer, so we can be served more advertising which, of course, makes more money for these platforms.

One of the primary methods used to extend our engagement is to show us content that is similar to what we have already expressed an interest in. This "echo chamber" plays on our confirmation bias to reinforce that what we already know (and what we already do) is the best, if not only option available.

Too much exposure to this artificially narrow view of the world changes us, making us hesitant (if not downright scared) to step out of our bubble and try something new.

Think of these algorithms as a swarm of "yes-men," only telling us what we want to hear. And, just like real-world yes-men, they only say what they think will make you like them more.

And don't forget, not only is all this content "nonthreatening," it's also free. What's not to like?

As someone once told me, "If you don't pay for something, you're not the customer — you're the product." In this case, we're the product sold to advertisers by content platforms.

The more data we give the platforms (either actively or passively), the more they're able to "improve" the quality of that product. That is, they can better determine what we're more likely to buy and then show us ads for those types of products.

Of course, this more "highly qualified" audience is worth more to an advertiser, so the platform can charge more money for those ads.

Our only role in this process is to provide the data upstream and consume the content transmitted downstream. Any participation beyond that, such as trying to influence how our data is used, is completely unwanted.

After all, we're not the customer.

Entrepreneur, author, and journalist John Battelle compares this relationship to the "dumb" computer terminals that were prevalent before the PC revolution of the 1980s.[33] These "dumb" terminals were little more than a monitor and keyboard, with all the real processing (i.e., the thinking) handled at a remote centralized server. All the terminal did was send data up to the server and display what came back.

Unfortunately, our current technological mass subservience is the exact opposite of the mass participation required for individuals and societies to innovate and flourish.

Indeed, economist and Nobel Laureate Edmund Phelps notes that "mass flourishing" (that is, when there is prosperity on a national scale) only comes from "broad involvement of people in the processes of innovation: the conception, development, and spread of new methods and products — indigenous innovation down to the grass roots."[34]

He points out that this type of participatory "dynamism" doesn't just lead to economic prosperity, but also to human prosperity; a system and society that encourages innovation (and not just lower-cost imitation) generates both satisfaction and financial success.

By Phelps' estimation, we haven't seen "mass flourishing" in any society since the 1960s.

That decade, of course, was when millions of people were engaged and involved: acting with shared purpose to change the status quo and make things better. This was a society that was relatively undaunted by the scale of such enormous goals as civil rights, saving the environment, and even going to the moon.

As John F. Kennedy said in 1962, "We choose to go to the Moon in this decade and do the other things, not because they are easy, but because they are hard."[35]

Our moon shot for this decade will be to change the nature and purpose of business from one where we serve the corporation, to one where corporations serve us; to harness the great power we have bestowed on companies and redirect it to satisfy all the needs of all the people; and to make this change before exponential growth in technology locks the current relationship in place.

Transforming the institution of business will be hard. But hard doesn't mean impossible.

Climbing any mountain is only accomplished through a series of tiny steps. Similarly, climbing this mountain will take many, many small steps made by both people and companies.

Arriving at the summit will also be beneficial for both.

We will find ourselves living more satisfied lives. And companies will realize a sustainable, acceptable way to earn a profit. One that relies on creating value, rather than extracting it.

But first, we have to get there. And that requires a route.

7

SIX STEPS FOR BUSINESS LEADERS

"A goal without a plan is just a wish."

— ANTOINE DE SAINT-EXUPÉRY (ATTRIBUTED)

As much as we like to personify brands, they're not real people like you and me.

You can't invite a brand out for coffee, sit across the table, and say, "Look, you're acting like a jerk."

The companies behind the brands aren't "natural persons" either. As we've seen, they're only persons in a legal sense, with, as Edward Thurlow said, "no body to jail, no soul to damn."[1]

Yet, these phantoms have a very real impact on our corporeal world thanks, in large part, to the very real human beings who work for the companies.

So, if we want to change the way a company acts, we have to change the way its people act.

That change can come from many places, although it goes by different names, depending on where it originates:

- Change which comes from senior management is usually

called "strategy," which implies the endorsement of hierarchy.

- Change from workers is called "initiative" (when management likes it) or "insubordination" (when they don't).
- Change from outside is often called "pressure." As a general rule, change is much harder to bring about from the outside than from the inside. On the outside, you don't have direct access or input into decisions. You can only encourage or try to force those on the inside to make decisions that lead to change.

No matter where it starts, corporate change is usually driven, at least in part, by an individual's desire to personally benefit from their ideas and actions. Whether it's a promotion, a raise, recognition from co-workers, or the satisfaction that comes from "making a difference," we all want a dividend when we invest our time and expertise in an enterprise.

That's one reason why everyone, not just senior management, is constantly trying to answer the question "what's next?" What's going to give the enterprise a competitive advantage? What's going to drive more revenue? What's going to make us more profitable?

If you're interested in any (or all) of these, then you should probably focus less on cutting costs, and more on building your company's brand. And by "brand," I don't mean the minutiae of names, logos, and advertising taglines over which businesses often obsess.

The best definition I've heard of what a "brand" actually is came from the head of my graduate program, Tom Duncan. During the first week of class, he declared, "A brand is a relationship."

Brilliant in its simplicity, the aggregate concept of a "relationship" is something all of us can easily understand. A brand is not just the goods or services the company sells. It's not just an amusing commercial we see on TV. It's the sum total of all the actions, interactions, and transactions that involve the company.

All of them. Even those that don't include the company.

For example, a customer may tell her friend how much she loves your company's product or vent about how frustrated she is with your customer service. The company isn't there, has no idea what was said, but its brand is enhanced or damaged, respectively, by the conversation.

This sort of third-party chatter has always been there and has always been out of the company's control. But the explosion of easily accessible information created by technological advances has super-charged these conversations, so that they now dominate the discussion, drowning out the once-commanding voice of the company.

Needless to say, what's being discussed isn't always favorable, so the company would prefer the information had never been discovered in the first place. Some of the information is true. Some of it is fake, or at least out of context. Either way, when negative information conflicts with the rosy marketing messages a company sends out, it creates cognitive dissonance, mistrust, and a weaker brand.

This schism is the most pressing concern for the future of business.

The ultra-transparency of today's society means there can no longer be two corporate narratives — one external and one internal.

- You can't just say you're customer-centric when we can see that you put shareholders first.
- You can't just say you care about your employees when we can see that you don't provide paid family leave.
- You can't just say you protect the environment when we can see you build planned obsolescence into your products.

In short, you can't just say you care about my needs and then not address them.

These disparate messages must be reconciled. Otherwise, companies will remain hamstrung because they're too busy trying to defend themselves.

And since companies won't stop saying good things about themselves and their products, the only choice is to change how the company acts so that the "do" actually matches the "say."

Think of the company as an automotive assembly plant that needs to retool so it can produce a newer model. It's not giving up what it does, just updating its products and the way they're made.

Of course, retooling a whole company is more complicated than modernizing a factory. But both aims require the same commitment, investment and, above all, a clear idea of where you're going.

Retooling Your Company (in six not-so-easy steps)

Step One: Make Your Choice

Actually, the first step is quite easy. All you have to do is answer this question:

What type of brand do you want your company to have?

Do you want it to be seen as:

The psychopath who, after telling a person whatever they want to hear, is discovered to have been quietly stealing everything that person holds dear and giving it to someone else?

Or

The best friend who listens, asks questions, and considers the consequences before doing or saying anything, knowing that whatever it does or says must have the other person's best interests at heart?

If you've made it this far in this book, my hope is you'll choose "best friend." And not just because no one, not even a company, wants to be considered a psychopath, but because you see that a company acting like a best friend isn't just the best thing for people, but also for companies like yours.

Step Two: Figure Out Which Friend You're Going to Be

Saying you want your company to act like a best friend is easy. Doing it is something else entirely. Not only is there significant internal inertia to overcome, but there's pressure from just about everywhere else to keep your company acting like a psychopath.

Such is the uphill slog of a revolutionary.

Your best ally in this journey is a crystal-clear vision of exactly *who* your brand is trying to be.

Start with the basics. Best friend brands all live by a singular tenet: *Companies should serve people, not the other way around.*

This principle reflects the fact that, regardless of today's inverted relationship, corporations were originally created by people to benefit people. They were a way to harness our collective energy, knowledge, and resources, knowing that, synergistically, we can have a greater impact on human lives than we could as individuals.

It's a "subordinate," as opposed to "superior," role, one that reflects the inherent difference between "natural" and "legal" persons.

In many ways, a company in this subservient role is like a robot, something which is also created by people to serve people. As such, best friend brands might also be governed by the Three Laws of Robotics, as described by science fiction author Isaac Asimov in his famous 1950 collection of short stories, *I, Robot:*[2]

> **First Law:** A robot may not injure a human being or, through inaction, allow a human being to come to harm.
> **Second Law:** A robot must obey the orders given it by human beings except where such orders would conflict with the
> First Law.
> **Third Law:** A robot must protect its own existence as long as such protection does not conflict with the First or
> Second Law.

Just swap out the word "robot" for the word "company" and you get:

> **First Law:** A company may not injure a human being or, through inaction, allow a human being to come to harm.

Second Law: A company must obey the orders given it by human beings except where such orders would conflict with the First Law.

Third Law: A company must protect its own existence as long as such protection does not conflict with the First or Second Law.

In Asimov's stories, how the Three Laws are interpreted changes their application. Strict interpretation of the word "harm" would have a robot sacrifice its own existence to stop a human being from getting even a minor scratch. A more relaxed interpretation would only have the robot intervene when the perceived harm was significant.

Similar decisions will need to be made on how the Three Laws apply to a company, since one wouldn't want an enterprise to entirely cease operations just to protect one tree on one piece of property that one person thought was beautiful.

But, as a general principle, a corporate version of the Three Laws does properly prioritize the needs of humans over the needs of companies, providing a fundamental grounding for decisions and behavior.

Building on this foundation, the next step is to determine, specifically, *which* friend your brand is going to be.

In the real world, most of us have a variety of friends. Each one offers us a unique combination of experiences, knowledge, and perspectives that, together, fulfill different needs we have.

There's the friend who knows how to repair stuff. The friend who knows everything about food. Or the friend who has lived in a city that we're about to visit.

When we have one of these needs, we reach out to that particular friend for help. Now, these functional roles aren't the only reason we're friends, but they do help to define who they are in our minds.

So, beyond just being selfless, identifying which friend your brand can be will also help define what functional role it can play in people's lives.

Historically, businesses have equated their functional role with the category or industry that they're in. For example, if they're in the widget industry, the company believes its role is to create the best darned widget out there, knowing that when people need a widget, they will buy theirs. The company strives to beat its competitors in that same category, hoping they will ultimately succeed in becoming the "number one" company in that industry.

This worldview is reinforced from all sides, by a variety of stakeholders.

Most of the federal government categorizes companies using the North American Industry Classification System (NAICS). This standardized carve-up of the economy separates businesses into more than 3,500 different types of production, ranging from "Soybean Farming" (NAICS 11111) to "International Affairs" (NAICS 92812).

The structure is quite specific, for example, differentiating between the manufacture of "Bread and Bakery Products" (NAICS 31181), "Cookie, Cracker, and Pasta" (NAICS 31182), and "Tortillas" (NAICS 31183); or between "Automotive Parts and Accessories Stores" (NAICS 44131) and "Tire Dealers" (NAICS 44132).

Similarly, the finance and investment community, including the Securities and Exchange Commission, uses Standard Industry Classification (SIC) codes to categorize businesses. The predecessor to NAICS, SIC separates the economy into 439 industries. While not as narrow as NAICS definitions, SIC codes still force companies into competitive sets based on production, encouraging shareholders to rank companies using this type of label.

Even natural persons like you bolster the role that business categories play in our world. Many people regularly introduce themselves by not just stating their name, but also by saying what industry they work in. (It's not quite as bad as the 12th century, when people *took* their surname from their occupation, with barrel makers named "Cooper," those who ground grain named "Miller," and metal workers named "Smith.")[3]

The problem with this focus on categories is that it's all based on the perspective of the *companies* that produce satisfiers, not the *human beings* who acquire and use them. It's a misalignment that means a company's category will never be a good way to define what role its brand can play in our lives. Business categories just aren't customer-centric.

The human condition is much more likely to be perpendicular to industry verticals, with us crossing multiple categories (like stepping-stones) during a journey to satisfy our needs.

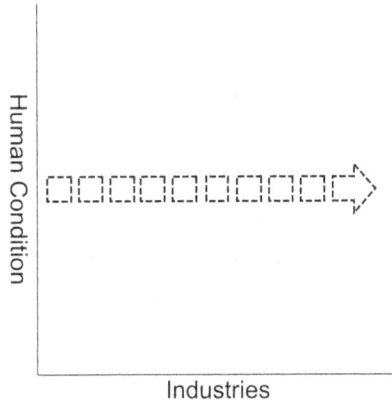

The resulting offset creates a "fragmentation of satisfaction" which is bad for both people and companies.

For people, it forces us to engage with multiple companies as we try to secure a "complete solution" for our problems. That means more research, more negotiation, and more coordination between providers, all of which significantly increases the likelihood of frustration along the way.

For companies, this fragmentation artificially limits the length of the customer engagement, so that companies routinely say "goodbye" when they could be saying "and then..." This, in turn, restricts potential revenue while increasing the likelihood of customer dissatisfaction and churn.

But what if companies stopped defining themselves by a category and instead chose a particular human condition? In essence, what if a company was organized around "which friend" their brand was going to be?

It's a pivot that would allow a business to own not just one "stepping-stone," but the whole "sidewalk" of satisfaction for a particular set of human needs.

Such a vertically integrated customer experience (V.I.C.E.) would have many benefits including more revenue, increased affinity, and a longer customer engagement, all from providing an end-to-end, turnkey solution that satisfies a person's human needs.

Let's take a look at an example of how a company could transform its functional role from the category to the human condition.

Self Storage

The self-storage category is a $39.5 billion business, offering 1.9 billion square feet of rentable space spread across over 49,000 U.S. facilities. The industry is highly fragmented, with the largest six players only accounting for 20% of facilities. Almost one in ten Americans pays for self-storage, averaging $89/month.[4]

The heart of the self-storage category: storage units. (Photo by Joshua Coleman, Unsplash)

Officially classified by the federal government as NAICS 53113, the self-storage category is defined as *"establishments primarily engaged in renting or leasing space for self-storage. These establishments provide secure space (i.e., rooms, compartments, lockers, containers, or outdoor space) where clients can store and retrieve their goods.*"[5]

True to form, businesses in this category focus a great deal on the "secure spaces" part, where to locate them, and how much to charge for them.

But anyone who has ever used self-storage knows "secure spaces where clients can store and retrieve their goods" is only a small part of the solution to the human condition known as "having too much stuff in my house."

So, what you really need when you realize that you "have too much stuff" is a friend who knows about more than just the "secure spaces" part of the solution. They also need to know everything about boxes, tape, and moving trucks. Someone who has personally experienced the self-loathing, procrastination, and physical exhaustion involved with trying to clean up your house. Not to mention someone who appreciates pizza and cold beer at the end of moving day.

"Having Too Much Stuff In My House"

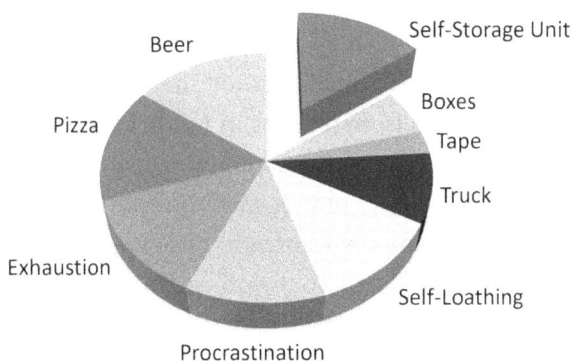

The pie chart of self-storage opportunity.

If a self-storage company could recognize this, it would find itself with many opportunities to expand its role in someone's life. It could lengthen customer engagement by providing people with everything they need, rather than just one piece of the puzzle.

To put it another way, the self-storage company should stop trying to be all about the "self-storage" category and start trying to be the friend who understands what it's like to have "too much stuff."

To be fair, most self-storage companies understand the front part of this journey. That is, the "on ramp" that gets customers to their door. That's why many also sell boxes, tape, and access to trucks. These make it easier for people to move their stuff into their facilities.

But the moment a customer signs the rental agreement, the company's focus shifts dramatically, from apparently helping the person to clearly helping itself.

This change is most evident when you look at the satisfiers the company does *not* offer. These omissions are often justified under the heading of "efficiency" or because the satisfiers aren't seen as necessary to close the initial sale.

In reality, these "extras" could be avenues to incremental revenue, a better brand, or both.

For instance, anyone who has ever moved things into a self-storage unit knows it is physically exhausting. You get tired, hungry, and thirsty pretty quickly. Yet most self-storage companies don't offer solutions to these very real human needs. The manager of one self-storage facility I visited pointed out that they did have a water fountain near the bathrooms. She also noted that if I wanted to sit down, they had a sidewalk out front (as long as I didn't stay there too long).

Really? How hard is it to put in a couple of vending machines and some folding chairs? The vending machines pay a commission, for heaven's sake. If the company wanted to be aggressive, it could open a small pizza and beer café next to the office. If that's too much, it could contract with a local food truck to come by the facility on nights and weekends (the busiest times for self-storage). All these options keep the customer on-site, where the company can make some more revenue by satisfying human needs, while also providing an opportunity for staff to offer self-storage advice, building better relationships with customers.

Self-storage companies also exclude satisfiers that might make it easier for people to move their stuff out of the facility. This, of course, would reduce rental income, but this decision denies the reality that, at some point, virtually every self-storage customer grows weary of paying for storage and will want to end their lease. And that being unhelpful at the end of the relationship will leave a bad taste in the customer's mouth.

For example, if someone decides they do want to take their stuff out of storage, once they get there, they'll probably find there's a lot of stuff in the storage unit that they really don't want anymore. But self-storage companies aren't in the disposal business. They keep their trash dumpsters padlocked, instead telling customers to haul away the stuff they don't want and find another way to get rid of it.

But what if the company did expand into the disposal business? After all, "disposal" is inherently part of "having too much stuff." The company could install an industrial floor scale and charge customers a price-per-pound to throw away their unwanted things (or even to have some recycled).

Better still, the company could arrange for a local Goodwill donation truck to take a spot in the parking lot. That way, if the customer has something of value that they don't want anymore, they could donate it to charity (and get a tax deduction) on the spot.

Of course, if the company really wanted to embrace the idea of "having too much stuff" they could offer satisfiers that help people reduce the amount of stuff they need to store in the first place. This may seem counterintuitive since it would result in a smaller storage unit and less monthly rent, but it would also send a strong signal that the company is on the customer's side, helping them pay only for the storage they need, which would lead to better customer satisfaction and potentially a longer stay (which means more months of rent collected).

For example, the company could partner with local antiques appraisers to help people understand if any of the "stuff" they are considering moving out of their house is valuable. Providing this consulting service — branded with the name of the self-storage company, of course — would allow the company to provide additional value to the customer while also building a preference for the company for the things that will eventually go into storage.

———————

SURVEYING the landscape to determine where your company's V.I.C.E. "sidewalk" should go may seem difficult, at least at first. Old habits die hard, especially those that have become as much second nature as viewing the world through a company's "category" focus.

Fortunately, if you're reading this, you're a person. And, as a real, live human being, you are innately familiar with the natural progression of human experiences that best define where your company's "sidewalk" should lead.

All you need to do is translate your understanding of the human condition to the customer journey.

Think of it as a type of segmentation analysis. But rather than trying to decide which type of person best matches the company's needs, the objective is to decide which type of company best matches the person's needs. And, instead of using demographics and psychographics to help define the target, you use human needs (such as those identified by Manfred Max-Neef) to define the company.

Specifically, as you lay out the "sidewalk" that follows the path of a human experience, ensure that each step satisfies at least one fundamental human need.

You'll remember that Max-Neef identified nine fundamental human needs: subsistence, protection, affection, understanding, participation, idleness, creation, identity, and freedom.

In the self-storage example, above, the core human need that the industry satisfies is "protection" for our things (that are, of course, an extension of ourselves and our "identity"). Satisfiers that meet this need include the storage unit (of course) as well as goods such as boxes, Bubble Wrap, and tape, not to mention services such as security cameras and climate control systems that keep our stuff from getting too hot or freezing.

But beyond this core offering, the ancillary satisfiers described above would also help to solve other human needs.

An area where you can take a break or enjoy some food and drink satisfies the need for "idleness" as well as "subsistence." If you have friends or family helping you move, this service also helps satisfy the need for "affection," providing a place to interact and reinforce these interpersonal relationships.

Offering to dispose of, or recycle, unwanted items helps satisfy the need for "protection" of the customer's home (by preventing the junk from coming back) as well as of the environment (by ensuring any unwanted items are properly disposed of, recycled, or reused by someone else (via a charitable donation). Allowing for donations also helps satisfy the need for "participation" in the local community and the lives of others, which also helps build the person's "identity."

Finally, the company's partnership with local antiques appraisers is a selfless act that endears the company to the customer, helping to satisfy the person's need for "affection." Interestingly, this affection arises not from the company creating a space for natural persons to interact (as with the break/snack area), but from the company itself. As such, it directly builds legitimacy into the company's best friend brand, showing that it can put others first, just like a natural person.

Obviously, it's not just the self-storage companies that could benefit from shifting their focus from categories to human needs. Here are some other examples of industries and the type of best friends they could decide to become.

Airlines

Long focused on the technology that defines their industry, airlines spend a lot of time and effort on their planes: getting them to fly farther and faster; ensuring they depart and arrive on time; and filling them with the latest entertainment options (perhaps to distract us from our ever-shrinking seats and legroom).

But being on the plane is only a very small part of a travel day. So, what if the airline tried to own not just the flight, but the whole day?

To be the best friend brand that is the perfect traveling companion, fluent in every step of the process. From getting you to the airport and through security on time, to finding a place near the gate where you can sit and charge your phone. That's not to mention knowing where the nearest bathroom is and where you can buy a snack and your favorite beverage.

Even after you land, a travel day continues, so a best friend airline could use its logistical expertise to help you navigate the unfamiliar destination airport, retrieve your luggage, and get you to wherever you're spending the night.

Many of these additional offerings would help satisfy the need for "understanding," which is significant when you're in an unfamiliar place. But this information also leads to the satisfaction of other needs, whether it is "subsistence" (a seat, snack, and bathroom) or "protection" (ensuring you make it safely to your final destination).

This expanded "companion" role is something many cruise lines embraced a long time ago. When you go on a cruise, it's not uncommon for representatives from the cruise line to meet you at the airport and get you to the ship. It's also standard practice to help arrange for excursions away from the ship at various ports of call, knowing that these, too, are part of the cruising experience, even if they don't take place on board.

Hardware Stores

The rise of big-box hardware stores, such as Home Depot and Lowe's Home Improvement, is the story of wider selection and lower price, two things that smaller neighborhood hardware stores couldn't compete against. After all, what's the point of a hardware store that doesn't have the thing you need? And why pay more if you don't have to?

But it's also the story of loss. Because, as America shifted its business to these massive warehouses, it lost the ability to ask someone a question. Not just about where you might find a particular product, but broader questions about how things in your house work and how you can build or repair them. This is what local hardware stores used to offer. A friendly, knowledgeable store clerk who became almost a quasi-partner on your project. One who would ask you what you're working on, steer you to the right supplies, and then discuss with you the best way to move forward.

Can you even imagine that level of engagement in today's hardware warehouse stores? Of course not. Yet, it's not like homeowners have genetically evolved to innately understand carpentry, plumbing, and electricity, among other skills.

That leaves a significant opportunity for hardware warehouse stores to not just be huge, but helpful. To be the best friend brand that knows how everything in your home works and helps satisfy a homeowner's inherent need for "understanding." This education then enables you to satisfy other needs that come from working on your own home, such as "creation" and "identity."

Along the way, you might even satisfy the need for "affection" by building a casual friendship with the trusted expert at the store. This, of course, brings you back every time something in your house breaks. (Which, if you've ever owned a home, you know is *all* the time.) And that's something that no number of online "how-to" videos can provide.

Coffee Beans

Globally, we drink an estimated 2.25 billion cups of coffee every single day.[6] In general, we do so to satisfy our human need for "subsistence." More specifically, most of us consume coffee for two reasons: caffeine and taste, with each of us determining which is more important, and to what degree.

For those who care more about kick than flavor, the goal is maximum caffeine for the dollar. This usually translates into either instant coffee or a mass-produced pre-ground coffee, both of which are more likely to include beans from the *coffea canephora* species of coffee tree. Commonly known as Robusta, it is cheaper and contains more caffeine (2.7%) than its less hearty cousin, *coffea arabica*.[7]

For those who prioritize taste, Arabica coffee is the preferred choice. While containing only 1.5% caffeine, it makes up for this deficit with 60% more lipids and almost twice the sugars, which make it less bitter and more flavorful than Robusta.[8] These qualities are also what make Arabica beans so expensive, more than twice as much on the commodities market.[9] But coffee connoisseurs don't mind paying this premium for taste. Nor do they mind paying even more to have an expert (i.e., a barista) regularly make their coffee for them.

This quest for flavor often drives aficionados down the rabbit hole of trying to recreate this "perfect cup" at home. And it's this journey that creates a real opportunity for companies that sell coffee beans.

That's because making better-tasting coffee at home starts with buying better beans. Not just Arabica, but whole (not pre-ground) beans, vacuum-sealed in a bag or can. Why? Coffee gets its amazing flavor from the essential oils locked inside a roasted coffee bean. But these compounds are highly volatile and start to deteriorate the moment they come in contact with oxygen. So, the best way to preserve coffee's flavor is to keep the beans whole until you're ready to brew a cup.

It's something a best friend who worked as a barista would tell you. And it's something a coffee bean company would tell you when it's acting like a best friend brand. Because it realizes the company's role in satisfying human needs doesn't end once the beans are purchased. It's just beginning.

For many people, preparing a cup of coffee is less of a chore and more of a craft. And like any artist, those who perform the ritual of making coffee are always looking for better materials and techniques. And who better to offer them than the best friend barista brand?

Start with home coffee grinders. At a minimum, a best friend brand would recommend burr grinders instead of blade grinders, explaining how they create more uniformly sized granules of coffee (which promotes better flavor extraction). A stronger approach would be for the company to actually sell high-quality burr grinders, perhaps co-branded with the manufacturer.

The same holds true for coffee brewers, which utilize a variety of methods, including drip, immersion, percolation, and high-pressure steam. Each of these approaches creates a different flavor profile and each requires education to use properly. Again, the best friend barista brand can provide this expertise, helping the home enthusiast dial in the perfect grind size, coffee-to-water ratio, temperature, and brew time, all of which vary based on the extraction technique and desired result.

Acting as this "coffee co-pilot" helps to satisfy many needs beyond mere "subsistence." Most obviously, it addresses the need for "understanding," but also the broader needs for "idleness" and "creation" that subsequently contribute to the connoisseur's personal "identity."

The best friend barista brand could also expand its V.I.C.E. "sidewalk" upstream from the moment of bean purchase to other opportunities to satisfy human needs and increase revenue.

For example, one step above packaging coffee beans is roasting them. Like brewing, this too is a complex craft, with a master roaster relying on multiple senses and years of experience to transform raw "green" coffee beans into the dark brown nuggets of flavor we buy in the store. Also, like brewing, roasting is a craft that can be practiced at home, with hot-air home roasters selling from around $60.

So, the opportunity already exists for the best friend coffee bean brand to sell unroasted versions of its beans, in essence challenging the enthusiast to roast them at home to see if they can match the flavor profile of the roasted beans they already enjoy. Ancillary offerings could include roasters and roasting classes, either online or at the company's commercial facility. Whether as a value-add or for a fee, giving access to the upstream production process allows the amateur to feel more like a professional, satisfying the human need for "participation" in the broader coffee culture.

The same holds true when the best friend coffee bean brand participates in "fair trade" and "organic" certification programs that ensure the company isn't exploiting the coffee farmers or using chemicals and methods that are bad for the environment or the end consumer. These practices can be promoted as helping to satisfy the purchaser's human need for "protection" or even marketed in conjunction with trips to the coffee plantations where the company buys their beans, allowing people to learn even more about coffee production while earning the company incremental income.

DEFINING which best friend brand your company represents creates a natural path of engagement between it and your customers, no matter which industry you're in.

This decision also aligns your company with other "non-customer" stakeholder roles that people play, helping to satisfy their human needs as well.

For employees, aligning around the satisfaction of human needs instead of share price elevates and ennobles the nature of work from something that benefits just a fortunate few to something that benefits everyone, inherently increasing job satisfaction. This is especially true for customer-facing personnel, for whom decreased conflict between the company and the customer can dramatically improve the work environment.

For shareholders, the extended customer engagement period and ancillary offerings provide opportunities for increased revenue and stronger brand loyalty, both of which can legitimately increase the value of the company and its share price.

For suppliers, the company's expanded V.I.C.E. "sidewalk" provides more opportunities for a symbiotic partnership where a supplier provides expertise and products that aren't in the company's core competency, but which still flesh out the company's overall best friend brand offering.

A company that focuses on satisfying human needs (as opposed to maximizing shareholder value) will also benefit other members of the community, even if they don't have a direct relationship with the company as a customer, employee, shareholder, or supplier. That's because the impact of many satisfiers isn't limited to just one stakeholder role. For example, when customers demand better environmental practices from the company as a condition of purchase, the resulting improvements are enjoyed by everyone who uses this common resource.

It's further proof that attempting to favor one stakeholder group over another — to build a stool with only one leg — is a misguided, artificial, and futile exercise.

Stakeholder groups are not mutually exclusive. They are merely different facets of the same human beings. As a result, sustained success can come from embracing the human being at the core of these facets and trying to satisfy as many of their human needs as possible, regardless of what stakeholder role they happen to be playing.

If you're still doubting that your company can profit by serving multiple stakeholders, consider this: every year since 2015, the non-profit organization Just Capital has analyzed the 1,000 largest publicly traded companies in America, comparing their performance across 339 data points to measure their impact on five key stakeholder groups: customers, employees, shareholders, communities, and the environment.[10]

Companies that scored higher in this analysis (what it calls the "Just 100") have many things in common:[11]

- They pay their median U.S. employee a third more than other companies.
- They paid no consumer product safety commission fines over the past three years and no U.S. Food and Drug Administration fines.
- They donate 3.8 times more to charity per dollar of revenue.
- They emit 72% fewer greenhouse gases per dollar of revenue.
- They face 74% fewer employment discrimination cases per dollar of revenue.
- They use 80% less fossil fuel per dollar of revenue.

And while they're doing all of that, they also deliver an *eight percent higher* return on equity.

That's "doing well by doing good."

Step Three: Assemble the Components of Satisfaction

The way our economy satisfies human needs has evolved significantly over the last 200 years, moving through three distinct phases, as described by economists Allan Fisher, Colin Clark, and Jean Fourastié in their Three-Sector Model.

Before the industrial revolution, the main focus of activity was on the extraction and production of raw materials, including farming, fishing, hunting, logging, and mining. These "primary sector" activities employed most people and composed the largest portion of the U.S. GDP.

As technology advanced, fewer people were needed in the primary sector, allowing employment and GDP to shift to the "secondary sector," which involves the manufacture of finished, tangible goods that can be purchased to satisfy needs.

However, as manufacturing itself became more and more automated, the workforce was freed up again, this time moving to the "tertiary sector" of the economy, which delivers satisfaction via services and intangible goods, such as information (which is sometimes called the "quaternary sector").

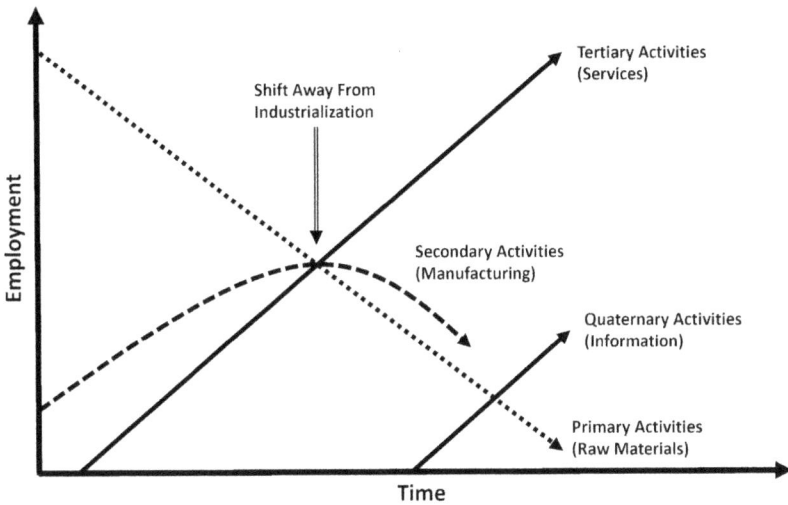

Three-Sector Model (expanded to include Quaternary Activities)

Today, Americans live in an economy dominated by the tertiary sector, with 71% of employment[12] and 66% of GDP[13] coming from services. For comparison, in 1950, services accounted for just 46% of U.S. employment[14] and 39% of U.S. GDP,[15] percentages that are roughly equivalent to the economy of present-day Iran.[16]

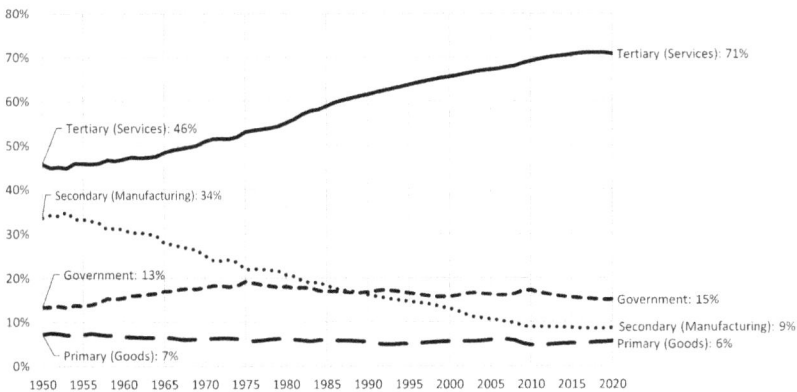

Percentage of Employees (non-agricultural payrolls), by Major Industry, 1950-2020 (Source: Council of Economic Advisors, Economic Report of the President, 2000, 2011, 2021.)

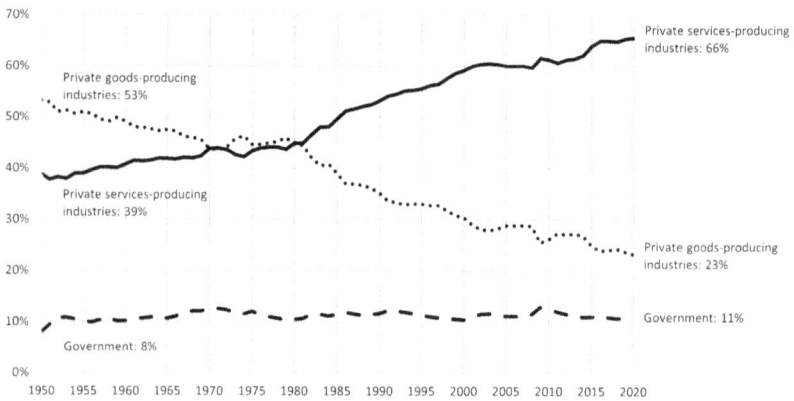

Percentage of Gross Domestic Product Output by Sector, 1950-2020 (Source: Bureau of Economic Activity (BEA))

This dominance by services isn't the result of fewer goods being made for sale. (One visit to Amazon will prove that.) It's due to the expansion of services offered in addition to goods.

In fact, there are very few products that are either "pure goods" or "pure services." Most are a mixture of both, with the proportions varying along a continuum.

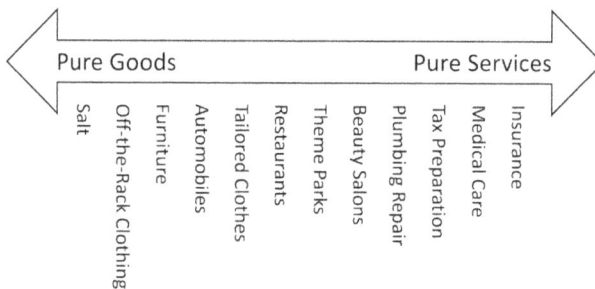

But for your company, how do you determine exactly which goods and services it should offer to best satisfy human needs? It's such an all-encompassing question that it can be difficult to wrap your head around it.

Fortunately, Manfred Max-Neef's "Fundamental Human Needs"

provides a bit of structure that can help make this problem more manageable.

As you'll recall, he stated that the nine needs he identified could be satisfied at their intersection with four existential needs (types of needs inherent to human existence): being, having, doing, and interacting.

(For our purposes, we can set aside the need for "being" since it is, well, a "state of being" and not something that a company can directly offer. Instead, think of "being" as the result of experiencing the satisfiers that are accessed through "having" people or things, "doing" actions or activities, or "interacting" in certain places.)

When you put all these together, you get a recipe for how to satisfy any of the nine axiological needs with some combination of people, things, actions or activities, and a particular place.

Of course, like any good recipe, you can't just mix random ingredients together. You need to decide what you're trying to create and then start assembling your *mise en place*.

If you prefer, think of it as theater with you being the one putting on the show. Any good play needs a set (the place), actors and props (people and things) and a script (the actions or activities, including dialogue). Only, instead of the plot unfolding through a series of scenes, the satisfaction of human needs unfolds along the steps of the V.I.C.E. sidewalk.

As an example, here's how one "scene" for a self-storage company could begin:

TITLE: "I've got too much stuff in my house"
 ACT 2: Moving day
 SCENE 3: Taking a break
 SETTING: A small café space next to the storage facility office. At the front of the room is a counter where patrons can order food. On the wall behind the counter is a sign reading "Moving Day Café" along with a small menu. Today's specialty, just like every day, is the perfect moving day meal: pizza. Not too many choices. Just a few, such as cheese, pepperoni, and veggie. But all of them are freshly baked in a small commercial

oven behind the counter. Also on the menu are bottles of ice-cold water and soft drinks, available from a serve-yourself fridge next to the counter, and, of course, fresh chocolate chip cookies for those with a sweet tooth.

Spread around the room is a handful of round tables and chairs. Nothing fancy, but certainly a welcome place to sit down and rest your back after hauling too many boxes that were much heavier than they should have been. On the walls are posters offering helpful hints for how to store things in a storage space. For example, "Leave an empty space down the middle of your storage unit. This creates an aisle, making it easier to get things from the back without moving everything out."

Running this little slice of relaxation is SANDY, the co-manager of this self-storage location. SANDY has been helping people store their stuff for over a dozen years and knows many of the "tricks of the trade" used to maximize space while keeping things safe. She also understands that putting things into storage can be a surprisingly emotional experience. That's because people tend to put things into storage after one of the four Ds: death, divorce, downsizing, or displacement. All of these are times of change, and change is tough for us human beings. SANDY knows this, so she has a kind soul and a willing ear to hear the backstory that led people to her door (and her café) today.

Once this part of the "script" is written, it's relatively easy to extract the specific people, things, places, and actions that the company needs to offer to satisfy relevant human needs.

		Existential needs		
		Having	Doing	Interacting
		People	Things	Actions	Places
Axiological needs	Subsistence	Co-Manager	Pizza, soft drinks, cookies	Eating and drinking	Café
	Protection				
	Affection	Co-Manager		Sharing stories	Café
	Understanding		"Storage Tips" posters	Reading	Café
	Participation				
	Idleness		Chairs and tables	Resting	Café
	Creation				
	Identity				
	Freedom				

In this case, a self-storage company setting up a small break room that also serves simple food and drinks can lead to the satisfaction of several ancillary human needs associated with the usage of "self-storage." Specifically, the need for "subsistence" and "idleness," not to mention "understanding" (e.g., the best ways to use self-storage), and a tiny bit of "affection" (which comes from an employee of the company empathizing with your emotional backstory.)

At a higher level, the satisfaction of ancillary needs builds a broader, deeper, and longer relationship with customers than just trying to satisfy their primary need for the "protection" of their stuff. Simultaneously, it also reinforces the perception that the company isn't just there to make money, demonstrating that it is a best friend brand that can help people navigate multiple aspects of "having too much stuff."

And that's something worth paying for.

Of course, the setting for a scene doesn't need to be a "brick-and-mortar" store location. The "place" can also be the customer's house (especially for a company that provides in-home services, such as appliance repair). Alternately, it could be at some third-party location, such as when a company has an "experiential" presence at a festival, park, or other public space. Or the place could be entirely virtual, taking place on the company's website or other online platform. Regardless, the choice of setting brings a significant amount of context to the scene, so it needs to be actively crafted to ensure that it helps with satisfaction, rather than hinders it.

The same holds true for the things (i.e., the "props") your company has on hand for a scene. Some of them (such as the pizza, soft drinks, and cookies from the self-storage example) may be goods for sale. Others (such as the tables and chairs) are just necessary elements of the overall experience. Regardless, it's up to you to decide which should be for sale, which are for rent, and which are free of charge.

For example, should the self-storage company restrict use of the café seating to only those customers who buy food? Or can any person with a storage unit use them to rest for a few minutes? How about people who don't even have a storage unit? Can the general public come to the café space? Clearly, everything can't be free. But the other extreme, where the customer has to pay for everything, flies in the face of the concept of a best friend brand.

As important as the "place" and "things" are to providing satisfaction, nothing is more important than the "people" your company puts on stage. After all, your people are the characters who interact with customers during the scene. And, as people themselves, customers will more easily build relationships with people than with places or things.

Your people, quite literally, personify your company's best friend brand, so casting them is enormously important. And while industry knowledge and experience are necessary to ensure your company is providing high-quality goods and services, it's hard to overestimate the value of empathy in the paradigm of satisfying human needs.

This ability to identify and understand another person's situation and feelings can provide huge insights into how best to satisfy their needs, even when the other person can't articulate them.

That's because emotions, like rational thoughts, arise from the brain in response to a perceived need. However, instead of coming from the cerebral cortex, emotions arise from the brain's limbic system. The limbic system is much older from an evolutionary standpoint, so the messages it sends are more primitive and vague. But they still alert us, just like they did for our ancestors, when our brains sense something that threatens or enhances our survival prospects.

Psychologist and professor Robert Plutchik detailed this mechanism in his 1980 "psychoevolutionary" theory of emotions.[17] It all starts with our senses relaying information to our brains. For example, we may see a bear emerging from the trees, running toward us. Our brains recognize this visual pattern as a bear and, based on the bear's size, speed, proximity, and our previous experience, our brains quickly calculate that the bear is a threat. Our limbic system floods our bodies with electrochemical messages that we interpret as the feeling of "fear," which causes a behavior (running away) which, hopefully, results in protection from death or serious injury.

Nowhere in this sequence do we stop to consider the rational concept of "danger." Nor do we use our cerebral cortex to "decide" to run away. Our response is automatic and immediate — two traits that served us well during millions of years of evolutionary history. And, while most of us don't come across charging bears on a regular basis, the physiology of emotions is still present, still functioning, and still sending messages designed to help us.

Plutchik believed there were only eight primary emotions, which existed as four pairs of opposites: joy and sadness; anger and fear; trust and disgust; and surprise and anticipation. Each of these core emotions is correlated with a different evolutionarily beneficial behavior.

Stimulus event ⇒	Feeling ⇒	Behavior ⇒	Effect
Find a valuable object	Joy	Retain and repeat	Gain resources
Loss of valued object	Sadness	Cry	Seek help
Obstacle/enemy	Anger	Attack	Destroy obstacle
Threat	Fear	Escape	Safety
Recognize a friend	Trust	Groom and share	Mutual support
Unpalatable object	Disgust	Vomit	Eject poison
Unexpected event	Surprise	Stop	Orientation
New territory	Anticipation	Explore	Gain knowledge

Furthermore, primary emotions can be felt with different intensities. For instance, "serenity" is just a lesser feeling of "joy," while an extreme version is what we might call "ecstasy."

Finally, when we experience more than one primary emotion at the same time (what he called a "dyad"), we interpret it as a different, more complex emotion. For example, "love" is a combination of "joy" and "trust," or "optimism" is a combination of "joy" and "anticipation."

The relationships between the various aspects of Plutchik's theory can be illustrated as a wheel of emotions.

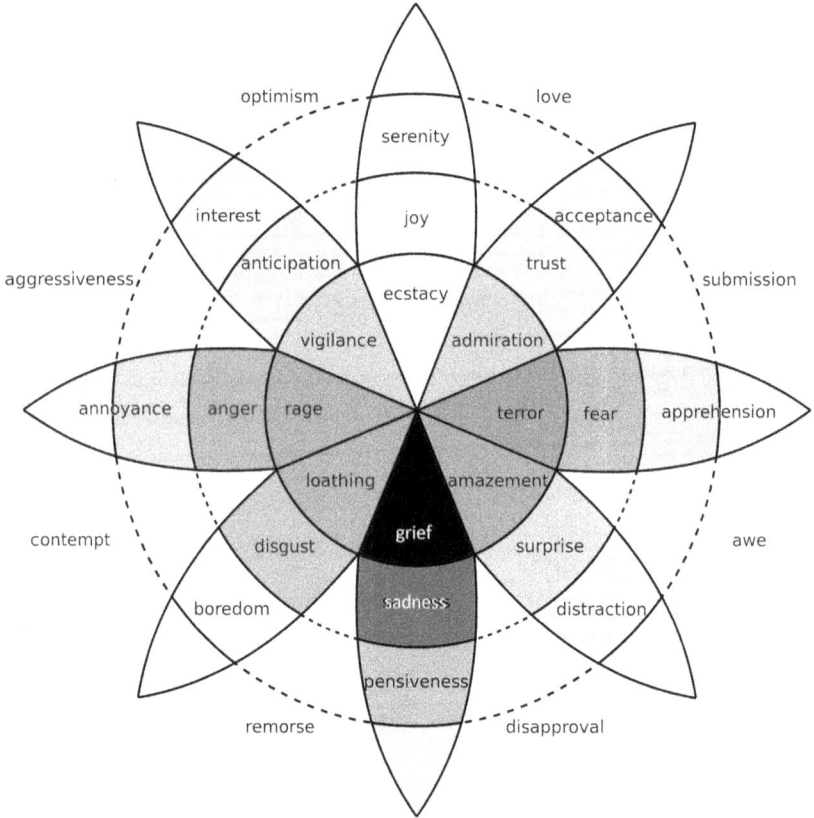

Robert Plutchik's Wheel of Emotions. (Public domain)

While most of us inherently understand portions of this theory, holistically understanding how emotions work allows us to not only identify an emotion, but also "reverse-engineer" its potential cause.

This diagnostic capability, when added to the ability to satisfy human needs, creates a complete framework that any company can adopt, customizing it into a formalized system for serving human beings as a best friend brand.

But this whole system falls apart if your company can't identify your customers' emotions. That's where your people come in. People can navigate the complex, subtle vocabulary of emotions better than any technology — even cutting-edge algorithms that try to decipher emotions from facial expressions.

This human ability isn't surprising. Each of us has been learning to read emotions since the first moment we gazed into our parents' eyes. Of course, some of us are better at it than others, but the average adult is remarkably adept at quickly and accurately identifying what someone else is feeling.

Just look at the results of the "eyes test," a simple tool developed by psychologists at the University of Cambridge to measure a person's ability to "mentalize," or predict another person's feelings.[18] For the test, subjects are shown a black-and-white photo of just the eye region of 36 different people's faces and asked to select which emotion the person in each photo is feeling.

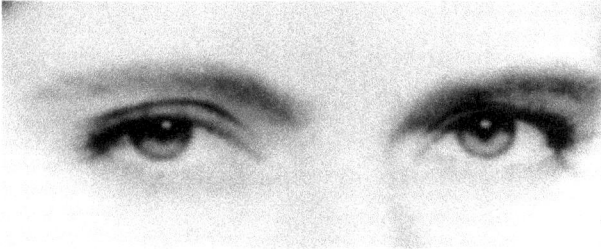

An example from the "Eyes Test." Is this person feeling doubtful, affectionate, playful, or aghast? The correct answer is "doubtful." (Source: "The 'Reading the Mind in the Eyes' Test, Revised Version.)

The researchers found that, even with such limited information (a static, black-and-white photo of just a person's eyes), the average adult is able to correctly identify the person's emotion a remarkable 73% of the time. Interestingly, the test was developed to help diagnose high-functioning autism or Asperger syndrome, since individuals with these conditions often struggle with social understanding and empathy.

The benefits of empathy are obvious when it comes to customer interactions. But since all stakeholders are human beings, emotional intelligence can be equally valuable when applied to all of a company's relationships. Empathy enhances communication, which leads to better understanding and the subsequent ability to satisfy the diverse, yet convergent human needs of employees, shareholders, communities, and the environment.

Universally applied empathy also makes it easier for the company to "keep its story straight" compared to a communication strategy that tells each stakeholder group they are more important than the rest. Knowing that no messages are truly discrete, there is, instead, just one message: we are here to satisfy human needs, regardless of what role that human plays. It's a single, consistent focus that manifests as a stronger and more trustworthy brand.

In short, your people already know how to help other people. All you need to do is to give them the information and empowerment to make it happen.

That brings us to the final component of the play you're staging: the script. In theater, the actions and dialog in the script are the verbs that bring all the nouns (i.e., characters, props, and set) to life. The same holds true when you're animating the elements of your company's best friend brand. Except, unlike a play, the show needs to be different every time.

After all, you don't control all the actors in this play. Sure, some are your employees, but at least half the script is delivered by customers, suppliers, shareholders, or other members of society. So, you don't know what they're going to say or do. Not to mention the fact that, with every "performance," the setting and props may be different.

All this uncertainty means your company's actions and dialog just can't be tightly scripted. Instead, you should embrace a looser approach that enables your people to improvise in this dynamic reality.

Think of your company as Disneyland. On any given day, you control certain aspects of the theme park, but not the visitors you welcome through the gates. As a result, your cast members need to have the freedom and flexibility to handle any interaction as they see fit, as long as they do so "in character." What defines "in character" is determined in advance, aligning with your company's best friend brand.

Lastly, as you're assembling your company's components of satisfaction, remember that you don't need to provide them all yourself. If a particular element falls outside your area of expertise, partner or co-brand with a qualified company that is also compatible with your best friend brand. Not only can this help to mitigate risk as you test out new satisfiers, but it will also demonstrate that your best friend brand is all about providing the best solution for people, rather than just serving itself.

Step Four: Determine How Much Satisfaction Will Cost

The ability to satisfy such a wide variety of human needs creates a lot of potential value. So, one of the first questions you'll need to answer is, "how much does it cost?" Traditionally, this question refers to the amount of money that will be exchanged at the time of purchase.

Money is awesome. I love money and would love some more right now. (It's so much better than the barter system where you had to carry around chickens to pay for everything.) Money is not only a standardized medium of exchange, but also a store of value, so I can stockpile it now and use it later.

But today, the term "cost" certainly includes more than just money. Take, for example, "time." Most of us consider time a type of currency and dislike it when we have to spend too much on something. Time spent researching solutions or slogging through online product reviews. Time spent wandering around a warehouse store (or website) looking for a particular item. Time spent standing in line at checkout. Time spent waiting for delivery of our purchase (or for a technician to show up during a dreaded "four-hour window").

That's one reason why companies work so hard to speed up every step of the purchase cycle. To help remove some of the "friction" that stops customers from buying (or buying again.)

Another cost that most of us keep an eye on is data. Specifically, information about ourselves and our behavior that individuals, companies, governments, and other institutions can use to identify, track, and profile us. While data on us has always been available, the rise of technology has exponentially increased the amount of information gathered (often without our knowledge) as well as the speed and ease with which it can be analyzed and applied.

Examples of this type of personal data include our name, address, phone number, email address, age, gender, race or ethnicity, fingerprints, DNA profile, medical history, salary, credit history, search history, websites we've visited, videos we've watched, GPS location history, purchase history, photos of us, and recordings of our voice.

At best, these data can be used to customize an experience or recommend products to us. At worst, they can be used to increase the prices we pay, deny us services altogether, or even allow someone else to assume our identities. So, it's no wonder there has been so much focus on data privacy and the ability of individuals to control the collection, sale, and use of data about them: in other words, their ability to treat their data as a currency and how to empower them to spend it as they see fit.

Together, these three costs (money, time, and data) make up the bulk of "transactional" costs — things that we surrender *during* a purchase in exchange for goods and/or services. Transactional costs are usually visible. We know how much money we're handing over, how much time we've spent during the purchase process, and (to some degree) what data we're sharing.

We're also familiar with how these costs can be exchanged for one another. You can make a trade to spend less time waiting for your purchase to be delivered if you're willing to pay more money for overnight delivery. Some websites will give you a ten percent discount off your first order when you give them your email address. Or you could avoid paying any money at all to instantaneously communicate with your friends as long as you're willing to let a social media or email provider monitor everything you do on their app and show you ads.

The point is, when you pay less of something, you're probably paying more of something else.

Even when you don't know what that "something else" is.

Obviously, all the costs related to a purchase aren't evident at the moment of the transaction. Nor can all costs related to a transaction be accurately measured solely in terms of money, time, or data. For example, when you purchase a cheap "fast fashion" t-shirt, you have no real idea of the related environmental, health, and societal costs (as discussed in Chapter 5) that have already been incurred.

But that doesn't make those costs any less real.

Similarly, when you purchase a pair of Apple AirPods wireless earbuds, you have no idea that their lithium-ion batteries won't hold a useful charge after as little as 18 months. You also have no idea that, instead of making these batteries replaceable, Apple has chosen to seal them in with glue, effectively meaning you'll need to throw the whole earbud away and buy a new pair every two to three years. And you also don't know that, because of the way the batteries are glued in place, AirPods are incredibly difficult to recycle.[19]

Again, this doesn't make these costs any less real. And, certainly, these costs aren't fully captured in the outlay of money, time, and data currencies.

These are "consequential" costs: the costs that are a direct consequence of a purchase but aren't apparent at the time of transaction. Consequential costs can be incurred before the purchase (i.e., during production) or after the purchase (i.e., during consumption).

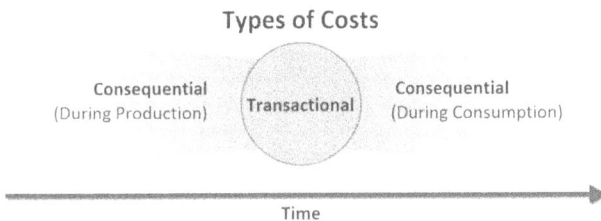

Types of Costs

Consequential
(During Production)

Transactional

Consequential
(During Consumption)

Time

Either way, because consequential costs are tied to the transaction, the customer is responsible for them the moment the transaction occurs. Conversely, if the transaction never takes place, the consequential costs are not the customer's responsibility. Moreover, if the transaction never happens, the corresponding consequential costs won't even be incurred since systemically reduced demand will drive a reduction in both production and consumption.

If consequential costs sound a little like externalities, you're right. Both are market failures. But whereas externalities are a failure to *capture* costs imposed on *third parties*, consequential costs arise from a failure to *disclose* costs to *a party involved in the transaction.*

To be fair, the failure to disclose consequential costs isn't usually due to maleficence. Companies simply don't know what the consequential costs are or how to measure and report them. After all, traditional business metrics are exceedingly poor at assessing non-monetary costs.

But that doesn't mean people haven't tried.

The concept of a "double bottom line" (DBL), where a company tries to measure its impact on society as well as its financial performance, goes back to the corporate social responsibility movement of the 1960s.

By the mid-1980s, social justice wasn't the only mainstream concern, and DBL was replaced by the "triple bottom line" (TBL), which also added the company's impact on the environment. Often summarized as "people, planet, and profit," the TBL concept illustrates the overlapping components of sustainability and is widely accepted, even playing a part in the United Nations' Sustainable Development initiative.

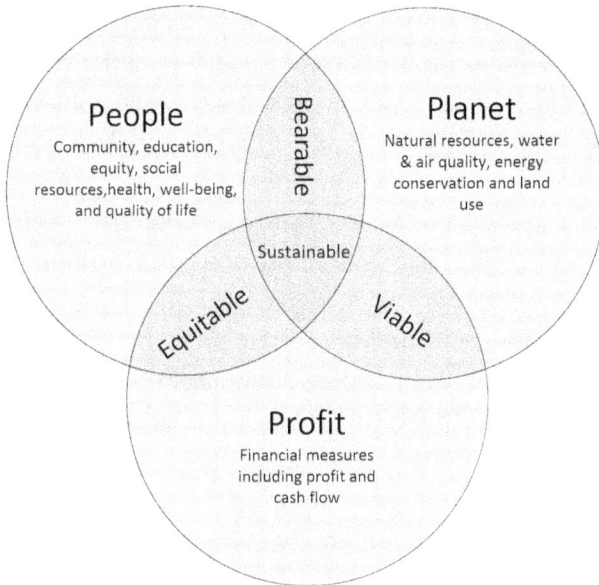

Foci of the Triple Bottom Line (TBL)

But putting the theory into practice has been challenging. Quantification of complex social and environmental costs is difficult. As a result, the TBL has primarily remained in the abstract — a perspective to help guide decision making rather than precisely accounting for the impact of those decisions.

However, as technological advances have made information easier and cheaper to access and manipulate, there have been advances in our ability to calculate social and environmental consequences.

Notably, Harvard Business School recently launched the Impact-Weighted Accounts Initiative (IWAI), an accounting methodology that attempts to translate social and environmental costs (and benefits) into dollars, which can then be added as line items in a company's financials, ultimately yielding a single, all-encompassing profit or loss.

For example, the IWAI estimated and monetized the impact of dozens of metrics related to airline travel, including the affordability of tickets, route availability, injuries sustained in airline accidents, the consequences of human trafficking, delays from late departures and arrivals, air pollution from jet engines, and even the recyclability of onboard water bottles.[20] When these were taken into account, the IWAI found that airlines such as Lufthansa and American Airlines, which regularly reported healthy pre-COVID profits, would actually have posted significant losses ($2.3 and $4.8 billion, respectively).[21]

Such a situation is also seen in other sectors. A limited review of 1,694 companies across a wide range of industries showed that, in 2018, 15% of firms (252) would see their profit (EBITDA) completely wiped out just by the environmental damage they caused, while 543 firms (32%) would see their EBITDA reduced by 25% or more.[22]

To be clear, the IWAI methodology doesn't just include negative impacts (costs). It also attempts to quantify positive impacts (benefits), including job creation, higher wages, diversity, and equal opportunity.

Certainly, this type of quantification is an improvement over other corporate impact metrics. Environmental, Social, and Governance (ESG) ratings, currently used by the investment industry to assess over $22 trillion of assets, are rarely based on "hard" outputs and impacts, instead utilizing "softer," subjective factors such as policies, management systems, and disclosures.[23]

So, while this type of "full cost accounting" is a step in the right direction, it is hardly a panacea and, in fact, suffers from some significant issues.

First and foremost, utilizing the landscape of corporate accounting inherently focuses these efforts on just one stakeholder: investors. After all, results are calculated and phrased in terms of corporate profit and loss (rather than costs and benefits to human beings), which limits the availability and usefulness of this information to the assessment of the company by its managers and by investors.

Even Harvard notes this in its IWAI executive summary, stating "the aspiration is an integrated view of performance which allows **investors and managers** to make informed decisions based not only on monetized private gains or losses, but also on the broader impact a company has on society and the environment." (Emphasis mine.)

Sure, potential customers or employees could look up the corporate performance data and make broad decisions about whether or not they wanted to be associated with these companies, but the aggregate nature of the data precludes any practical use in assessing individual purchases or job opportunities, for example.

Even the name "Impact-Weighted Accounts Initiative" is derived from the "Impact Investing" movement, championed by (among others) Sir Ronald Cohen, a British politician and businessman who has been described as both "the father of British venture capital"[24] and "the father of social investment"[25] (and who is also the chair of the IWAI).

This level of investor-centricity isn't surprising given that these methods were developed during the era of shareholder primacy. But if we're truly interested in changing how companies behave, shouldn't we also marshal the assistance of other stakeholder groups?

To do that, we need to create and distribute impact information in formats and ways that are also useful to customers, employees, and members of the community as they make decisions from their perspectives.

———

LOCATED at Haarlemmerplein 2 in Amsterdam's Haarlemmerbuurt neighborhood, the True Price Store tries to do just that. When it first opened in February 2020, this unique grocery offered only a handful of staples (coffee, chocolate, and bread), but the prices of these products were marked up to account for some of the social and environmental costs of producing them.

For example, a chocolate bar retails for $4.45 instead of $3.35, a coffee costs $4.50 instead of $4.20, and a loaf of bread will set you back $4.11 instead of $3.89. The price tags for all the products include line items showing how much of the markup goes to pay for which outside cost, such as a living wage for the farmers or offsetting green-house gas emissions.[26]

Providing this information on the shelf empowers customers to make a more informed decision about the "true price" of their purchase before they buy it. It's an interaction that, if repeated with every purchase at every store, could transform what we buy and what we don't, rewarding or punishing companies based on their overall behavior.

The True Price Store is, in all honesty, just a prototype, created by a social and environmental organization of the same name to illustrate how you could provide impact information to customers. As a prototype, one can't expect it to fully represent the concept at scale.

For instance, the store has an extremely limited offering. This is due to the enormous and painstaking effort it takes to research all the external costs related to each product, after the fact. Such a small number of choices would make it hard to attract shoppers, who are used to the selection and convenience of a supermarket (which typically carries over 31,000 items).[27] Additionally, if not every store charged the increased "true price," market pressures would encourage customers to seek out nonparticipating outlets in order to pay less money.

But even if one could achieve universal adoption of "true" pricing for every product in every store, there are still fundamental issues with its methodology.

First, incremental proceeds from higher prices don't go back to the makers of the products to compensate them for having changed their behavior. Instead, it goes to fund third-party organizations involved in reforestation as well as assisting individuals who are extremely poor.[28]

Consequently, the original upstream behavior doesn't change and is only addressed downstream, after it has already occurred. It's sort of like paying someone to fill in a hole after you paid someone else to dig it in the first place.

So, why not just give the incremental funds directly to the companies and individuals who produced the products?

Well, as we've seen, increasing revenue to a company without requiring them to provide additional value would most likely lead to profit-taking without any real change. Almost certainly, the company that received the extra income wouldn't pass it along to its upstream suppliers, opting instead to keep it all for itself. There's also a good chance that, after a while, the efficiencies of competitive market pricing would squeeze out this extra margin, with the incremental proceeds instead going to cover the hard costs to produce the products.

So, if you're going to give this extra revenue directly to the company, there would have to be conditions attached. But who would specify those conditions?

Certainly, the government has a long history of issuing regulations, so it could assume this role, too, specifying a myriad of corporate behaviors in excruciating detail. But the government can't be an expert in all the specifics of how millions of different products are produced, so many of these new regulations, while well-intentioned, would probably end up being convoluted or even counterproductive.

The heavy hand of government is at its best when it advances societal change in order to protect human beings from certain harm. For example, the EPA banned asbestos in 1989 because it had become clear that this common insulator caused cancer.[29] Similarly, in 1981 the U.S. Occupational Safety and Health Administration (OSHA) mandated hearing protection for workers exposed to sustained noises louder than 85 decibels after research showed it led to permanent hearing loss.[30] Government's legal intervention forced a relatively quick change to the status quo in order to protect life and limb.

The cause and effect of these physical harms isn't subjective or open to debate. It's scientifically proven, with the impacts indiscriminately affecting any human being who is exposed.

But the same clear-cut relationship can't be applied to all human needs. Human needs not related to our physical health are "soft" and subjective, less able to be defined by a singular standard for every person in every situation.

Once we recognize this, perhaps a better person to levy conditions on companies is the customer. That way, actual human beings could define what is important to them, individually, and purchase products that best satisfy *their* wish lists.

In this scenario, government's role would be reduced to that of a mere referee, determining how these conditions could be accurately and consistently assessed, ensuring that no one is cheating on their measurements, and acting as a transparent storehouse for the results.

This leaves it up to *companies* to find the best way to reduce the broader metrics that offend consumers and increase those metrics that consumers like. Consumer pressure would be translated via sales, as it always has been, just as companies would still seek to satisfy these broader customer needs in order to "get the sale." The only difference from today's paradigm is the broader list of costs that the company would be reporting and managing.

Conceptually, it's similar to the nutrition labels found on packaged foods. These labels, which have been required by the FDA since 1990,[31] communicate specific information about what actually went into the product. The information listed, including ingredients and key nutrients, would otherwise be virtually impossible for the customer to determine before making the purchase (or, for that matter, even after eating the contents).

Nutrition Facts	
8 servings per container	
Serving size	**2/3 cup (55g)**
Amount per serving	
Calories	**230**
	% Daily Value*
Total Fat 8g	**10%**
Saturated Fat 1g	**5%**
Trans Fat 0g	
Cholesterol 0mg	**0%**
Sodium 160mg	**7%**
Total Carbohydrate 37g	**13%**
Dietary Fiber 4g	**14%**
Total Sugars 12g	
Includes 10g Added Sugars	**20%**
Protein 3g	
Vitamin D 2mcg	10%
Calcium 260mg	20%
Iron 8mg	45%
Potassium 235mg	6%

* The % Daily Value (DV) tells you how much a nutrient in a serving of food contributes to a daily diet. 2,000 calories a day is used for general nutrition advice.

Since what's inside the package is also what's going inside our bodies, this disclosure is incredibly important, for example, giving people trying to avoid sodium or eat more whole grains the information they need to make a more informed purchase decision.

Yes, the monetary price of the food is still important, as is the size of the package. But, when these traditional metrics are combined with the "invisible" information about nutrition, customers get a much more holistic idea of what they're actually buying.

This nutritional transparency has allowed customers, *en masse*, to change the food industry. Back in 2003, the FDA updated nutritional labeling requirements to include the amount of "trans fat" in a serving.[32] These unhealthy fats, used by manufacturers to extend shelf life and give some foods a more desirable texture and taste, are quite inexpensive. Unfortunately, they also increase bad cholesterol (LDL) in the body and decrease good cholesterol (HDL), while also increasing the risk of stroke, heart disease and type 2 diabetes.[33]

Once updated, these labels showed consumers just how much trans fat was in the food they were eating, which allowed them to actively avoid those products. For their part, manufacturers, who were suddenly forced to show a hidden health cost of their products, quickly moved to reformulate them, eliminating trans fats and substituting healthier ingredients.

Note that this change in society didn't happen because the government suddenly made trans fats illegal. (That formality didn't happen until 2018.[34]) All it did was mandate that companies had to tell people how much of it was in their food. Consumers took that information and changed their behavior which, in turn, caused companies to change theirs.

Also note that, in this disclosure, the information was communicated in its "native" unit (i.e., "grams of trans fat"). This is quite different from how "full cost accounting" methodologies (including True Price, triple bottom line, ESG investment ratings, and the Impact-Weighted Accounts Initiative) would handle this cost. They would first convert it into a financial cost, expressed in dollars and cents.

While that type of monetization does have some benefits, such as the ease and simplicity of having a single total expressed in a familiar unit, a lot is lost in this translation.

Practically speaking, you can't directly convert between different categories of units. For instance, while you can easily convert inches into centimeters — just multiply times 2.54 — you can't convert inches into minutes. Similarly, there's no exchange rate between "dollars" and "grams of trans fat," so you're forced to find a unit that you can convert.

In this case, grams of trans fat could be converted into a numerically higher likelihood of developing heart disease, which could then be translated into the estimated medical costs to treat that condition over someone's lifetime. Makes sense, right?

But this path requires a multitude of assumptions and generalizations, including the person's age, how many servings they will eat, their genetic predisposition to heart disease, medical insurance premium and co-pay amounts, etc. Each of these steps lessens the information's accuracy and applicability to a specific individual.

And then there's the problem of variable valuation. Even if you decide that you're okay representing a nonmonetary impact using an "average" monetary cost, the meaning of that cost would vary based on the individual.

Let's say you determine that eating a certain product with trans fats would eventually cost an average person $8,000 in additional medical expenses. Now, $8,000 is a lot of money to many people, but not everyone. So, it's more likely that an affluent person might rationalize that cost in the moment and say, "yeah, I can afford that," whereas a poorer individual would be more likely balk at the significant expense they'd be signing up for — even if both individuals had the same age and medical propensities.

This variability of valuation only gets worse when you move into the more subjective realm of human needs beyond those related to our physical bodies.

For example, one fundamental human need is that of "understanding," with all of us human beings trying to make sense of our lives and our places in the world. One tool we use to help us understand those is art. But art is clearly subjective, resonating differently with different individuals.

So, I ask you, how much would you pay for this particular piece of art?

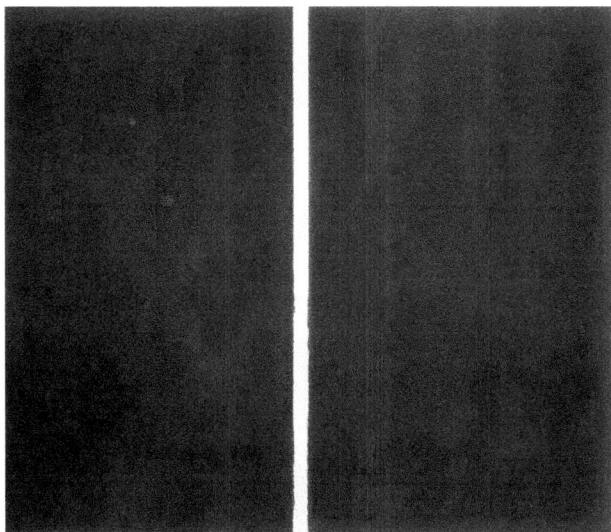

*"Onement VI," by Barnett Newman (Fair Use, from https://
www.wikiart.org/en/barnett-newman/onement-vi-1953.)*

You might look at it and think, "Wow, that is amazing!" and be willing to pay \$43 million for it, like someone did back in 2013.[35] Or you might look at it and think, "What's the big deal? It's a blue square with a white line on it" and wouldn't want it, even if it was free.

Either way, you'd be right. And that's the point. You can't put a singular monetary value on *everything* that satisfies a human need.

Monetizing nonfinancial costs into a single currency also encourages us to oversimplify. After all, since all costs are expressed in a shared unit (dollars), there will most certainly be a grand total somewhere at the bottom. And, given our propensity for "quicker and easier," the chances are we'll just focus on that total, instead of considering the contributions of each of the line items above it. Unfortunately, this self-inflicted reduction to a single bottom line eliminates the transparency of details that empowers us as customers to change corporate behavior through our purchase decisions.

Trying to reduce all costs to a single currency isn't just counterproductive, it's unnecessary. Human beings are quite capable of making decisions based on "mixed" information. We do it all the time, even in commerce.

Consider product labels such as "organic" or "cruelty-free" or "fair trade." All of these are nonmonetary declarations of environmental and social costs incurred (or not incurred) during production. Similarly, labels such as "Energy Star" or "recyclable" communicate costs that can be anticipated during consumption.

As shoppers, we include these consequential costs in our purchase calculus, along with transactional costs such as time and money, to determine if the product in question is a good value.

To put it another way, publishing consequential costs at the point of purchase makes them more like transactional costs, available for a customer to use in their purchase decisions.

Unfortunately, most current consequential cost labels are "binary" in nature. That is, they communicate either "100%" this or "zero" of that, with very few providing information about consequential costs that don't fall at either end of the spectrum.

One notable exception is the EnergyGuide label. Introduced in 1979 as part of the Energy Policy and Conservation Act,[36] EnergyGuide labels show consumers how much energy a major appliance (such as a clothes washer, refrigerator, or television) is expected to use every year. This information is listed in its native unit (kilowatt hours). As an example, check out this label for a standard size, top-loading GE clothes washer.

EnergyGuide label for a GE top-loading washing machine.

It shows that this particular model is expected to use 797 kilowatt hours (kWh) per year (a consequential cost incurred after purchase). But since most of us have no idea if 797 kWh/year is considered "good" or "bad," the label takes the additional genius step of plotting that value along a simple scale, allowing a shopper to see, in a glance, how this model compares to others in the same category.

In our example, the most efficient comparable model only uses 177 kWh/year, while the least efficient one uses 1,298 kWh/year, placing this particular GE clothes washer just about in the middle of the pack.

Since these labels appear on all clothes washers, it's easy for customers to do a side-by-side comparison, along with features and the monetary price, before they make up their mind on which model they're going to buy.

(Interestingly, the bottom of the EnergyGuide label also includes a dollar estimate of how much money this amount of energy might cost. But since this dollar amount is based on the national average cost of electricity, it's not especially accurate for an individual. For reference, in September of 2021, the average cost per kWh ranged from 9.37 cents in Louisiana up to 32.76 cents in Hawaii,[37] so where you live can make a real difference.)

Again, it's important to point out that, through this program, the government doesn't dictate how much energy appliances can use or tell manufacturers how to make their appliances more energy efficient. It simply requires that manufactures tell consumers what they can expect in terms of energy usage *before* they buy the product. To aid in this communication, the government (via the U.S. Department of Energy) defines how energy consumption should be measured so that everyone is using the same standard, and it compiles all the results so that the comparison scale is possible.

The real pressure to change comes from human beings, who have consistently rewarded companies that produce more energy-efficient appliances by buying more of them.

The EnergyGuide program is one standout. But all in all, our society does a poor job of defining and sharing consequential costs. Different labels utilize different methodologies administered by a hodgepodge of public and private entities. The resulting information is inconsistent and piecemeal at best.

But if the goal is to fundamentally change the way business operates so it better serves a broader set of human needs, presenting only a handful of consequential costs some of the time won't work. What's needed is a single and consistent methodology that provides customers with a holistic idea of everything they're agreeing to, no matter what they're buying.

That sort of fundamental change may sound impossible. After all, given the interconnected nature of our economy, even the simplest product is made from the contributions of dozens, if not hundreds of suppliers. And any effort to accurately report consequential costs will require near-unanimous participation of all those companies and individuals.

But fundamental change isn't as hard as you think.

By definition, fundamentals are basics. Small, simple things such as accepted beliefs or actions that are more like habits. Their significance only comes from the fact that we repeat them over and over, without question.

But when we do question them, and decide they need to change, even one simple alteration can have a massive impact.

The one simple change your company can make right now? Ask your suppliers for their consequential costs.

That's it.

Just ask them.

Companies like yours are customers, just like human beings, so you can use your company's purchasing power just like a human customer. Your suppliers really want your business and will go quite a long way to get it and keep it.

Walmart is famous for this type of pressure, requiring companies to meet a long list of conditions[38] to become one of their suppliers, and stay one. So, if it's good enough for Walmart, it's good enough for you.

Negotiate it into your contracts and purchase orders. Stipulate that your business is contingent on them delivering an accounting of consequential costs associated with the products you purchase from them. Not just the costs your direct supplier added, but the accumulated total of all consequential costs added by all the indirect suppliers in the supply chain, going all the back to when the raw materials were extracted from the ground.

Of course, to report this total to you, your supplier has to make a similar request to their suppliers who, in turn, have to secure the same information from their sources. And so on.

It's akin to the concept of "provenance" in fine art. From the French word *provenir*, meaning "to come from," provenance is an ownership history that helps to authenticate and value a particular piece of art. For example, here is the provenance published for *Onement VI*, the blue and white painting we referred to above, when it was auctioned in 2013:[39]

- Collection Annalee Newman (gift of the artist, December 1953)
- Mr. and Mrs. Frederick R. Weisman, Beverly Hills, California (purchased 1961)
- Weisman Family Collection, Richard L. Weisman, New York
- Private Collection, New York (acquired from the above in 1990)
- Acquired by the present owner in 2000

Provenance is sort of like the baton in a relay race, with one person handing it off to the next. But in our case, the baton isn't a running list of art owners, it's a running tab of consequential costs.

At each step along the supply chain, a supplier takes the consequential costs for the inputs it receives and adds in its own consequential costs before passing along the updated totals (along with its outputs) to its customers. One step at time, a grand total is accumulated until it reaches the end consumer.

One major benefit of this type of "running tab" is accuracy. If you've ever filled out an expense report or tried to itemize deductions on your taxes, you know it's much more accurate to gather receipts as you go, rather than trying to reconstruct things after the fact. To create, instead of trying to re-create.

Yes, you'll need to give your suppliers (both direct and indirect) time to figure out how to calculate their consequential cost contributions. But give them a deadline. And if they don't (or won't) hit it, find another direct supplier who will.

Conceptually, the request shouldn't be foreign to them (or to you). Many companies already utilize a Life Cycle Assessment (LCA) process to understand environmental impacts. Standardized terminology and methods are well-established in the ISO 14000 Environmental Management standards.[40]

Social Life Cycle Assessments (S-LCAs) aren't quite as well-defined, but a framework for understanding social and socio-economic impacts is described in both the ISO 26000 Guidance on Social Responsibility[41] and as part of the United Nations Environment Programme's Life Cycle Initiative.[42]

Importantly, these methodologies don't just explain how to measure costs incurred during production, but also during consumption, including future energy usage and "end of life" impacts such as demolition, waste disposal, and/or recycling.

In aggregate, it's way too much information for any one entity to compile on its own. But, as the saying goes, "many hands make light work." So, distributing the effort so that each company is only responsible for calculating and inputting the consequential costs that *they* contribute makes it much more manageable.

On the other hand, the Herculean task of integrating the data from all of these contributions will need to be centralized to ensure consistency, accuracy, and availability.

Consequential costs associated with one company's outputs will need to "travel" with their products to various other companies, where they'll need to be carved up as those products become individual inputs for the second company's products. As these subsequent products are assembled, the disparate sub-costs will then need to be re-totaled so they can travel with the second company's outputs to the next step in the supply chain, where the whole cycle begins again.

Consider, for example, the way that consequential costs related to a cup of coffee travel along the life cycle from "cradle to grave."

Consequential costs related to the coffee life cycle (simplified)

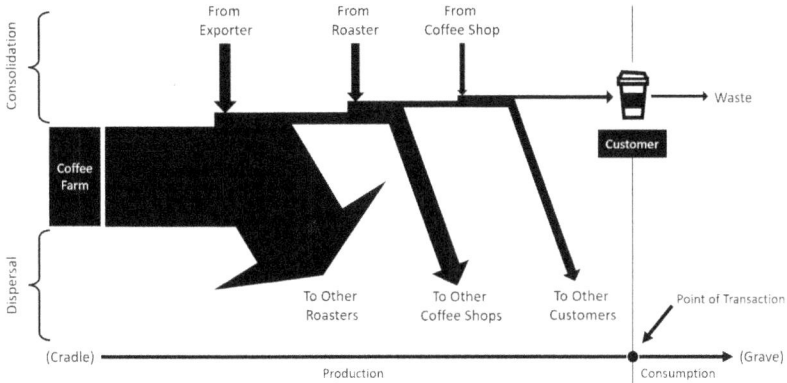

For coffee, the "cradle" is a coffee farm, which accumulates various consequential costs as it grows coffee beans. If their entire crop is sold to a single exporter, then the exporter assumes all of these costs at the time of purchase. The exporter then adds its own consequential costs as it transports these "green" coffee beans, before selling them once they reach their destination.

At this point, because the exporter is selling coffee beans to multiple coffee roasters, the consolidated consequential costs are dispersed to each of the roasters in proportion to how much of the shipment they buy. That way, each roaster is only responsible for the consequential costs associated with the beans they purchased.

This cycle of consolidation and dispersal continues as the roaster adds in the consequential costs it produces before selling roasted beans to multiple customers, including (in this illustration) a coffee shop, which inherits only its portion of the total consequential costs forwarded by the roaster. The coffee shop, in turn, adds in the consequential costs related to grinding and brewing the coffee, as well as serving it in a cup. The consolidated consequential costs for each cup of coffee are then attached to the cup before being transferred to a human customer at the time of purchase.

Up until this moment, the consequential costs are all related to production. However, after the customer buys a cup of coffee, any additional consequential costs are related to consumption. For a cup of coffee, these are relatively minor and are associated with waste (i.e., the "grave" in this product life cycle). Specifically, consumption consequential costs are primarily related to the paper coffee cup (which is either thrown away or recycled) and the customer's urine (which will probably be processed by a local water treatment facility before being returned to the local ecosystem).

That's just a simplified illustration; the complexities of the real world are exponentially more complicated.

Too bad we haven't invented some sort of machine that could quickly manipulate really large amounts of data, analyze the results for insights on outliers or lower overall cost paths, and effortlessly share the information with virtually anyone, anywhere around the world.

Oh wait. We have.

The same computers, algorithms, and interconnectivity that companies currently use to profile and stalk their customers can just as easily be used to trace and calculate the consequential costs associated with their products.

Data gathering and transmission could piggyback on top of the existing logistics infrastructure, which already uses a sophisticated network of barcodes, RFID tags, GPS receivers, and other technologies to know exactly what is where and when it can be where it needs to be. (Not to mention how much it costs in dollars.) So, the same systems used to provide "just-in-time" inventory or to recall a bad batch of medicine could also be used to accurately determine the consequential costs of an individual product.

Given that publishing consequential cost data could significantly increase or decrease sales, there will be a strong desire by companies to either cheat on their reporting or keep their cost data to themselves. That's why the data should be reported into (and warehoused in) databases managed by an independent third party, such as the government which, as we've seen, is uniquely positioned to stand up to business for the benefit of natural human beings.

Just like a lot of information reported to (and generated by) the government, all consequential cost data should be considered public, available to any person, company, or other entity. This unbiased transparency will not only ensure consequential cost information is available to customers when they need it, but it will also mean it can be further analyzed by companies seeking the competitive advantage that will come from further reducing their negative impacts on society and the environment.

So, exactly which consequential cost data should be tracked? That's a great question.

There are hundreds, if not thousands, of legitimate consequential costs stretching backward through production and forward through consumption. But clearly, you can't include all of them. The more metrics you ask a company to provide, the greater their resistance to doing so, thanks to the increasing effort required. Similarly, the more consequential costs you publish, the less likely customers are to read them all, let alone consider them during their purchase process.

On the other hand, if you consolidate the information too much, you lose the precision and detail that paints a clear picture of what's actually going on. This broader communication is also less credible than directly reported metrics, since rolling up any data inherently requires some amount of subjectivity in how it's done.

So, once again, what's called for is balance — that Goldilocks middle ground where information is relatable without being overwhelming.

One shortcut to relatability is metaphor. Metaphors allow a person who already understands a specific relationship or structure to transfer that understanding to a new set of circumstances, much like I did above when I used the word "Goldilocks." Most Americans know the 19th-century British fairy tale and can instantly transfer the concept of "just right" from baby bear's bed to something entirely different. In this case, I'm talking about not having too much detail, or too little detail, but just the right amount.

Astronomers also use the term "Goldilocks" to describe a planetary orbit around a star that is just the right distance to allow water to exist in a liquid state. Too close to the star and the water would all boil off. Too far and the water would be ice. This "Goldilocks" zone is critical in determining whether or not the planet could support life as we know it.

Back in 2012, economist Kate Raworth was looking for a way to describe a similar relationship between human society and planet Earth. Society utilizes Earth's natural resources to improve our human quality of life. Insufficient or disproportionate use of these resources can cause real hardship for our species. But utilizing too many resources causes real damage to our planet which, in turn, will eventually cause hardship for us. Raworth theorized that balance was possible, even within such a complex system, but she needed a simple way to communicate it.

Given that the story of Goldilocks is verbal, she opted for something more visual. And delicious. A doughnut.

Raworth imagined two concentric circles. The inner circle represents the social foundation below which you would see critical human deprivations. The outer circle represents the ecological ceiling beyond which critical planetary degradation occurs. Between the two circles is the doughnut — "a safe and just space for humanity" where "we can meet the needs of all within the means of the planet."[43]

climate
change

ozone layer
depletion

ECOLOGICAL CEILING

ocean
acidification

the safe and just space for humanity

SOCIAL FOUNDATION

OVERSHOOT

water food

energy health

air pollution

SHORTFALL

networks education

housing income
& work

chemical
pollution

gender
equality

peace &
justice

social political
equity voice

biodiversity
loss

REGENERATIVE AND DISTRIBUTIVE ECONOMY

nitrogen &
phosphorus loading

land
conversion

freshwater
withdrawals

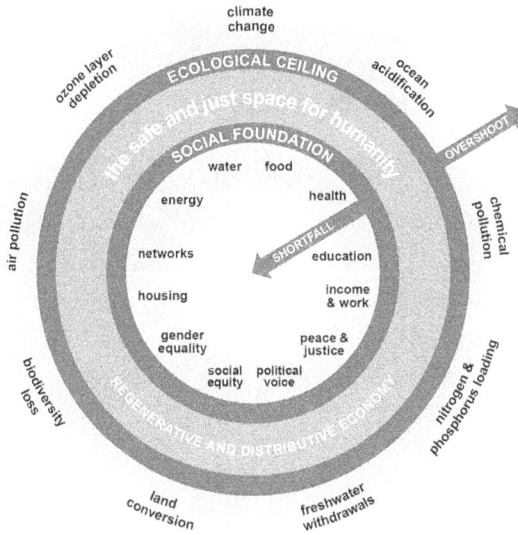

Doughnut Economics visual model. Created by Wikipedia user DoughnutEconomics. Creative Commons license: CC BY-SA 4.0

While Raworth's focus is on society in general, rather than just commerce, her "doughnut" relationship between societal and environmental impacts effortlessly translates to the concept of consequential costs, providing a simple dual structure on which to base our efforts.

The social foundation can be fleshed out to measure a product's contributions to key factors of a just society, such as ethics, diversity, equity, health, transparency, and community. Similarly, the environmental ceiling can be categorized to assess impacts to basic components of our planet, such as the air, water, land, plants, animals, and energy. Collectively, these dozen or so elements provide a fairly good snapshot of the consequential costs you're supporting with a purchase.

Subsequently, each of these social and environmental elements can be populated with just a handful of key data points — aspects of an element that are relatively easy to measure and define in simple, comprehensible terms.

For social, it could work like this:

1. Ethical Labor Practices

- Percentage of workforce that are under the age of 18 or are prisoners/forced labor — [smaller is better]
- Percentage of workforce that are ineligible for company paid benefits (including health insurance) — [smaller is better]
- Median hours worked per week (all labor) — [smaller is better]

2. Management Diversity

- Percentage of senior management/board of directors that is non-white — [larger is better]
- Percentage of senior management/board of directors that is female — [larger is better]

3. Equitable Compensation

- Percentage of workers who are paid at least a living wage relative to their community — [larger is better]
- Ratio of lowest-paid employee to highest-paid employee (including all compensation) — [larger is better]
- Ratio of median female income to median male income (all employees) — [larger is better]
- Ratio of median non-white income to median white income (all employees) — [larger is better]

4. Health & Safety

- Percentage of employees ineligible for at least one hour of paid sick leave for every 40 hours worked — [smaller is better]

- Number of significant worker injuries/deaths per worker — [smaller is better]
- Number of consumer injuries/deaths per units sold — [smaller is better]

5. Data Transparency

- Percentage of all customer data points gathered via direct customer submission — [larger is better]

6. Shareholder Dominance

- Percentage of annual gross profit paid to shareholders (e.g., dividends or stock buybacks) — [smaller is better]

7. Local Community Benefit

- Percentage of all production inputs sourced within 100 miles of where they're used — [larger is better]
- Percentage of all payroll paid to workers whose primary residence is less than ten miles from where they work — [larger is better]
- Percentage of annual gross profit dispersed to those living less than ten miles from a company location — [larger is better]

For environmental factors, it could work like this (note that smaller is better for all of these metrics):

1. Air Pollution

- Tons of CO_2 and climate change equivalents emitted
- Tons of SO_2 (acid rain pollutant) emitted
- Tons of particulate matter (2.5 microns) emitted

2. Water Usage & Pollution

- Hundred cubic feet (HCF) of water used
- HCF of untreated wastewater output
- Tons of fertilizing nitrogen applied to farmland
- Tons of fertilizing phosphorus applied to farmland

3. Land Usage & Pollution

- Acres of land occupied or used
- Tons of solid waste output
- Percentage of solid waste volume not recycled

4. Impact on Vegetation

- Percentage of yield that is genetically modified
- Tons of pesticide applied to farmland

5. Impact on Animals

- Percentage of output units that utilized animal testing
- Percentage of output that was genetically modified

6. Energy Usage

- Kilowatt hours (or equivalent) of energy used

In addition, you'll also want to know the estimated life expectancy of a product. This is so you can account for the impact of replacing the product when it is used up or when it wears out. One simple way of accounting for the "time" element is to treat the product's life expectancy as a divisor to calculate the number of products that would need to be purchased over the course of an average human lifetime (approximately 80 years.) Think of it as a common denominator.

For example, if you buy a coffee maker for your home and the estimated life expectancy for the model you buy is only five years, then you'll need to purchase 15 *more* of those same coffee makers to last you an average lifetime. Knowing this, both the financial cost (in dollars) and the consequential costs related to production can be multiplied by 16 to allow for an "apples-to-apples" comparison across all brands and models of coffee makers.

It's a step that rewards companies whose products are "built to last" (which minimizes consequential production costs over the long term) while punishing those who opt for inexpensive materials, poor design, or planned obsolescence — decisions which increase the number of production cycles (and related consequential costs) required to meet someone's long-term needs.

In total, that's 13 consequential costs that paint a fairly good picture of a product's overall footprint, based on the weighted averages of just 33 data points.

Is it exhaustive? No. But that's by design. Going for "exhaustive" is, well, exhausting for everyone involved. Companies will balk at the information collection effort and customers will tune out if there's too much to read and consider.

Is it perfect? Of course not. I'm sure this methodology can and will be improved as more people get involved, just as businesses will spring up to help companies measure and even reduce their consequential costs.

What's presented here isn't a finish line, it's a starting point. Which is what we need to get started.

To ensure that consequential cost data has the greatest impact at the point of purchase, the information will need to be presented in a way that is easy to understand and compare with data about other, similar products.

One way to do this is to take a page from the EnergyGuide labels, above. That is, for each consequential cost, display the score for the product in question along a visual scale dynamically defined by the best- and worst-performing similar products, like this:

Product with   This Product's   Product with
Best Behavior   Behavior   Worst Behavior
XX |_____|XX_____|XX
              Type of Behavior

This allows consumers to quickly see a numeric score (represented by the XXs, above), but also to see graphically how the product in question stacks up against other options.

For a specific instance, let's say a product doesn't perform as well as other similar products when it comes to having women and minorities in senior management involved in the production process. That fact might be displayed like this:

84 |_____34|_____|24
           Management Diversity

In this case, the best-performing similar product scored 84, the worst-performing one scored 24, and the product in question scored 34, placing it closer to the "bad" end of the scale.

Conversely, if the product in question scored better in this metric, it would move toward the "good" end of the scale, like this (with the product scoring 64):

84 |_____64|_____|24
           Management Diversity

For other consequential costs, where a smaller score indicates better performance (such as shareholder dominance of companies involved with the production of the product), the scale simply flips, with smaller numbers on the left and larger numbers on the right, like this:

22 |___|34_____|94
         Shareholder Dominance

Always having the "better" end of the scale on one side (the left) allows customers to quickly scan down multiple rating scales, knowing that scores that are closer to the left are always considered "better."

Put it all together and you get a supplemental label or tag that can be attached to any product, allowing customers to compare the consequential costs in addition to the financial costs before they make a purchase.

Product: Acme Single Kup 200
Category: Home coffee maker

By buying this product you are also encouraging these behaviors

How to read this tag to compare
this product to similar products

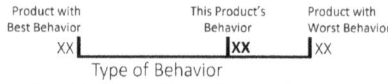

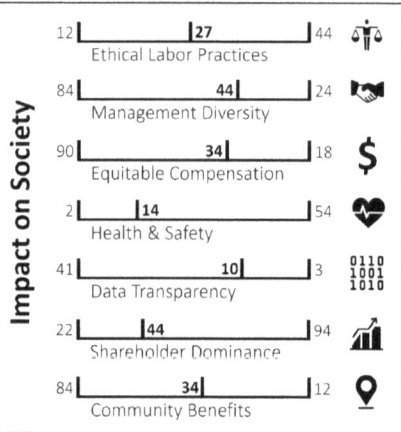

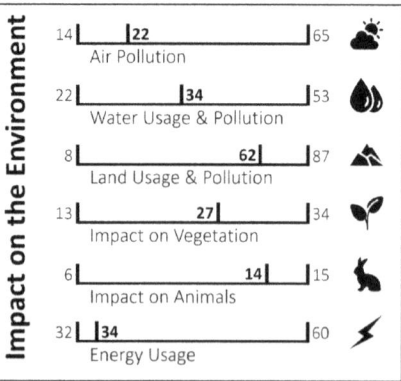

Product with Best Behavior	This Product's Behavior	Product with Worst Behavior
XX	XX	XX

Type of Behavior

Impact on Society

12 |————27————| 44 Ethical Labor Practices

84 |————44——| 24 Management Diversity

90 |————34———| 18 Equitable Compensation

2 |——14——————| 54 Health & Safety

41 |————10—| 3 Data Transparency

22 |——44————————| 94 Shareholder Dominance

84 |————34———| 12 Community Benefits

Impact on the Environment

14 |——22—————————| 65 Air Pollution

22 |———34————| 53 Water Usage & Pollution

8 |——————62—| 87 Land Usage & Pollution

13 |———27———| 34 Impact on Vegetation

6 |——————14—| 15 Impact on Animals

32 |—34————————| 60 Energy Usage

Estimated Product Life Expectancy: 5 years	
Average Human Lifespan: 80 years	
Products Needed Over Human Lifespan: 16	
Cumulative Price Over Human Lifespan: $1,440	Scan for more details

Information valid through September 2023

In the end, all this label or tag provides is disclosure of information. It's up to the individual customer to decide how important that information is to them. For people who really care about the environment, they may look for products that score better in those aspects, even if they cost more money. Those who aren't as worried about the environment may choose to favor other aspects, or even ignore everything but the monetary price.

And that's okay.

The whole point of reporting consequential costs is to put human beings into the driver's seat, rather than companies or the government — to empower them to make the decisions about what's best for them.

And not just as customers. The same consequential cost data can empower human beings to make more informed decisions in other stakeholder roles that they play — to understand more about a company before becoming an employee, allowing a company to build a plant in a community, or even whether or not to invest money in that company as a stockholder.

The flip side of this, of course, is that companies that have better scores will enjoy a competitive advantage in sales, recruiting, community relations, and in raising capital.

Finally, by reporting this information voluntarily, companies can avoid more intrusive government regulation that may be imposed if the problems our society and environment face aren't solved in some other way.

When it comes to costs, I'm reminded of the oath a witness takes when they testify in a trial, to "tell the truth, the whole truth, and nothing but the truth." Including consequential costs is telling the whole truth. And it's good for everyone.

Step Five: Show Everyone You Mean It

Business has always had a difficult relationship with the truth. It is quick to embrace the truth when it is positive and will help make a sale, but a company often has to be compelled to share the truth when it is negative.

This isn't surprising. Human nature responds more to benefits than costs. (Just imagine a television commercial for a pharmaceutical that started with warnings such as "serious illness or death.") But while we're first attracted to the "good" parts, we also know that nothing is free, so we want companies to be upfront with the "bad" parts before we make a purchase.

Once again, this type of balance is where business seems to struggle. The desire to maximize profits leads companies to shout about the pros and whisper the cons. To quote Tom Waits in his song "Step Right Up," "The large print giveth and the small print taketh away."

Even this would be okay with most of us, as long as the small print was actually there and written in a way that was as clear and as conversational as the large print. Unfortunately, this is not always the case, with negatives not disclosed at all or buried inside massive "terms and conditions" documents, drafted in impenetrable legalese.

Words not read are the same as words not written, which leads to nasty surprises discovered by customers only after the transaction. This, in turn, damages the trust people have in companies and business in general.

So, it's important to point out that some of the steps previously mentioned in this chapter could be easily abused if the companies only embrace the lingo without doing the work. After all, what company wouldn't want to say that it is a "Best Friend Brand?" Or that everything they do is to "satisfy your human needs?"

I've been in marketing for over three decades. I get it. Those phrases *sound* really good. I'd want to use them, too.

But if companies only use the phrases and don't change the way they operate, then the words become buzzwords, creating a façade that quickly fails to deliver on its promises.

And that's a recipe for more lost trust.

However, if you offer up a fuller picture of the costs of your products (including consequential costs), this proactive honesty can actually build trust in a brand.

But overcoming the inertia of mistrust that currently plagues business will take more than just owning up to consequential costs. To show all your stakeholders (including employees, shareholders, communities, and customers) that your company's new focus is genuine (and not just another marketing campaign), there's one more big step you should take.

Your company should put its life on the line. Literally.

As you may remember, a company only exists because the state grants it a charter, giving this legal person enormous power in exchange for benefiting the natural persons it serves. Without this charter, the company cannot do business and would, essentially, die.

Part of this charter is a commitment from the company to pursue a designated purpose. Hundreds of years ago, when companies and charters were first created, this purpose was quite specific, such as sailing to India in order bring back spices. Any activity outside of this purpose (for example, sailing to the New World to bring back beaver pelts) was prohibited.

Today, most companies have moved to an extremely broad "catch-all" purpose in their charters, such as to pursue "any lawful purpose." This not only avoids restrictions on what goods and services the company can offer, but it also makes it much harder for the state to revoke its charter for breaking its promise.

In fact, the handful of companies that do have their charters revoked each year suffer this corporate "death" mainly because they fail to pay taxes to the state, not because they deviated from their chartered purpose.

So, while mostly dormant, the power of the charter's "purpose" is still present and offers a real opportunity for companies that want to show they're serious about how they operate.

Specifically, a company could single-handedly reinstate this power by changing its chartered purpose to one that specifically commits to benefiting human beings in nonfinancial measures. This self-imposed submission would be a voluntary and very public admission that the company can't do whatever it wants — that it exists to improve the lives of all natural persons. And that, if it can't do that, there will be serious consequences.

To facilitate just this behavior, 37 states (including Delaware, where many major corporations are chartered) currently offer companies the ability to charter themselves as "benefit corporations" (also known as "B" corporations.) While specific requirements vary by state, these for-profit enterprises are virtually identical to traditional "C" or "S" corporations with just a few exceptions.[44]

Firstly, the charter of a B corporation defines the "best interest of the corporation" to include its impacts on one or more specific public benefits. This is in contrast to most C or S corporate charters, where this term remains undefined, and thus has been interpreted as implying the goal of maximizing profit and shareholder value.

Again, what constitutes a "specific public benefit" varies by state, but the model legislation (adopted by many states) offers seven options:[45]

1. Providing low-income or underserved individuals or communities with beneficial products or services;
2. Promoting economic opportunity for individuals or communities beyond the creation of jobs in the normal course of business;
3. Protecting or restoring the environment;
4. Improving human health;
5. Promoting the arts, sciences, or advancement of knowledge;
6. Increasing the flow of capital to entities with a purpose to benefit society or the environment;
7. Conferring any other particular benefit on society or the environment.

Second, a B corporation is required to publish an annual "benefit report" that assesses the company's performance against its commitments. Most states follow the best practice and require that these reports utilize accepted, third-party standards and are shared publicly.

Some B corporations take the additional, optional step of having their impact certified by a third party, such as B Labs, to further demonstrate that they are living up to their commitment and not just "cooking the books."

Because a corporate charter is legally binding, being a B corporation sends a strong message to all stakeholders, including shareholders. In fact, being upfront about your company's purpose will help attract investors who are looking for more than just a financial return.

Certified

Ⓑ

Corporation

That's not to say that investors won't want money. And that's fine. ROI is a valid expectation and actually related to item six on the list of specific public benefits above.

But to help ensure that the company doesn't revert to the practice of measuring success solely by financial metrics, some states (including Connecticut), include a "preservation" clause in their benefit corporation statute.[46] This "one-way door" prevents companies from reverting back to a C or S corporation simply because shareholders vote to do so. It's further proof that your company is serious about benefiting human beings and it's not going back.

If your company is an LLC, rather than a C or S corporation, you probably have fewer concerns about outside shareholders driving your company's focus. But you can still take advantage of a benefit-oriented charter by converting to a "low-profit limited liability" corporation (L3C). While currently offered by only ten states, the L3C entity has the additional benefit of potentially attracting grants from nonprofit foundations, since an investment in a L3C qualifies as a "program-related investment" (PRI) under IRS regulations.[47]

However you do it, fundamentally changing your company's charter (rather than just changing what your company makes) shows

that you're truly serious. You're putting your company's very existence on the line. And that's a commitment that is hard to question.

Step Six: Tell Everyone About It

This may sound obvious, but after you make all these changes, you'll need to tell people about them.

Now, most companies I know don't have a problem talking. On the contrary, they are nonstop chatterboxes because they realize (correctly) that talking (i.e., marketing) drives sales. And when you stop talking, sales slow down.

The problem with always talking, of course, is that you always have to have something to say. From the company's perspective, it would *love* to talk about itself, its "brand purpose," and its products all day long. But, just as we're turned off when a real person does nothing but talk about themselves and how great they are, we dislike it when companies are similarly self-centered. We want people to engage with us and learn about us and the things we find interesting.

So, companies try to weigh in on any number of current topics and issues to build "engagement." But they have shown us time and time again that they're not real people. They're businesses which are primarily out to make money, so their attempts at empathy, no matter how sincere, often come across as hollow and self-serving.

If you don't remember the examples of how badly this can go from way back in Chapter 1, here's another one:

Gillette is America's largest razor and shaving brand, known by its advertising tagline, "the best a man can get." In January 2019, with popular culture focusing on the #MeToo movement and calling out men for sexual harassment and sexual assault, Gillette decided to enter that conversation by launching a new advertising campaign.

The campaign, titled "the best men can be," challenged men (their primary target audience) to change the accepted norms for how men behave — to help eliminate bullying and the objectification of women by correcting those behaviors in their male friends and in their sons. Importantly, the ads did not show or specifically promote any Gillette product, merely ending with a Gillette logo.

While this message may sound positive (or, at worst, innocuous), Gillette was widely criticized for taking this stance,[48] and not just by those who opposed the #MeToo movement.

Gillette's misstep was that it was a company (a legal person) weighing in on an issue that concerned people (natural persons). This fundamental difference meant the company had no standing in the debate and was, therefore, not welcome to participate in the discussion, especially since everything a company says or does tends to be connected with commerce. As a result, the effort was seen by many as an attempt to monetize social justice.

Such is the problem when a company tries to talk about a brand purpose it borrowed or backed into, rather than one it cultivated organically.

The good news is that, if your company decides to become a best friend brand and takes the steps necessary to serve a specific set of human needs, you won't need to borrow or back into a brand purpose. You'll already have one — a genuine brand purpose (to serve human beings in a specific way) that you can talk about, knowing it is more than just words.

But, again, if you don't tell people about it, they won't know.

So, the last step in the retooling of your business is to spread the word. To show members of each of your stakeholder groups that your company has changed. That it truly recognizes the value of *all* of the legs of the stool and has something to offer each of them — not just in a singular stakeholder role, but as holistic human beings.

And since you'll finally have something powerful to say, don't be shy. Hold meetings with your employees, send letters to shareholders, launch an advertising campaign to your customers, talk with the press and members of the local community.

Better yet, involve them in the process as you retool your company. After all, they are the natural persons you're doing this for, so it would be more than a little foolish (and arrogant) to not ask for their input and opinions along the way.

Remember, you're not just changing your company. You're changing society.

Society is a bit like a rugby scrum, with people all pushing to move the ball where they think it should go. And, like many team sports, if you can get more people aligned and pushing in the same direction, you can really move the ball.

Shareholder primacy aligned people with the allure of simplicity. "Just focus on increasing the stock price and everything else will follow," it promised. That simplicity was, and is, a powerful argument. So powerful that, even today, as technology has made it much easier to see that putting one group above all others hasn't taken care of "everything else," most of us still don't question the gospel of simplicity.

Those who do question it know the truth: life isn't that simple. That business, like society, is a team sport, needing the contributions of many different stakeholders to be successful.

That a stool with all of its legs lifts all of us up.

And that's why the concepts in this book, which I guess you could collectively call "human primacy," can win out over "shareholder primacy." What human primacy lacks in simplicity, it more than makes up for in inclusivity. The size of its constituency is everyone. Eight billion people all pushing the scrum of society the same way.

The problem, of course, is that not everyone sees the issues with the current system. They either benefit from it or think that's "just how it is." This isn't surprising given that a whole generation has been raised to believe that shareholders should be their focus. But until people see the disadvantages of shareholder primacy, there's no way they'll be open to alternatives.

And that, in essence, is why I wrote this book.

To empower you with a cogent, detailed argument against the status quo as well as a clear articulation of a better path forward. Not just to convince you, but so that you can convince others.

With every person who agrees, not only will you find a potential customer who will reward you for your company's new focus, but we'll add an ally to this side of the scrum. These allies will be strong ones because, when people believe in something, they tend to push harder than when they're just following orders. In fact, some of our teammates will find new ways to push, coming up with even better ideas and solutions than those you've read here.

After a while, we'll reach a tipping point. We'll realize we're not pushing as hard as we were and find the scrum is actually pulling us along. That's when we will know that there is such buy-in and alignment that the new culture is taking over.

Please don't mistake my enthusiasm for naïveté.

Clearly, the changes I'm talking about are massive in both scope and scale. But the same could be said about the concept of shareholder primacy when it was first introduced 50 years ago. Yet, here we are, living in a society that routinely favors a small percentage of our population, even though it has adverse side effects for everyone.

So have faith. You're a human being. This is *your* company. This is *your* society.

Start pushing.

8

FOUR ROLES FOR ALL OF US

"If you think you are too small to make a difference, try sleeping with a mosquito."

— TENZIN GYATSO, THE 14TH DALAI LAMA

One person can't change a company, even if that person is the CEO. That's because, while the CEO is the most powerful person inside the company, they still work *for* the company, a separate and more powerful legal person.

Sure, a CEO can take significant or even revolutionary steps to alter the company and what it does, but if those changes don't prove beneficial to the company itself, those changes will quickly be rolled back, and the CEO will find themselves out the door.

This is a defensive move. The company knows its success depends on an interconnected ecosystem of stakeholders including customers, employees, shareholders, and communities, so it is rightfully hesitant to abandon the status quo. That said, if the ecosystem migrates, the company will follow in order to stay successful.

While the company is more powerful than any one person, the ecosystem is more powerful than the company, meaning it's the *ecosystem* that ultimately sets the terms of engagement for how businesses operate.

It's an important point to remember because harnessing this "power of everyone" is the best hope for changing the way companies behave — which makes companies not that different from human beings.

When a human being exhibits destructive behavior, such as drug or alcohol addiction, they may not see the problems they are causing for themselves and others. As a result, they may resist change, even when it's suggested by someone they trust, such as a friend or family member.

After individual efforts fail, friends and family may come together to stage an intervention, or confrontation by the whole group. The reason an intervention often works is that the person who needs help has nowhere to hide. They are confronted by seemingly everyone they know, with everyone saying the same thing: "You have a problem. You need to acknowledge that problem and make changes. We're here to support you if you change but, if you can't, then here are the consequences."

So, if you personally want companies to change, realize that engaging a company wearing only one of your stakeholder hats isn't going to work. For example, saying, "I'm not going to support you as a customer, but I'm still going to own your stock" sends a mixed message.

Instead, you need to present yourself as a one-person intervention, sending the same, unified message as a customer and an employee and a shareholder and a citizen — in other words, all the roles you are able to play.

Importantly, the purpose of an intervention is to help someone you genuinely care about, not someone you hate (or blindly follow). The same holds true for companies. So, for your intervention to work, you can't view companies as evil (nor as saviors). Recognize them for what they are: groups of people acting together around a shared purpose.

If that shared purpose is beneficial, then a company's size and power can improve all our lives. But if that purpose is causing harm, then it's up to you to provide a little "tough love" and tell the company three things:

1. What behavior you expect it to change.
2. What the reward will be if it does.
3. What the consequences will be if it doesn't.

These three things will, of course, vary based on the stakeholder role you are playing at any given time so, like any successful intervention, you'll need to prepare beforehand.

As a Customer

When acting as a customer, the leverage you hold is obvious: the transaction. If you like what you see, then you'll make a purchase, trading your money (as well as time and data) for the company's product. Conversely, if you don't like what you see, the transaction won't happen.

What's not so obvious is what you want from the company in exchange for your payment. Sure, there are the features and benefits of the product itself but, as described in the previous chapter, there are so many more things you, as a customer, can ask for, such as:

- Request that the company offer a vertically integrated customer experience (V.I.C.E.), providing satisfiers for every facet of a particular human condition.
- Select those companies that include all four components (people, things, places, and actions) that help satisfy human needs.
- Require the company to list not just a monetary price at the point of purchase, but also significant consequential costs that impact society and the environment. If more than one company offers this information, you can choose the products that have lower consequential costs.

- Reward companies that are structured as a benefit corporation (B corp) or low-profit limited liability corporation (L3C), which indicates a legal commitment to benefit all human beings, rather than just shareholders.

But *how* you ask for these things is just as important as what you're asking for.

First and foremost, you actually have to ask. Yes, no one likes confrontation. It takes more time and effort than just ghosting a company or product you find lacking. But, while saying nothing is easier and more efficient, it's also horribly ineffective at solving the problem. After all, if you don't tell the company what you want, how can they give it you?

That's not to say that all companies will want to hear from you. Some, that are still consumed by the short term and gaining efficiencies, probably won't. But there are many, many companies that are desperate to hear what you want because they realize that satisfying customer needs is the key to long-term customer retention and overall success.

Second, you have to ensure the person you're asking is actually in a position to do something with the information. This is particularly problematic in the retail environment where the person working on the sales floor isn't usually informed or empowered enough to give you a response. Or, sometimes, even pass along your message to someone who is. Seeking out a dedicated customer service representative or manager is a slightly better option, but even these avenues, by themselves, are no guarantee of success since what you're asking for may be out of their control as well.

The same holds true for online shopping. Most e-commerce sites are engineered to funnel customer communication directly to a trained customer service representative, but their authority also only goes so far.

That's not to say that you shouldn't talk about what you want to your local store manager or chat real-time with an online customer service rep. Theoretically, all of these employees are supposed to escalate significant requests. It's just that you shouldn't count on one conversation to be effective. A better strategy is to also communicate directly with "corporate," where there's a shorter path to the executives who will need to address the changes you're seeking.

And not just the corporate offices of retailers, but also the corporate offices of the companies who actually manufacture the products you're considering. These are upstream of the retailers and also where many of the changes, especially involving consequential costs, will need to be made.

Third, consider the tone of how you ask for change. While it's true that companies aren't human beings with feelings, when you ask the company for something, you're not actually talking to the company. You're talking to a human being *about* the company. And it's a fact of life that people (even employees) are more willing to help you when they don't feel attacked.

Besides, you don't need any attitude. Your power is in your resolve. That, unless the company gives you what you want, you're going to walk away. Your best chance of success, therefore, is to clearly and succinctly describe what you're asking for as well as what's at stake.

Engaging with companies in public forums such as social media can actually help your cause. Social media — not to mention old-school in-person conversations with your friends and family — will multiply the number of people asking for the same changes, offering the same rewards, and threatening the same consequences. So, your one-person intervention can become even bigger.

The public visibility of social postings also gives competitive companies a chance to step in, step up, and "steal your business" by offering what you're asking for.

Lastly, after all of these communications, be sure to follow up to show that you're serious. You'll need to give them some time to make the changes, or at least respond to you, but if they miss your deadline, follow through with the consequences you promised and take your business elsewhere.

As an Investor

If you're part of the 50% of Americans who are fortunate enough to own stock in a company (either directly or through a mutual fund), you're in luck. The current dynamic of shareholder primacy means the company is already predisposed to listening to you and hearing what you want.

Unfortunately, most of what they've heard from shareholders for the last 50 years is that all they really want is money. So, when you do tell the company that you want something more than a financial return, they may not know how to respond. That's okay. They'll figure it out because, even though what you want is different, the stakes remain the same. If you don't get what you want, you'll sell your shares (or not buy them in the first place) — both of which are bad outcomes for a publicly traded company.

One of the easiest ways for an investor to ask for change is to vote at the annual shareholders meeting. By law, this ballot includes a "say-on-pay" question that allows you, the shareholder, to advise the company on whether or not you agree with the executive compensation plan, details of which are included in the proxy statement. So, take five minutes and educate yourself on how the company is paying the people who make the decisions.

Most companies use a pay-for-performance model that awards executives cash and/or stock if they reach certain goals. But exactly what are the goals the company has to meet? Are they entirely based on appreciation of the stock price and other financial metrics? Or are massive rewards only paid out if the company also meets other specific objectives related to the company's societal and environmental impact? The chances are, it's all about the former.

If it's all about increasing shareholder value, vote "against" the compensation package. While this vote on executive compensation is not legally binding, even a slight reduction in the approval percentage can be enough to get the company's attention, encouraging it to find out what shareholders want, especially since the word "against" doesn't exactly explain the rationale behind your vote.

So, also send a letter or email to the company's compensation committee, letting them know how you think executive compensation should change to include non-stock-related performance goals and that executive compensation shouldn't be so heavily weighted toward stock options and other stock-related benefits. And, since this committee is usually composed of members of the board of directors, let them know that, if you don't see improvement on this, you will vote against them the next time their name is on ballot.

If you've owned at least $2,000 worth of the company's securities for at least three years, then you're also eligible to submit a shareholder proposal to the company.[1] Based on SEC regulations, this proposal must be presented to all the company's shareholders at the next annual meeting, where they can vote to either accept or reject it.

As such, you could submit a proposal that would require the company to make specific changes to itself and its focus on maximizing shareholder value. For example, you could propose that the company convert its charter from a C corporation to B corporation, which would legally require it to provide one or more specific public benefits. (Note: You're probably more likely to succeed if, instead of putting such a change to a simple yes/no vote, you propose that the company study how it could best convert to a B corporation and report back to the shareholders and vote on the broader change at the following year's meeting.)

Don't think this sort of "shareholder activism" can work? Guess again. In May 2021, 61% of Chevron shareholders voted to force the company to reduce its "scope 3" carbon emissions — those that are generated by Chevron's upstream suppliers and downstream users.[2] And, during the same month, ExxonMobil shareholders voted to replace three of the company's 12 board members with independent nominees more committed to addressing climate change and ExxonMobil's role in it.[3]

You don't have to wait for the annual meeting to flex your power as a stockholder. Anytime you like, you can write a letter or email to the company's leadership, sharing your thoughts on how, as a shareholder, you want the company to focus on more than money. This type of "back door" correspondence doesn't have the formality of a proxy vote, but precisely because it's not in the public eye, the executives may not feel like you're putting them "on the spot," and be more receptive to your logic.

If all of these attempts to change the company fail, as a shareholder, you have one final option. Sell your stock and reinvest the proceeds in a company that does satisfy your broader needs. If you do this, let the company know. Send them a letter or email that says you're selling your stock and why. Without this final communication, the company will have no real idea that you've given up on them and left.

When researching new stocks, look into companies and mutual funds that have a good ESG (Environmental, Social, and Governance) rating. Since these ratings rely more on a company's declarations than data about outcomes, they're not perfect. But they do at least give you an idea of which companies realize there's more to life than shareholder value.

Alternately, look into holding companies that have subsidiaries chartered and certified as B corporations. Examples include Unilever, Proctor & Gamble, and Danone (which is now composed of approximately 50% B corporations).[4] While not nearly as common as traditional C corporations, B corporations will become more available for investment as more investors say that's what they want.

Once companies start tracking and reporting consequential costs to customers, they can also recut the same data to show investors a more accurate quantitative analysis of the company's impact on society and the environment so that investment decisions can be based on that, as well as financial returns.

Now, at this point, you might be having second thoughts about walking away from an "otherwise good investment" just because the company doesn't focus on its nonfinancial impacts.

That's not surprising. You've been told for the last 50 years that a stock's financial return is all that matters — that if you don't go for the best financial return, you're a chump or an idiot, or both. And you've been told that your goal should be to get as much money in your hands as soon as possible so you can retire early and do what you want, even if that is to give all that money away to charities that save the world.

The problem with this worldview is that the financial return on your investment doesn't just magically appear. The company is doing *something* to make all that money. What is it? Is it curing cancer? Is it defrauding grandmothers? Do you know?

You should. Because while the financial return on your investment may be showing up at your front door, the collateral damage is being dumped in your backyard. Greater environmental pollution, income inequality, discrimination, disease, and death are just a few of the costs routinely incurred in exchange for more profit. They are consequences that don't just disappear because you ignore them.

But if you take a broader view of your investment, you'll realize that your return on it doesn't just have to arrive in dollars. It can also materialize in a better society and environment for you, personally, and for your children and grandchildren. So, when you invest in companies that actively manage their nonfinancial impacts, you're simply choosing to get paid in a multitude of currencies.

As an Employee

Being a customer or investor isn't really about you. It's about your money. Sure, you control how your money is spent or invested, but that's pretty much the limit of your participation. After the decision is made, your money is the one that goes off and does the work.

As an employee, it's the exact opposite. The role cares very little about your money but is all about you and the value *you* can bring to the inner workings of the company.

Part of that value is how well you follow orders, especially when you're in an entry-level position. But most jobs quickly demand judgment. That is, the ability to make decisions, no matter how small, that don't require approval first. And it's these decisions that truly define your value to the company.

If you are only able to make good tactical decisions, based on the immediate situation at hand, then you'll likewise be given only limited tactical responsibilities. But if you're able to consider the bigger picture and make strategic decisions that lead the company to long-term success, then chances are you'll be given more responsibility, not to mention more money to compensate you for this valuable skill.

So, as you make decisions in your job at your company, remember that satisfying human needs is the key to any company's long-term success. And remember that the company is merely a legal person, incapable of understanding human beings and how to satisfy their needs. For that, it needs real, live, natural persons — like you.

As empowering as that is, also bear in mind that lasting change rarely happens quickly. Revolutions tend to be overturned by the next revolution, but evolution tends to be a one-way street. So, take your time and try not to overstep your authority. What you're trying to do is show that the decisions within your purview can be made better — that if the company takes tiny steps toward satisfying human needs as its purpose, the stakeholder ecosystem is there and values that behavior.

Then, tiny steps can be followed by further tiny steps, which add up to big steps over time. The company will see that it's not a threat to focus on satisfying human needs. On the contrary, it's a sustainable and profitable path forward. And the company will also see that your perspective is quite valuable.

Because change is a marathon rather than a sprint, it's good to prepare for a long engagement with your coworkers and your bosses. For that, try following these 3 Es:

1. **Educate** yourself — not just on the broader theory (which I hope this book has covered), but also on the specifics of your industry, your company, and your customers.
2. **Evangelize** to others — not in a forceful or arrogant way, but find casual opportunities to discuss your perspective with others and ask what they think.
3. **Exemplify** the idea — talking theory is great, but also

show people how to put it into practice, every day with everything you do. Show everyone how it works.

In the end, the only way to change a company is to change the minds of the people who work there. And there's no better person to do that than someone else who works there.

Being a part of change can be immensely satisfying. After all, it was *you* that did it, not just your money. But after a while, if your coworkers or bosses don't want to change, give your notice and take your value somewhere else. Find another company that is more in alignment with you and satisfying human needs.

As a Citizen

There's one more major stakeholder role that needs to be part of your corporate intervention. It's a role you play even if you don't buy a company's products, own their stock, or work there.

You become a citizen of our planet the moment you're born and remain one until the day you die. In between, you're expected to actively participate in managing the components of our shared society. Some of these components, of course, are corporations.

We created corporations, legal persons designed to serve *our* needs, so it's our responsibility to guide them, teach them, and help them reach their full potential.

Unfortunately, many of us have neglected this duty, assuming our corporate "children" have reached the age of their majority and don't need our help. But parents often have a blind spot where their children are concerned, so here are a few things you can do as a citizen to help companies behave better.

First, get to know the companies near you; they are your neighbors, after all. I'm not saying you have to bring them a pie (although it couldn't hurt), but go visit them, introduce yourself, and find out what they're doing.

If the location is a retail outlet, just walk on in during business hours and look around. Examine the products that are for sale. In what country are they made? What are the ingredients or materials?

If the company is more office-based, call first to make an appointment. Just say that you live in the area and would like to come see the office and learn more about what they do there. If you get an appointment, they'll probably want to show off their facilities so, while you're walking around, take in the floor plan. Is it full of cubicles? Are there closed-door offices? Is there a break room or other common areas for employees? Are there recycling bins?

If the location is a factory or other industrial site, call them to see if they offer tours. If so, while you're being shown around, ask questions about where they get their raw materials from and what they do with their waste. Keep an eye out for a hazmat diamond that displays how dangerous the chemicals inside the facility are.

No matter what type of facility you visit, pay attention to the employees. Are they a diverse group or are they mostly white, male, and/or young? Given the chance, ask the people who work there why they chose to work for that particular company, what they like about it, what they don't like about it, and why they stay.

Hazmat diamond (a.k.a., NFPA 704), often displayed at the entrance to a facility that uses chemicals.

To be clear, most of what you see and hear on your visits will probably be positive. Stores are designed to impress you, managers don't want to share dirty laundry, and factory tours are curated to only show the highlights. That's just human (and corporate) nature, so take what you learn with a grain of salt.

But also remember that you're not there to dig up dirt. You're there to build a relationship with them so that you can have productive conversations in the long run. So, be polite with any questions you ask and be appreciative that they welcomed you into their space. The last person anyone wants to help is a nosy neighbor.

Besides, after you're home, you can research more about the company online. Its own website, again, will probably be mostly (if not entirely) positive, but there's a lot of third-party information out there to balance things out. The internet is filled with sites that share the opinions of current and former employees, customers, rating agencies and, of course, the government — also to be taken with a grain of salt.

Second, after you've learned a little about a company, reach out to them to share your thoughts on what you've discovered. If you're concerned about something you saw, heard, or read, say so along with any thoughts you have on what they could do instead. But don't focus entirely on what's wrong. Share what you found positive or encouraging. An open, honest relationship involves supporting the company when it acts appropriately, but also letting them know when you think they aren't.

Third, realize that there are a lot of companies out there, and you can't get to know them all. But this is okay too, because we live in a representative democracy where we elect full-time representatives to, well, represent us on important issues like this.

Since corporations can't vote, make the best of this purely human right. Vote for government officials who put human needs above corporate needs. That doesn't mean voting for candidates who are adamantly anti-business. Nor does it mean supporting those who are blindly pro-business. Companies are inherently neutral entities that can be used for good or evil. It's the priorities that make the difference.

Heck, if you're *really* passionate about changing our world, run for office yourself. And do so on a platform of "humans first."

In addition to voting, regularly communicate with your elected officials, so they know how to best represent you and your beliefs, especially when it comes to oversight of the companies in their jurisdiction. This includes not just existing businesses, but those that want to locate in your area.

Government frequently gives special treatment to larger corporations looking to set up shop. Politicians are eager to bring jobs and tax revenue to their constituents and are willing to offer a lot in return. Take, for example, Amazon's famous contest to see where it would locate its secondary headquarters (labeled "HQ2") back in 2018.

In exchange for a promise to create 50,000 high-paying jobs, 238 cities submitted proposals to this $1 trillion company.[5] Offerings included the usual tax breaks, job training grants, and infrastructure improvements, but also nontraditional perks such as a private airport lounge for Amazon executives, renaming local streets, and even setting up a task force to lower the murder rate in the neighborhood where Amazon was expected to be located.[6]

In the end, Amazon chose to split its HQ2 among three locations (New York, Virginia, and Tennessee) in exchange for more than $2.4 billion in incentives.[7] That's $48,000 per job promised.

As large as that sounds, it's nowhere near as big as the $8.7 billion Washington state offered Boeing to keep jobs in Seattle, the $5.6 billion New York offered Alcoa, or the $4.8 billion President Trump offered Foxconn to move from China to Wisconsin.[8]

Incentives themselves aren't necessarily a problem. They are simply value offered to attract other value. So, the question is, what are these municipalities getting for these incentives? Job creation and tax revenues are nice, but could the screening process be expanded to ensure that the size of the incentive is correlated with how much the company is focused on satisfying human needs concerning overall society and the environment?

It's a "carrot" that could be used alongside the "stick" of oversight and regulation to help encourage companies to live up to their purpose of making people's lives better.

To a great degree, this book has tried to argue that many of the problems with corporate behavior can be fixed by the companies themselves, utilizing enlightened market forces instead of being forced to change by government involvement. But a modicum of legislation could accelerate the widespread adoption of the strategies, helping them gain critical mass more quickly.

Given the interstate nature of commerce, some of this involvement should be at the national level. This will ensure there is one, consistent standard for certain initiatives (such as the reporting requirements for the consequential cost label discussed in Chapter 7), rather than a patchwork of requirements that differ from city to city and state to state.

Finally, remember that, when you're playing the role of citizen, you're not just a citizen of one particular city, state, or country. Companies certainly view the whole planet as their backyard, and you should, too. So, the goal of having a corporate intervention isn't to just shift bad behavior to someplace you can't see it. It's to eliminate the behavior altogether.

INTERVENTIONS ARE MOST effective when the subject has nowhere to hide: when they hear the same demand from everyone, from every corner of the room — from every leg of the stool.

You can be *all* of those voices. Confronting a company with a harmony of humanity, no matter where it turns. Demanding that it stop serving itself, stop playing favorites, and satisfy the human needs of all of its stakeholders. Explaining that if it doesn't, it will cease to exist.

Or, you can decide to say nothing at all.

It's entirely up to you.

You are the protagonist in your own story. But remember, it's the actions a character takes that determine whether the character ends up a victor or a victim.

A FINAL THOUGHT

The acquisition of knowledge is liberating.

Like turning on a light, knowledge means you are no longer constrained by the darkness of ignorance or the optical illusions of falsehoods. Rather, you can see the world for how it really is and stride around with confidence.

For me, researching this book was just such a light switch. It helped to dispel the myriad of excuses, delusions, and misperceptions that we have collectively used to rationalize shareholder primacy for the last fifty years.

But as liberating as my journey has been, it has also been binding. Understanding the problems with shareholder primacy and its underlying causes has compelled me to do something about it, starting with writing this book.

My hope is that this book has helped you "see some light" and that you will feel similarly inclined to share it with those you know. Because, unlike a light, once knowledge gets turned on, it can't just be turned off.

Or, as the Indian author Arundhati Roy wrote in her book *Power Politics*, "The trouble is that once you see it, you can't unsee it. And

once you've seen it, keeping quiet, saying nothing, becomes as political an act as speaking out. There's no innocence. Either way, you're
accountable."

———

-Ed Chambliss
ed@aoneleggedstool.com

NOTES

Introduction

1. Milton Friedman, "The Social Responsibility of Business Is to Increase its Profits," *The New York Times Magazine*, September 13, 1970.
2. Lynn A. Stout, *The Shareholder Value Myth: How Putting Shareholders First Harms Investors, Corporations, and the Public* (San Francisco: Berrett-Koehler Publishers, Inc., 2012), 67, Kindle.
3. Atkinson, Hasell, Morelli, and Roser, "The Chartbook of Economic Inequality," (2017), https://www.chartbookofeconomicinequality.com/inequality-by-country/usa/.
4. Ibid.
5. Lynn A. Stout, "On the Rise of Shareholder Primacy, Signs of Its Fall, and the Return of Managerialism (in the Closet)" (2013), Cornell Law Faculty Publications, Paper 865, 1171.
6. Ibid.
7. U.S. Department of Commerce, Bureau of Economic Analysis, "Gross Output by Industry," revised June 24, 2021, www.bea.gov.

1. A Loss of Trust

1. SurveyMonkey, "Global Consumer Trust Survey," 2018, https://docs.google.com/spreadsheets/d/1VtOsQMlLMtoaUrBEkFkUYq-dvT56dnN27EsPahfi-CAs/edit#gid=1299500645.
2. Edelman, Global Trust Barometer, 2016, https://www.edelman.com/trust/2016-trust-barometer.
3. Robert Wollan, Rachel Barton, Masataka Ishikawa, Kevin Quiring, "Accenture Global Consumer Pulse Survey," 2017.
4. Kelsey Sutton, "What's the State of Brand Safety in 2018?" *Adweek*, July 23, 2018.
5. Ocean Tomo, LLC., Intangible Asset Market Value Study, 2017.
6. The World Bank, "Market Capitalization of Listed Domestic Companies," 2018, https://data.worldbank.org/indicator/CM.MKT.LCAP.CD?locations=US, (calculated using Ocean Tomo percentages.)
7. Ibid.
8. Wollan et al., "Accenture Global Consumer Pulse Survey."
9. Judann Pollack, "Hey, Brands: Almost Half of Americans Don't Find You Honest," *Ad Age*, April 3, 2017.
10. Rebecca Stewart, "Only 4% of People Trust What Influencers Say Online," *The Drum*, May 9,2019, https://www.thedrum.com/news/2019/05/09/only-4-people-

trust-what-influencers-say-online.

11. Gallup, Inc., "Confidence in Institutions Poll," 2021, https://news.gallup.com/poll/1597/confidenceinstitutions.aspx.

12. Forrester Research, "2017 Predictions: Dynamics That Will Shape The Future In The Age Of The Customer," October 27, 2016, https://www.forrester.com/blogs/16-10-27-predictions_2017_the_year_of_action/.

13. Ibid.

14. Wollan et al., "Accenture Global Consumer Pulse Survey."

15. Ibid.

16. SurveyMonkey, "Global Consumer Trust Survey."

17. Ibid.

18. Wollan et al., "Accenture Global Consumer Pulse Survey."

19. SurveyMonkey, "Global Consumer Trust Survey."

20. Erica Perry, "Lack Of Trust Costs Brands $2.5 Trillion Per Year: Study," *Social Media Week*, February 6, 2018.

21. Wollan et al., "Accenture Global Consumer Pulse Survey."

22. SurveyMonkey, "Global Consumer Trust Survey."

23. Amy B. Wang, "Nivea's 'White Is Purity' Ad Campaign Didn't End Well," *The Washington Post*, April 5, 2017.

24. Samantha West, "H&M Faced Backlash over Its 'Monkey' Sweatshirt Ad. It Isn't the Company's Only Controversy." *The Washington Post*, January 19, 2018.

25. Cleve R. Wootson Jr., "A Dove Ad Showed a Black Woman Turning Herself White. The Backlash Is Growing." *The Washington Post*, October 9, 2017.

26. Caitlin Dewey, "McDonald's Flipped Its Logo to 'Celebrate' Women. Then Came the Backlash." *The Washington Post*, March 8, 2018.

27. Rose Hackman, "Are You Beach Body Ready? Controversial Weight Loss Ad Sparks Varied Reactions," *The Guardian*, June 27, 2015.

28. David Gianatasio, "Huggies Flunks Dad Test, Alters Campaign," *Adweek*, March 13, 2012.

29. Sarah Pulliam Bailey, "Martin Luther King Jr. Sermon Used in a Ram Trucks Super Bowl Commercial Draws Backlash," *The Washington Post*, February 5, 2018.

30. Daniel D'Addario, "Why the Kendall Jenner Pepsi Ad Was Such a Glaring Misstep," *Time*, April 5, 2017.

31. Wikimedia Foundation, "Let's Talk About The North Face Defacing Wikipedia," May 29, 2019, https://wikimediafoundation.org/news/2019/05/29/lets-talk-about-the-north-face-defacing-wikipedia/

32. Jon Simpson, "Finding Brand Success In the Digital World," *Forbes*, August 25, 2017.

33. Rani Molla, "Mary Meeker's Most Important Trends on the Internet," *Vox*, June 11, 2019.

34. Nicole Perrin, "Demanding a Better Ad Experience (US Internet Users' Attitudes Toward Ads Today)," eMarketer, December 4, 2018, https://www.emarketer.com/content/demanding-a-better-ad-experience.

35. Ibid.

36. Ibid.

37. Ibid.
38. Ibid.
39. Ibid.
40. Ibid.
41. Ibid.
42. Frank Maguire, "Reaching Consumers with Video: the Interruptibility Myth," *Ad Age*, June 21, 2018.
43. Ibid.
44. Perrin, "Demanding a Better Ad Experience."
45. Ibid.
46. SurveyMonkey, "Global Consumer Trust Survey."
47. Hannah Ritchie and Max Roser, "Technology Adoption," 2017, https://ourworldindata.org/technology-adoption
48. Ibid.
49. Ibid.
50. Ibid.
51. Leigh Ann Anderson, "FDA Drug Approval Process," Drugs.com, April 13, 2020, https://www.drugs.com/fda-approval-process.html.

2. Who's to Blame?

1. Fernando M. Pinguelo, Timothy D. Cedrone, "Morals? Who Cares About Morals? An Examination of Morals Clauses in Talent Contracts and What Talent Needs to Know," *Journal of Sports And Entertainment Law*, Seton Hall University School of Law, Vol. 19.2 (2009): 347-380.
2. Jane Leavy, "Being Babe Ruth's Daughter," *Grantland*, January 3, 2012.
3. Ben Curren, "The Response to Elon Musk's Cannabis Use Shows that We Have a Giant Double Standard to Overcome." *Forbes*, September 12, 2018.
4. Alex Hern, "Silicon Valley Ad Boss Gurbaksh Chalal Fired Over Abuse Convictions," *The Guardian*, April 28, 2014.
5. Jeff Green, "CEOs Fired for Ethical Lapses Hit New High as Complaints Soar," *Bloomberg*, May 14, 2019.
6. *The Corporation*. Directed by Mark Achbar and Jennifer Abbott. Zeitgeist Films, 2003, 44:10.
7. Ibid.
8. Ibid., 43:40.
9. Government of Madhya Pradesh, "Immediate Relief Provided by the State Government," http://www.bgtrrdmp.mp.gov.in/Immediate_Relief.html, Accessed September 28, 2021.
10. A.K. Dubey, "Bhopal Gas Tragedy: 92% Injuries Termed 'Minor,'" *First14.News*, June 21, 2010, accessed via archive.org, Accessed September 28, 2021.
11. National Oceanic and Atmospheric Administration (NOAA), "On Scene Coordinator Report: Deepwater Horizon Oil Spill," September 2011.
12. Agustino Fontevecchia, "BP Fighting a Two-Front War as Macondo Continues to Bite and Production Drops," *Forbes*, February 5, 2013.

13. Bill Chappell, "'It Was Installed for This Purpose,' VW's U.S. CEO Tells Congress about Defeat Device," *National Public Radio*, October 8, 2015.
14. Joel Bakan, *The Corporation: The Pathological Pursuit of Profit and Power* (New York: Free Press, 2004), 56-57.
15. *The Corporation,* Achbar and Abbott, 41:35.
16. Bakan, *The Corporation*, 60.
17. Ibid., 61.
18. Katie Jennings, Dino Grandoni, and Susanne Rust, "How Exxon Went from Leader to Skeptic on Climate Change Research," *The Los Angeles Times*, October 23, 2015.
19. Exxon Research and Engineering Company, Coordination and Planning Division, "CO_2 Greenhouse Effect: A Technical Review," April 1, 1982.
20. Nicola Jones, "How the World Passed a Carbon Threshold and Why It Matters," *Yale Environment 360*, January 26, 2017.
21. Union of Concerned Scientists, "Smoke, Mirrors & Hot Air: How ExxonMobil Uses Big Tobacco's Tactics to Manufacture Uncertainty on Climate Science," 2007.
22. Sybille van den Hove, Marc Le Menestrel, and Henri-Claude de Bettignies, "The Oil Industry and Climate Change: Strategies and Ethical Dilemmas," *Climate Policy*, May 2002.
23. Suraje Dessai, "The Climate Regime from The Hague to Marrakech: Saving or Sinking the Kyoto Protocol?" Tyndall Centre for Climate Change Research, December 2001.
24. United Nations Framework Convention on Climate Change, "The Kyoto Protocol - Chapter XXVII, 7.a" - Ratification Status as of September 28, 2021.
25. National Aeronautics and Space Administration (NASA), "Scientific Consensus: Earth's Climate Is Warming," July 12, 2019.
26. Exxon Mobil Corporation, "Form 10-K, for the Year Ending December 31, 2007," filed with the Securities and Exchange Commission.
27. ExxonMobil website - Climate Change, Accessed September 28, 2021, https://corporate.exxonmobil.com/Sustainability/Environmental-protection/Climate-change.
28. Tim McDonnell, "Exxon Has 25 Billion Barrels of Fossil Fuel and Plans to Extract It All," *Mother Jones*, April 2, 2014.
29. ExxonMobil website - Policy, Accessed September 28, 2021, https://corporate.exxonmobil.com/About-us/Policy
30. Gilbert Metcalf, "Carbon Taxes: What Can We Learn from International Experience?" *Econofact*, Tufts University, May 3, 2019.
31. "End of the Road for World's Oldest Firm," *The ChosunIlbo* (English Edition) Daily News from Korea - Business, December 15, 2005.
32. Bakan, *The Corporation*, 79.
33. Ibid., 150.
34. Ibid., 109-110.
35. Annelise G. Anderson, "The Development of Municipal Fire Departments in the United States," *The Journal of Libertarian Studies*, April 11, 2019.
36. Ibid.

37. Fran Spielman, "Parking Meter Deal Keeps Getting Worse for City as Meter Revenues Rise," *Chicago Sun Times*, May 14, 2018.
38. Michael Gerstein and Jonathan Oosting, "State Set to End Private Prison Food Service," *The Detroit News*, February 7, 2018.
39. Glyn Holton, "History of Corporations," June 12, 2013, https://www.glynholton.com/notes/corporation.
40. British History Online, "Amboyna Massacre," *A Calendar of State Papers Colonial - East Indies - China and Japan - Volume 4 - 1622-1624*.
41. Parliament of the United Kingdom, "An Act for the Registration, Incorporation, and Regulation of Joint Stock Companies," 1844 c. 110 7 & 8 Vict.
42. Brian Landers, "Corporations Are Only Human - at Least in Law," *OpenEconomy*, December 2, 2010.
43. Rayford Whittingham Logan, *The Betrayal of the Negro, from Rutherford B. Hayes to Woodrow Wilson* (New York: Collier Books, 1954), 107.
44. U.S. Supreme Court, "Marshall v. Barlow's, Inc. 436 U.S. 307 (1978)," Justia US Supreme Court Center.
45. U.S. Supreme Court, "PG&E v. Public Utilities Comm'n 475 U.S. 1 (1986)," Justia US Supreme Court Center.
46. U.S. Supreme Court, "Citizens United v. Federal Election Comm'n, 558 U.S. 310 (2010)," Justia US Supreme Court Center.
47. John Celock, "Steve Lavin, Montana Legislator, Didn't Mean to Give Corporations the Right to Vote," *The Huffington Post*, February 25, 2013.
48. Bureau of Economic Analysis, "Gross Output by Industry."
49. Adolf A. Berle and Gardiner C. Means, *The Modern Corporation and Private Property* (New York: Macmillian, 1932), 103.
50. Stout, "On the Rise of Shareholder Primacy," 1171.
51. Ibid.
52. Friedman, "The Social Responsibility of Business Is to Increase Its Profits."
53. Steve Denning, "The Origin of 'The World's Dumbest Idea': Milton Friedman." *Forbes*, June 26, 2013.
54. Stout, "On the Rise of Shareholder Primacy," 1172.
55. Denning, "The Origin of 'The World's Dumbest Idea': Milton Friedman."
56. Stout, *The Shareholder Value Myth*, 67.
57. Ibid., 66.
58. Ibid., 20.
59. Robert J. Samuelson, "A Beginner's Guide to Stock Buybacks (and Why They're Not All Bad)," *The Washington Post*, March 6, 2019.
60. William Lazonick, Matt Hopkins, Ken Jacobson, Mustafa Erdem Sakinç and Öner Tulum, "US Pharma's Financialized Business Model," Institute for New Economic Thinking, July 13, 2017.
61. PhRMA website - Our Mission, Accessed June 1, 2021, https://www.phrma.org/about/our-mission.
62. *This American Life*, episode 205, "Plan B," WBEZ Chicago, February 1, 2002,
63. Katy Milani and Devin Duffy, "Profit Over Patients: How the Rules of Our Economy Encourage the Pharmaceutical Industry's Extractive Behavior," The Roosevelt Institute, February 13, 2019.

64. "Why Do Americans Pay So Much for Prescription Drugs," BBC News, July 21, 2019.
65. Milani and Duffy, "Profit Over Patients."
66. Ibid.
67. Ibid.
68. Ibid.
69. Ibid.
70. Ibid.
71. Lazonick, et al., "US Pharma's Financialized Business Model."
72. Milani and Duffy, "Profit Over Patients."
73. Ibid.
74. Chris Baraniuk, "As Big Pharma Abandons Antibiotic Research, Scientists Turn to Graves, Lizards, and Fungus for New Cures," *OneZero*, May 1, 2019.
75. Centers for Disease Control and Prevention, "Antibiotic / Antimicrobial Resistance (AR / AMR)," July 20, 2020, https://www.cdc.gov/drugresistance/index.html.
76. Dylan Scott, "The Untold Story of TV's First Prescription Drug Ad," *STAT*, December 11, 2015.
77. Harvard Medical School, "Do Not Get Sold on Drug Advertising," *Harvard Health Publishing*, February 14, 2017.
78. Milani and Duffy, "Profit Over Patients."
79. Dan Mangan, "EpiPens Cost Just Several Dollars to Make. Customers Pay More Than $600 for Them," *CNBC*, August 25, 2016.
80. Lydia Ramsey and Andy Kiersz, "An EpiPen Is 500% More Expensive than It Was in 2007 — Here's How That Happened," *Business Insider*, August 24, 2016.
81. Milani and Duffy, "Profit Over Patients."
82. Ibid.
83. Wayne Drash, "Anatomy of a 97,000% Drug Price Hike: One Family's Fight to Save Their Son," *CNN* June 29, 2018.
84. Lisa Schencker, "Pharma Firm CEO Insists $89,000 Drug Is Affordable, But What's the True Cost?" *Chicago Tribune*, February 17, 2017.
85. Ibid.
86. Edward N. Wolff, "Household Wealth Trends in the United States, 1962 to 2016: Has Middle Class Wealth Recovered?" National Bureau of Economic Research, November 2017.
87. Robert Frank, "The Wealthiest 10% of Americans Own a Record 89% of All U.S. Stocks," *CNBC*, October 19, 2021.
88. Wolff, "Household Wealth Trends in the United States."
89. Lawrence Mishel, Elise Gould, and Josh Bivens, "Wage Stagnation in Nine Charts," Economic Policy Institute, January 6, 2015.
90. Ibid.
91. Ibid.
92. Ibid.
93. Jordan Valinsky, "Roy Disney's Granddaughter Thinks Bob Iger's Paycheck Is 'Insane,'" *CNN*, April 22, 2019.

94. Christina Starmans, Mark Sheskin and Paul Bloom, "Why People Prefer Unequal Societies," *Nature Human Behaviour,* Volume 1, Article 0082 (April 7, 2017.)
95. Alvin Chang, "This Cartoon Explains How the Rich Got Rich and the Poor Got Poor," *Vox*, May 23, 2016.
96. Ibid.
97. Warren E. Buffett, "Stop Coddling the Super-Rich," *The New York Times*, August 14, 2011.
98. Dylan Scott, "The GOP Tax Law's Lopsided Giveaway to Corporations, Explained in One Sentence," *Vox*, May 29, 2019.
99. Jane G. Gravelle and Donald J. Marples, "The Economic Effects of the 2017 Tax Revision: Preliminary Observations," U.S. Congressional Research Service, May 22, 2019.
100. Ibid.
101. Annie Lowrey, "Are Stock Buybacks Starving the Economy?" *The Atlantic*, July 31, 2018.
102. Ibid.
103. Gravelle and Marples, "The Economic Effects of the 2017 Tax Revision."
104. Robert J. Samuelson, "The $100 Trillion Question: What to Do About Wealth?" *The Washington Post*, May 5, 2019.
105. Michael Batty, Jesse Bricker, Joseph Briggs, Elizabeth Holmquist, Susan McIntosh, Kevin Moore, Eric Nielsen, Sarah Reber, Molly Shatto, Kamila Sommer, Tom Sweeney, and Alice Henriques Volz (2019). "Introducing the Distributional Financial Accounts of the United States," Finance and Economics Discussion Series 2019-017. Washington: Board of Governors of the Federal Reserve System, https://doi.org/10.17016/FEDS.2019.017.
106. Ibid.
107. Organisation for Economic Co-operation and Development (OECD), "Under Pressure: The Squeezed Middle Class. How Does the United States Compare?" 2019.
108. Timothy Noah, "White House — Here's Why You Have to Care About Inequality," *The New Republic*, January 12, 2012.
109. Kate E. Pickett and Richard G. Wilkinson, "Income Inequality and Health: A Causal Review," *Social Science & Medicine*, Volume 128, March 2015, Pages 316-326
110. Angus Deaton, *The Great Escape: Health, Wealth, and the Origins of Inequality* (Princeton: Princeton University Press, 2013), 213, Kindle.
111. Gary Standing, *The Precariat: The New Dangerous Class* (New York: Bloomsbury Academic, 2011), 8.
112. Mike Elgan, "Uh-Oh: Silicon Valley Is Building a Chinese-Style Social Credit System," *Fast Company*, August 26, 2019.
113. Melissa Locker, "China's Terrifying 'Social Credit' Surveillance System Is Expanding," *Fast Company*, April 24, 2018.
114. Elgan, "Uh-Oh: Silicon Valley Is Building a Chinese-Style Social Credit System,"
115. Ibid.

116. Jessica Baron, "Life Insurers Can Use Social Media Posts to Determine Premiums, as Long as They Don't Discriminate," *Forbes*, February 4, 2019.
117. Benjy Egel, "Hundreds of Bar Patrons in Sacramento on a Blacklist. Do Private ID Scanners Go Too Far?" *The Sacramento Bee*, July 8, 2019.
118. Jackson Cunningham, "Digital Exile: How I Got Banned for Life from AirBnB," *Medium*, July 13, 2018.
119. The Business Roundtable, "Statement on Corporate Governance," September 1997, 1 - Introduction.
120. The Business Roundtable, "Statement on the Purpose of a Corporation," September 6, 2019.

3. The 50-Year-Old Fallacy

1. ValuePenguin by Lending Tree, "Average Bank Interest Rates in 2021: Checking, Savings and Money Market Rates," Accessed September 30, 2021, https://www.valuepenguin.com/banking/average-bank-interest-rates.
2. Jim Chappelow, "Principal-Agent Problem," *Investopedia*, September 10, 2019.
3. Barry M. Mitnick, "Origin of the Theory of Agency," Katz Graduate School of Business, University of Pittsburgh, January 2006.
4. Ibid.
5. Chappelow, "Principal-Agent Problem."
6. Michael C. Jensen and William H. Meckling, "Theory of the Firm: Managerial Behavior, Agency Costs and Ownership Structure," *Journal of Financial Economics*, October 1976, V. 3, No. 4, pp. 305-360.
7. Margaret M. Blair, "Corporate Law and the Team Production Problem," Vanderbilt University Law School, April 9, 2012.
8. Amy Drury, "The Voting Rights of Common Stock Shareholders," *Investopedia*, April 30, 2021.
9. Armen A. Alchian and Harold Demsetz, "Production, Information Costs, and Economic Organization," *The American Economic Review*, Vol. 62, No. 5 (December 1972), pp. 777-795.
10. Margaret M. Blair and Lynn A. Stout, "A Team Production Theory of Corporate Law," Virginia Law Review, Vol. 85, No. 2 (March 1999), 316.
11. Ibid., 315.
12. Ibid.
13. Henry Hansmann, "The Role of Nonprofit Enterprise," Faculty Scholarship Series (5048), 1980, 838.
14. Friedman, "The Social Responsibility of Business Is to Increase Its Profits."
15. Stout, *The Shareholder Value Myth*, 23.
16. Ibid., 29.
17. "Transcript of Pacific Railway Act," CHAP. CXX., (1862), The National Archives and Records Administration. Accessed via https://www.ourdocuments.gov.
18. Linda O. Smiddy and Lawrence A. Cunningham, *Corporations and Other Business Organizations: Cases, Materials, Problems* (Seventh ed., 2010), LexisNexis, pp. 228–231, 241, ISBN 978-1-4224-7659-8

19. Peter F. Drucker, *The Practice of Management* (New York: Harper & Row, 1954), 37.
20. Stout, *The Shareholder Value Myth*, 87.
21. Ibid., 108.

4. The Upside of Progress

1. A. H. Maslow, "A Theory of Human Motivation," *Psychological Review*, 50, (1943), 370-396.
2. Uriel Abulof, "Introduction: Why We Need Maslow in the Twenty-First Century," *Society*, 54, (2017), 508–509.
3. Louis Tay and Ed Diener, "Needs and Subjective Well-Being Around the World," *Journal of Personality and Social Psychology*, Vol. 101, No. 2, (2011), 354–365.
4. Hans Villarica, "Maslow 2.0: A New and Improved Recipe for Happiness," *The Atlantic*, August 17, 2011.
5. Ibid.
6. ClickView Education, "Causes of the Industrial Revolution: The Agricultural Revolution," August 10, 2015, https://www.youtube.com/watch?v=6QKIts2_yJo.
7. Ibid.
8. Ibid.
9. Gordon Conway, *The Doubly Green Revolution: Food for All in the Twenty-First Century* (Ithaca, NY: Comstock Publishing Associates, 1998), 44-65.
10. U.S. Census Bureau, "Historical Estimates of World Population," July 5, 2018.
11. Patricia A. Daly, "Agricultural Employment: Has the Decline Ended?" Monthly Labor Review, Bureau of Labor Statistics, U.S. Department of Labor, November 1981, 12.
12. Max Roser, "Employment in Agriculture," July 30, 2021, https://ourworldindata.org/employment-in-agriculture.
13. Bryan Walsh, "Getting Real About the High Price of Cheap Food," *Time*, August 21, 2009.
14. "100 Years of U.S. Consumer Spending: Data for the Nation, New York City, and Boston," Bureau of Labor Statistics, U.S. Department of Labor, May 2006.
15. "Consumer Expenditure Survey," Bureau of Labor Statistics, U.S. Department of Labor, 2020.
16. Geoffrey Timmins, *The Last Shift: The Decline of Handloom Weaving in Nineteenth-Century Lancashire* (Manchester: Manchester University Press, 1993), 18.
17. Edward Baines, *History of the Cotton Manufacture in Great Britain* (London: H. Fisher, R. Fisher, and P. Jackson, 1835), 155.
18. Robert Longley, "The Biography of Eli Whitney, Inventor of the Cotton Gin," *Thoughtco*, September 24, 2019.
19. Museum of American Heritage, "Stitches in Time: 100 Years of Sewing and Machines - Impact," http://www.moah.org/stitches/impact.html, September 1, 2005.
20. "100 Years of U.S. Consumer Spending," Bureau of Labor Statistics.
21. "Consumer Expenditure Survey," Bureau of Labor Statistics.

22. Norman Ball, "Circular Saws and the History of Technology," *Bulletin of the Association for Preservation Technology*, Vol. 7, No. 3. (1975), 79-89.

23. Alex W. Bealer, *The Tools that Built America* (Mineola, NY: Dover Publications, 2004), 60-61.

24. Paul Fourshee, "A Two-Bit History of Nails," *The Blueprint*, Vol 1, No. 2, April 27, 1992.

25. Division of Historic Preservation and Archaeology, *Historic Building Research Handbook*, Indiana Department of Natural Resources, February 1, 2007.

26. Ibid.

27. Paul Belford, "Hot Blast Iron Smelting in the Early 19th Century: A Re-Appraisal," *Historical Metallurgy*, 46(1), 2012, 32–44.

28. Donald B. Wagner, *Science and Civilisation in China, Volume 5, Chemistry and Chemical Technology, Part 11, Ferrous Metallurgy* (New York: Cambridge University Press, 2008), 361.

29. Key to Metals AG, "Classification of Carbon and Low-Alloy Steels," *Total Materia*, November 2001.

30. Robert L. Heilbroner, *The Economic Transformation of America* (New York: Harcourt Brace Jovanovich, 1977), 88.

31. Sash Windows London, "The History of Window Glass Manufacture," Accessed September 30, 2021, https://www.sashwindowslondon.org.uk/info/history-of-glass-manufacture.html

32. P. Hopkins, "Pipelines: Past, Present, and Future," The 5th Asian Pacific IIW International Congress, March 7, 2007.

33. Steven J. Burian, Stephan J. Nix, Robert E. Pitt, and S. Rocky Durrans, "Urban Wastewater Management in the United States: Past, Present, and Future," *Journal of Urban Technology*, Volume 7, Number 3, 2000, pages 33-62.

34. Thomas A. Edison, "Electric Light Bulb - Patent US223898," United States Patent Office, January 27, 1880.

35. Louis C. Hunter, *A History of Industrial Power in the United States*, 1780-1930 (Charlottesville: University Press of Virginia, 1979), 191.

36. Amanda Green, "A Brief History of Air Conditioning," *Popular Mechanics*, January 1, 2015.

37. "100 Years of U.S. Consumer Spending," Bureau of Labor Statistics.

38. "Consumer Expenditure Survey," Bureau of Labor Statistics.

39. Charlie Giattino, Esteban Ortiz-Ospina and Max Roser, "Working Hours," 2019, https://ourworldindata.org/grapher/work-hours-per-week.

40. Max Roser, "Working Hours," 2019, Working Hours, https://ourworldindata.org/working-hours.

41. Max Roser, "The Short History of Global Living Conditions and Why It Matters that We Know It," 2020, https://ourworldindata.org/a-history-of-global-living-conditions-in-5-charts#health.

42. Max Roser, Esteban Ortiz-Ospina, and Hannah Ritchie, "Life Expectancy," 2019, https://ourworldindata.org/life-expectancy.

43. Don Phillips, "Flight of Boeing's 777 Breaks Distance Record," *The New York Times*, November 10, 2005.

44. Gordon E. Moore, "Cramming More Components onto Integrated Circuits," *Electronics*, Vol. 38, No. 8, April 19, 1965.

45. Ray Kurzweil, "The Law of Accelerating Returns," March 7, 2001, https://www.kurzweilai.net/the-law-of-accelerating-returns.

46. R. Buckminster Fuller, *Critical Path* (New York: St. Martin's Press, 1981.)

47. David Russell Schilling, "Knowledge Doubling Every 12 Months, Soon to Be Every 12 Hours," *Industry Tap*, April 19, 2013.

48. Dan Farber, "2010: Data Doubling Every 11 Hours," *ZDNet*, February 13, 2007.

49. Alvin Toffler, *Future Shock*, (New York: Random House, 1970), 4.

5. The Catastrophe of Efficiency

1. U.S. Bureau of Labor Statistics, Consumer Price Index, U.S. City Average, adjusted for inflation.

2. Tara Parker-Pope, "A High Price for Healthy Food," *The New York Times*, December 5, 2007.

3. Walsh, "Getting Real About the High Price of Cheap Food."

4. Michele Ver Ploeg, Vince Breneman, Paula Dutko, Ryan Williams, Samantha Snyder, Chris Dicken, and Phil Kaufman, "Access to Affordable and Nutritious Food: Updated Estimates of Distance to Supermarkets Using 2010 Data," Economic Research Service, U.S. Department of Agriculture, November 2012.

5. Rebecca A. Krukowski, Delia Smith West, Jean Harvey-Berino, and T. Elaine Prewitt, "Neighborhood Impact on Healthy Food Availability and Pricing in Food Stores," *Journal of Community Health*, 35(3), June 2010, 315–320.

6. Jenny Gustavsson, Christel Cederberg, Ulf Sonesson, Robert van Otterdijk, and Alexandre Meybeck, "Global Food Losses and Food Waste: Extent, Causes, and Prevention," Food and Agriculture Organization of the United Nations, 2011.

7. Heesu Lee, "Food Waste Is Worse Than We Thought and the Rich May Be to Blame," *Bloomberg*, February 12, 2020.

8. Monika van den Bos Verma, Linda de Vreede, Thom Achterbosch, and Martine M. Rutten, "Consumers Discard a Lot More Food than Widely Believed: Estimates of Global Food Waste Using an Energy Gap Approach and Affluence Elasticity of Food Waste," *PLoS ONE*, 15(2), February 12, 2020.

9. Max Roser and Hannah Ritchie, "Food Prices," 2013, https://ourworldindata.org/food-prices.

10. Diana Yates, "Study: Restaurant Meals Can Be as Bad for Your Waistline as Fast Food Is," *Illinois News Bureau*, July 1, 2015.

11. Ibid.

12. Drew Desilver, "What's on Your Table? How America's Diet Has Changed over the Decades," *Pew Research Center*, December 13, 2016.

13. National Center for Chronic Disease Prevention and Health Promotion (NCCD-PHP), "Poor Nutrition," Centers for Disease Control and Prevention (CDC), January 11, 2021.

14. Ibid.

15. National Center for Health Statistics, "FastStats: Obesity and Overweight," Centers for Disease Control and Prevention (CDC), March 1, 2021.
16. Division of Diabetes Translation, "Long-Term Trends in Diabetes," Centers for Disease Control and Prevention (CDC), April 2017.
17. Roser, Ortiz-Ospina, and Ritchie, "Life Expectancy."
18. Ibid.
19. Esteban Ortiz-Ospina and Max Roser, "Financing Healthcare," 2017, https://ourworldindata.org/financing-healthcare.
20. Jane Wheeler, "Clothing of The 1830s," *Conner Prairie Museum*, 2019.
21. Nancy Mitchell, "The Secret History of the Closet," *Apartment Therapy*, April 24, 2016.
22. Molly Millard, "A Brief History of Closets," *Alexandria Stylebook*, July 29, 2015.
23. Wanda Thibodeaux, "What Are Standard Closet Dimensions?" *Hunker*, March 19, 2018.
24. Mary Bellis, "The Invention of the Coat Hanger," *Thoughtco*, March 3, 2019.
25. Emma Johnson, "The Real Cost of Your Shopping Habits," *Forbes*, January 15, 2015.
26. Thibodeaux, "What Are Standard Closet Dimensions?"
27. Johnson, "The Real Cost of Your Shopping Habits."
28. Thibodeaux, "What Are Standard Closet Dimensions?"
29. Kyle Donash, "New Trunk Club Survey Finds Americans Experience 'Wardrobe Panic' 36 Times Annually," Nordstrom, March 12, 2018.
30. Ibid.
31. Ibid.
32. Stephanie Vatz, "Why America Stopped Making Its Own Clothes," *KQED*, May 24, 2013.
33. Marc Bain, "Americans Have Stopped Trying to Stuff More Clothes into Their Closets," *Quartz*, February 26, 2018.
34. "100 Years of U.S. Consumer Spending," Bureau of Labor Statistics.
35. Sara Idacavage, "Fashion History Lesson: The Origins of Fast Fashion," *Fashionista*, October 17, 2018.
36. Nathalie Remy, Eveline Speelman, and Steven Swartz, "Style That's Sustainable: A New Fast-Fashion Formula," *McKinsey & Company*, October 2016.
37. Ellen MacArthur Foundation, "A New Textiles Economy: Redesigning Fashion's Future," 2017.
38. Remy, Speelman, and Swartz, "Style That's Sustainable."
39. Ellen MacArthur Foundation, "A New Textiles Economy."
40. Louise R. Morgan and Grete Birtwistle, "An Investigation of Young Fashion Consumers' Disposal Habits," *International Journal of Consumer Studies, 33*, 2009, 190–198.
41. U.S. Environmental Protection Agency, "Nondurable Goods Product-Specific Data," Facts and Figures about Materials, Waste and Recycling, August 26, 2021.
42. Ibid.
43. Mattias Wallander, "Closet Cast-Offs Clogging Landfills," *The Huffington Post*, May 25, 2011.

44. U.S. Environmental Protection Agency, "Nondurable Goods Product-Specific Data."
45. Ibid.
46. Ellen MacArthur Foundation, "A New Textiles Economy."
47. Alasdair Carmichael, "Man-Made Fibers Continue to Grow," *Textile World*, February 3, 2015.
48. Ibid.
49. *Textile Today*, "Recycle Polyester: Way to Safe Environment and Energy," August 4, 2018.
50. Frequently Asked Questions (FAQs), "How Much Electricity Does an American Home Use?" U.S. Energy Information Administration (EIA), October 9, 2020.
51. Carmichael, "Man-Made Fibers Continue To Grow."
52. *Textile Today*, "Recycle Polyester."
53. Ibid.
54. Frequently Asked Questions, U.S. Energy Information Administration.
55. United Nations Economic Commission for Europe (UNECE), "Fashion and the SDGs: What Role for the UN?" March 1, 2018.
56. Craig Bednarz, Glen Ritchie, Jim Hook, Rad Yager, Sidney Cromer, Dudley Cook and Ivey Griner, "Cotton Crop Water Use and Irrigation Scheduling," University of Georgia, Department of Crop and Soil Sciences, October 27, 2004.
57. Randy Boman, "Estimating Cotton Yield Using Boll Counting," Oklahoma State University, Southwest Research and Extension Center, September 12, 2012.
58. Bonny Brown Jones, "How Much Cotton Does it Take to Make a Shirt?" *Sciencing*, October 31, 2018.
59. Deborah Drew and Genevieve Yehounme, "The Apparel Industry's Environmental Impact in 6 Graphics," *World Resources Institute*, July 5, 2017.
60. United Nations Economic Commission for Europe, "Fashion and the SDGs."
61. Ellen MacArthur Foundation, "A New Textiles Economy."
62. United Nations Economic Commission for Europe, "Fashion and the SDGs."
63. Ethical Fashion Group Ltd., "Fashion Industry Pollution | Sustainable Chemicals," *Common Objective*, February 1, 2018.
64. Greenpeace International, "Toxic Threads: The Big Fashion Stitch-Up," November 19, 2012.
65. Ethical Fashion Group Ltd., "Fashion Industry Pollution | Sustainable Chemicals."
66. Greenpeace International, "Toxic Threads."
67. Ibid.
68. Julien Boucher and Damien Friot, "Primary Microplastics in the Oceans: A Global Evaluation of Sources," International Union for Conservation of Nature, 2017.
69. Ellen MacArthur Foundation, "A New Textiles Economy."
70. Ibid.
71. Simon Marks, "Cambodian Factories Seek Eco-Friendly Power Alternatives," *The New York Times*, May 27, 2010.
72. Ibid.

73. Mike Lee, "The Truth About Where Your Donated Clothes End Up," *ABC News*, December 21, 2006.
74. Ibid.
75. Franck Kuwonu, "Protectionist Ban on Imported Used Clothing," *Africa Renewal*, United Nations, December 2017.
76. Ibid.
77. Vatz, "Why America Stopped Making Its Own Clothes."
78. Paul M. Barrett, Dorotheé Baumann-Pauly, and April Gu, "Five Years After Rana Plaza: The Way Forward," NYU Stern Center for Business and Human Rights, April 2018.
79. Ellen MacArthur Foundation, "A New Textiles Economy."
80. Barrett, Baumann-Pauly, and Gu, "Five Years After Rana Plaza."
81. Ibid.
82. ITV News, "Case Filed Against Owners of Collapsed Building in Dhaka," July 21, 2014.
83. Barrett, Baumann-Pauly, and Gu, "Five Years After Rana Plaza."
84. *The Daily Star*, "Finally, Rana on ACC Charge Sheet," July 15, 2014.
85. *Al Jazeera America*, "Murder Charges for Dhaka Garment Factory Chiefs," June 1, 2015.
86. Humayun Kabir, Myfanwy Maple, Md Shahidul Islam, and Kim Usher, "The Current Health and Wellbeing of the Survivors of the Rana Plaza Building Collapse in Bangladesh," *International Journal of Environmental Research and Public Health*, 16, 2019.
87. "Accord on Fire and Building Safety in Bangladesh," May 13, 2013.
88. "Accord on Fire and Building Safety in Bangladesh - Signatories," Accessed October 4, 2021, https://bangladeshaccord.org/signatories
89. Ibid.
90. Steven Greenhouse and Stephanie Clifford, "U.S. Retailers Offer Plan for Safety at Factories," *The New York Times*, July 10, 2013.
91. Michael Safi and Dominic Rushe, "Rana Plaza, Five Years On: Safety of Workers Hangs in Balance in Bangladesh," *The Guardian*, April 24, 2018.
92. Ibid.
93. *The Daily Mail*, "Women Spend Eight Years of Their Life Shopping," November 27, 2006.
94. "100 Years of U.S. Consumer Spending," Bureau of Labor Statistics.
95. "Consumer Expenditure Survey," Bureau of Labor Statistics.
96. Emmie Martin, "Here's How Much Housing Prices Have Skyrocketed over the Last 50 Years," *CNBC*, June 23, 2017.
97. Michael Bluejay, "Historical Real Estate Appreciation Rate in the United States," *How to Buy a House*, August 2009.
98. U.S. Census Bureau, "Average Population Per Household and Family: 1940 to Present," Accessed October 5, 2021, https://www.census.gov/data/tables/time-series/demo/families/households.html.
99. Alexander Harris, "U.S. Self-Storage Industry Statistics," *SpareFoot Storage Beat*, January 27, 2021.

100. Raul Amoros, "The Rising Cost of Land in the Past 40 Years," HowMuch.net, July 14, 2015.

101. U.S. Census Bureau, "Historical National Population Estimates (1900-1989)" and "Monthly Population Estimates (2000-2010)," Accessed October 5, 2021, https://www.census.gov/topics/population.html.

102. Len Kiefer, "State Population Growth and House Prices," lenkiefer.com, December 20, 2017.

103. United Nations, *Report of the Special Rapporteur on Adequate Housing as a Component of the Right to an Adequate Standard of Living, and on the Right to Non-Discrimination in this Context*, January 18, 2017.

104. Ibid.

105. Esteban Ortiz-Ospina, "Homelessness," *Our World in Data*, November 2016.

106. Tam Harbert, "Here's How Much the 2008 Bailouts Really Cost," MIT Sloan School of Management, February 21, 2019.

107. William J. Baumol and William G. Bowen, *Performing Arts, the Economic Dilemma; A Study of Problems Common to Theater, Opera, Music, and Dance* (New York: Twentieth Century Fund, 1966), 168.

108. "Consumer Price Index Data by Industry," Bureau of Labor Statistics, U.S. Department of Labor, 2020.

109. "Quarterly Census of Employment and Wages," Bureau of Labor Statistics, U.S. Department of Labor, 2020.

110. Ibid.

111. Ibid.

112. James Surowiecki, "Debt By Degrees," *The New Yorker*, November 14, 2011.

113. Ibid.

114. "Consumer Price Index Data by Industry," Bureau of Labor Statistics.

115. Charlie Giattino, Esteban Ortiz-Ospina and Max Roser, "Annual Working Hours Per Worker," *Our World in Data*, 2017.

116. Derek Thompson, "The Religion of Workism Is Making Americans Miserable," *The Atlantic*, February 24, 2019.

117. Adewale Maye, "No-Vacation Nation, Revised," *Center for Economic and Policy Research*, May 21, 2019.

118. Ibid.

119. U.S. Travel Association, "Paid Time Off Trends in the U.S." August 8, 2019.

120. Lydia Saad, "The '40-Hour' Workweek Is Actually Longer — by Seven Hours," Gallup, Inc., August 29, 2014.

121. Juliana Menasce Horowitz and Nikki Graf, "Most U.S. Teens See Anxiety and Depression as a Major Problem Among Their Peers," *Pew Research Center*, February 20, 2019.

122. John Maynard Keynes, "Economic Possibilities for Our Grandchildren," *Essays in Persuasion* (New York: W.W. Norton & Co., 1963), 358-373.

6. Understanding Satisfaction

1. Abraham H. Maslow, *Toward a Psychology of Being* (Princeton, NJ: Van Nostrand, 1968, 2e), 221.
2. Tom Wolfe, "The 'Me' Decade and the Third Great Awakening," *New York Magazine*, April 8, 2008.
3. Vikram Johri, "'Alexis de Tocqueville': The First French Critic of the US," *Christian Science Monitor*, April 10, 2007.
4. Alexis de Tocqueville, *Democracy in America* (New York: George Dearborn & Company, 1840), Volume 2, Chapter 8.
5. Ibid.
6. Bernardo J. Carducci, "Basic Processes of Mischel's Cognitive-Affective Perspective: Delay of Gratification and Conditions of Behavioral Consistency," *The Psychology of Personality: Viewpoints, Research, and Applications* (New York: John Wiley and Sons, 2009), 443–444.
7. Sharon Begley, "The New Science Behind Your Spending Addiction," *Newsweek*, October 30, 2011.
8. Kim I. Mills, "Can the Kids Wait? Today's Youngsters May Be Able to Delay Gratification Longer Than Those of the 1960s," *American Psychological Association*, June 25, 2018.
9. Shane Frederick, George Loewenstein, and Ted O'Donoghue. "Time Discounting and Time Preference: A Critical Review." *Journal of Economic Literature* 40, no. 2, 2002, 351–401.
10. Alfred E. Kahn, "The Tyranny of Small Decisions: Market Failures, Imperfections, and the Limits of Economics," *Kyklos*, Volume 19, Issue 1, February 1966.
11. Alfred E. Kahn, *The Economics of Regulation Principles and Institutions* (New York: Wiley, 1970) 237.
12. William Forster Lloyd, "Two Lectures on the Checks to Population," Lecture 1, The University of Oxford, 1832, Wikisource, December 16, 2017.
13. Farber, "2010: Data Doubling Every 11 Hours."
14. John Timmer, "World's Total CPU Power: One Human Brain," *WIRED*, February 11, 2011.
15. Kurzweil, "The Law of Accelerating Returns."
16. Ibid.
17. "About Supercomputers," National Weather Service, National Oceanic and Atmospheric Administration, Accessed October 5, 2021, https://www.weather.gov/about/supercomputers.
18. John Williamson, "What Washington Means by Policy Reform," *Peterson Institute for International Economics*, November 1, 2002.
19. Dani Rodrik, "Goodbye Washington Consensus, Hello Washington Confusion? A Review of the World Bank's *Economic Growth in the 1990s: Learning from a Decade of Reform*," *Journal of Economic Literature*, Vol. XLIV, December 2006, 973–987.
20. Amy Goodman, "Chilean Economist Manfred Max-Neef on Barefoot Economics, Poverty and Why The U.S. Is Becoming an 'Underdeveloping

Nation,'" *Democracy Now!* November 26, 2010.

21. Manfred Max-Neef, *Human Scale Development* (New York: The Apex Press, 1991), xi.

22. Ibid., 8.

23. Ibid, 16.

24. Ibid.

25. S. O'Dea, "Average Price of a Smartphone in the United States," *Statista*, October 6, 2020.

26. Travis Bradberry and Jean Greaves, *Emotional Intelligence 2.0* (San Diego, Talent-Smart, 2009), 13.

27. John F. Helliwell, Richard Layard, and Jeffrey D. Sachs, *World Happiness Report* (New York: United Nations Sustainable Development Solutions Network, 2019), 27.

28. Ibid., 22.

29. Kimberly Amadeo, "Unemployment Rate by Year Since 1929 Compared to Inflation and GDP," *The Balance*, September 17, 2020.

30. Andrew T. Jebb, Louis Tay, Ed Diener, and Shigehiro Oishi, "Happiness, Income Satiation and Turning Points Around the World," *Nature Human Behavior*, Vol. 2, January 2018, 33-38.

31. Ibid.

32. Todd B. Kashdan and Michael Steger, "Curiosity and Pathways to Well-Being and Meaning in Life: Traits, States, and Everyday Behaviors," *Motivation and Emotion,* 31, 159-173.

33. John Battelle, "Are We Dumb Terminals?" *NewCo Shift*, June 1, 2018.

34. Edmund S. Phelps, *Mass Flourishing: How Grassroots Innovation Created Jobs, Challenge, and Change* (Princeton: Princeton University Press, 2013), vii, Kindle.

35. John F. Kennedy, Speech at Rice Stadium, September 12, 1962, National Aeronautics and Space Administration.

7. Six Steps for Business Leaders

1. Bakan, *The Corporation*, 79.

2. Isaac Asimov, *I, Robot* (New York: New American Library, 1956), 6.

3. Kimberly Powell, "Surnames Derived from Occupations," *ThoughtCo*, May 03, 2019.

4. Harris, "U.S. Self-Storage Industry Statistics."

5. NAICS Association, "NAICS Code 531130 Lessors of Miniwarehouses and Self-Storage Units," Accessed October 6, 2021, https://www.naics.com/naics-code-description/?code=531130.

6. Matt Morrow, "Have the Coffee Wars Come Home?" *The Food Institute*, November 13, 2020.

7. "10 Differences Between Robusta & Arabica Coffee," *The Roasters Pack*, September 19, 2014.

8. Ibid.

9. Aaron O'Neill, "Average Prices for Arabica and Robusta Coffee Worldwide from 2014 to 2025," *Statista*, September 14, 2021.

10. JUST Capital, *2021 JUST Capital Rankings Methodology*, October 30, 2020.

11. Peter Georgescu, "Just 100 Do Well by Doing Good," *Forbes*, January 10, 2018.

12. Chairman of the Council of Economic Advisers, *Economic Report of the President*, Table B-29, January 2021.

13. Bureau of Economic Analysis, "Gross Output by Industry."

14. Chairman of the Council of Economic Advisers, *Economic Report of the President*.

15. Bureau of Economic Analysis, "Gross Output by Industry."

16. "Field Listing - Labor Force - by Occupation," *The World Factbook* (Washington, D.C.: Central Intelligence Agency, 2021.)

17. Robert Plutchik, *The Emotions*, Revised Edition (Lanham, Maryland, University Press of America,1991).

18. Simon Baron-Cohen, Sally Wheelwright, Jacqueline Hill, Yogini Raste, and Ian Plumb, "The 'Reading the Mind in the Eyes' Test Revised Version: A Study with Normal Adults, and Adults with Asperger Syndrome or High-functioning Autism," *Journal of Child Psychology and Psychiatry*, Vol. 42, No. 2, 2001, 241-251.

19. Will Oremus, "What Really Happens to AirPods When They Die," *OneZero*, May 28, 2019.

20. George Serafeim and Katie Trinh, "Accounting for Product Impact in the Airlines Industry," Harvard Business School, November 18, 2020.

21. Ronald Cohen and George Serafeim, "How to Measure a Company's Real Impact," *Harvard Business Review*, September 3, 2020.

22. Ibid.

23. George Serafeim, T. Robert Zochowski, and Jen Downing, "Impact-Weighted Financial Accounts: The Missing Piece for an Impact Economy," Harvard Business School, September 17, 2019.

24. Affairs Today, "An Interview with Sir Ronald Cohen, the Father of Venture Capital in the UK," October 9, 2014.

25. Gemma Hampson, "Good Deals 10: Bond and Bank are Vital to Sector's Growth, Says Cohen," *Social Enterprise*, November 16, 2010.

26. I Amsterdam, "New Amsterdam Store Sells Goods at the Price Required to Avoid Pollution, Exploitation and Climate Change," March 5, 2020.

27. FMI, The Food Industry Association, "Supermarket Facts," 2020, Accessed October 6, 2021, https://www.fmi.org/our-research/supermarket-facts.

28. I Amsterdam, "New Amsterdam Store Sells Goods at the Price Required to Avoid Pollution, Exploitation and Climate Change."

29. U.S. Environmental Protection Agency (EPA), "Asbestos Manufacture, Importation, Processing, and Distribution in Commerce Prohibitions - Final Rule," *Federal Register*, Vol. 54, No. 132, Rules and Regulations, July 12, 1989.

30. The Occupational Safety and Health Administration (OSHA) of the United States Department of Labor, "Occupational Noise Exposure; Hearing Conservation Amendment - Final Rule," *Federal Register*, Vol. 46, No. 11, Rules and Regulations, January 16, 1981.

31. U.S. Food and Drug Administration (FDA), "Milestones in U.S. Food and Drug Law History," January 31, 2018.

32. Ibid.
33. American Heart Association, "Trans Fats," March 23, 2017.
34. Caitlin Dewey, "Artificial Trans Fats, Widely Linked to Heart Disease, Are Officially Banned," *The Washington Post*, June 18, 2018.
35. Sotheby's, "Contemporary Art Evening Auction Catalogue," Lot 17, New York, May 13, 2013.
36. U.S. Congress, "Energy Policy and Conservation Act," Statute 89, 871, December 22, 1975.
37. Electric Choice, "Electricity Rates by State (September 2021)," Accessed October 6, 2021, https://www.electricchoice.com/electricity-prices-by-state/.
38. Walmart, "Walmart Standards For Suppliers," June 30, 2017.
39. Sotheby's, "Contemporary Art Evening Auction Catalogue."
40. Alan S. Morris, *ISO 14000 Environmental Management Standards: Engineering and Financial Aspects* (West Sussex: John Wiley & Sons, Ltd., 2004.)
41. International Organization for Standardization, *Discovering ISO 26000: Guidance on Social Responsibility* (Geneva: International Organization for Standardization, 2018.)
42. Catherine Benoît Norris, Editor, *The Methodological Sheets for Subcategories in Social Life Cycle Assessment (S-LCA)* (Nairobi, Kenya: United Nations Environment Programme, November 12, 2013.)
43. Kate Raworth, *Doughnut Economics: 7 Ways to Think Like a 21st Century Economist* (White River Junction, Vermont: Chelsea Green Publishing, 2017), 9.
44. Jaime Lee, "Benefit Corporations: A Proposal for Assessing Liability in Benefit Enforcement Proceedings," *Cornell Law Review*, Vol. 103, No. 4, May 2018, 1075-1100.
45. B Lab, "Model Benefit Corp Legislation," April 17, 2017.
46. Connecticut General Assembly, "Connecticut Benefit Corporation Act," February 2014.
47. Edward A. Haman, "What Is an L3C?" Accessed October 6, 2021, https://info.legalzoom.com/article/what-l3c.
48. Thomas Mitchelhill, "Why Did the New Gillette Ad Backfire So Horrendously?" *Noteworthy - The Journal Blog*, January 15, 2019.

8. Four Roles for All of Us

1. U.S. Securities and Exchange Commission, "SEC Adopts Amendments to Modernize Shareholder Proposal Rule," September 23, 2020, https://www.sec.gov/news/press-release/2020-220.
2. Christopher Helman, "Shareholders Rebuke Exxon Mobil on Climate, in a Wake-Up Call for Big Oil," *Forbes*, May 27, 2021.
3. Steven Mufson, "Dissident Shareholders Win a Third Seat on ExxonMobil Board," *The Washington Post*, June 2, 2021.
4. Danone S.A., "B Corp," Accessed October 7, 2021, https://www.danone.com/about-danone/sustainable-value-creation/BCorpAmbition.html.

5. Reid Wilson, "States, Cities Rethink Tax Incentives After Amazon HQ2 Backlash," *The Hill*, February 17, 2020.

6. Luticia Miranda, Nicole Nguyen, and Ryan Mac, "Here Are the Most Outrageous Incentives Cities Offered Amazon in Their HQ2 Bids," *BuzzFeed News*, November 14, 2018.

7. Robert McCartney, "Amazon HQ2 to Benefit from More than $2.4 Billion in Incentives from Virginia, New York and Tennessee," *The Washington Post*, November 13, 2018.

8. Wilson, "States, Cities Rethink Tax Incentives After Amazon HQ2 Backlash."

ACKNOWLEDGMENTS

So, one day, you glimpse an idea in your mind. It seems so simple, clear, and powerful that you decide to share it. But the moment you try to tell someone about it, you realize that your idea is only simple within the construct of your brain. And that untangling this beautiful rat's nest and laying it out in a linear progression of words, sentences, and paragraphs will be a Herculean task.

During my journey, I was guided by the words of many brilliant thinkers, each sharing their own perspective either in print or over the phone. While most of these people are included in the endnotes, there are a handful of extraordinary individuals who deserve special recognition. Without these people, this book simply would not exist: Lynn Stout, Margaret Blair, Joel Bakan, Manfred Max-Neef, Robert Plutchik, Max Roser, and the man who first got me thinking, James Burke. Immerse yourself in their thoughts.

As I was writing, I had a handful of friends who read each of my chapters as I finished them, offering encouragement and improvements — both of which are hugely appreciated since they helped me determine if the translation of thoughts into prose was working. So, to Caroline Dickey, David Tibbets, Debba White, Marisa Porto, and Myles Watling, a huge "thank you" for keeping me going.

Once the first draft was completed, a different group of friends read the entire manuscript to see how (or if) it held together, offering feedback on the macro view. To Bob Amundson, Fred Pfaff, and Hank Shaw, thank you for giving up hours of your time to travel down the bumpy road of a first draft. Glad you didn't get too carsick.

Given that this is my first book, I knew there was a lot I didn't know, so I was fortunate enough to find some experienced professionals to help me improve this book in many ways. Thanks to Shay Totten, my developmental editor, for helping me realize (among other things) that books, like freeways, need on-ramps and off-ramps to help people navigate them. Thanks also to Hugh Barker, my copy editor, who amazes me with his ability to consider every single detail before offering notes that are clear, candid, and kind. While you can't judge a book by its cover, a good one certainly doesn't hurt, so I feel especially lucky to have worked with Joe Montgomery. His impeccable design skills are only matched by his ability to understand what I was trying to do. Thanks, Joe. And, to Kate Victory Hannisian, my proofreader, thank you for your rigor and your willingness to keep engaging with me, despite a couple of false starts.

Finally, to my family. To my mom and dad for teaching me that knowledge is power and that, if you believe in something, you should never, ever give up. You are the primary reasons why I was able to attack such a huge problem. To my brother Carwin, who has embodied the twin roles of supporter and tormentor throughout my life, thank you for this balance (and I'm sorry about the pencil lead I jabbed into your arm when we were kids). To my mother-in-law, Janice, who has blindly supported me from day one, often reminding me of her faith in me with a simple comment or an inspirational book she saw on her travels, thank you.

Most importantly, my never-ending love and thanks to my wife, Laina, for always helping me be my best and accomplish what's important to me, even if it means being underfoot far too much for months on end. And to my daughters, Olive and Piper. In the end, I wrote this book for you, hoping it will transform (even just a little bit) the world you inherit, into one where you can be can be happy, healthy, and become the best "you" that you can be.

ABOUT THE AUTHOR

Ed Chambliss is, at heart, a teacher. Not just by title, but by nature. He is someone who is infinitely curious about the world — a student who loves to explore and to learn. But what transforms a student into a teacher is the love of sharing. Someone who, upon finding something amazing, desperately needs to tell others about it so they can experience the same rush of discovery that he did.

Professionally, Ed has focused his efforts for the last 35 years on the world of marketing, both at corporations and at universities, helping others understand how companies can best communicate with customers by recognizing their humanity.

Ed currently lives in Los Angeles with his wife and two daughters.

twitter.com/edchambliss
instagram.com/ed.chambliss
linkedin.com/in/edchambliss

www.ingramcontent.com/pod-product-compliance
Lightning Source LLC
Chambersburg PA
CBHW070100030426
42335CB00016B/1963